ECO-REPUBLIC

ECO-REPUBLIC

WHAT THE ANCIENTS CAN TEACH US ABOUT ETHICS, VIRTUE, AND SUSTAINABLE LIVING

MELISSA LANE

Princeton University Press
Princeton and Oxford

Published in the United States and Canada by Princeton University Press,
41 William Street, Princeton, New Jersey 08540

press.princeton.edu

This edition of *Eco-Republic* is published by arrangement with Peter Lang Ltd
First published in 2011 by Peter Lang Ltd

Peter Lang Ltd
International Academic Publishers
Evenlode Court, Main Road, Long Hanborough, Witney,
Oxfordshire OX29 8SZ
United Kingdom

www.peterlang.com

Library of Congress Control Number: 2011933429
ISBN: 978-0-691-15124-3

Printed on acid-free paper. ∞

Printed in the United States of America

1 3 5 7 9 10 8 6 4 2

Contents

vi

Acknowledgements

This book was conceived in Cambridge, England, and completed in Princeton, New Jersey, with sabbatical support provided by the University of Cambridge and King's College, Cambridge, in spring 2009; research support provided by Princeton University from the time of my moving there in the summer of 2009; and a return summer in Cambridge made easier by the hospitality of the Centre for History and Economics and the Lauterpacht Centre for International Law. I am grateful to all these institutions and to the colleagues and staff in them, with special thanks to John Dolan, Carole Frantzen, Inga Huld Markan, Doug Rosso, and Debra Wintjen for making my logistical transitions work.

In Cambridge, the idea for the book grew originally out of the confluence between my study of Plato and of political thought and ethics more broadly, and the many opportunities given to me for over a decade by the Cambridge Programme for Sustainability Leadership, HRH the Prince of Wales's Business and Sustainability Programme, and the Corporate Theatre, to convey why those ideas mattered to people in business, public policy, and charities in the UK, the US, and further afield. I can't begin to calculate my debt to Polly Courtice, Jonathon Porritt, Martin and Sue Best, and all staff and fellow faculty of these programmes, in particular Bill Adams, Bernie Bulkin and his partner Vivien Rose, Kate Owen, and Richard Newton. Thanks go to those who formed my knowledge of Greek thought – Myles Burnyeat, Malcolm Schofield, and Dominic Scott – and of political thought – the late Judith Shklar and Quentin Skinner; and to the many colleagues, friends, and students who continue such conversations, especially colleagues of the B Caucus in Cambridge and the Program in Classical Philosophy in Princeton, my longstanding interlocutors in Platonic matters Danielle

Allen and Verity Harte, and more recently Dimitri El Murr; and newer friends in the American academic community, especially Jill Frank, Sara Monoson, Arlene Saxonhouse, and John Wallach for their welcome. Conversations with Jimmy Doyle, Philippa Kelly, John Lambie, Gerry Mackie, Tori McGeer, Philip Pettit, Jeanne Safer, Stephanie Spink, and Richard Tuck were important. Environmentalists Tom Crompton, Jules Peck, and Joe Smith were challenging interlocutors in the UK, and my new environmental colleagues Bob Keohane, Michael Oppenheimer, and Rob Socolow have been similarly so in Princeton, where I am especially grateful to Steve Pacala for inviting me to join the Associated Faculty of the Princeton Environmental Institute.

Comments on various working papers related to the book were offered by seminar participants at the University of Cambridge, University of Utrecht, Hebrew University, Columbia University, LSE, University College London, and Princeton, with especially helpful written comments by George Kateb, and by readers of a *Guardian* article in 2009, especially Ian Christie. An earlier draft of the book was read with care and insight by Danielle Allen, Catherine Cameron, Dan Chandler, Antony Hatzistavrou, Jacob Lipton, and Jonathon Porritt, the latter especially generous given the demands on him at the time as Chair of the UK Sustainable Development Commission. A penultimate draft was read at speed and with philosophical acuity by Corey Brettschneider, Alex Guerrero, Antony Hatzistavrou, and Tim Mulgan. It was a special pleasure to write the beginning in Cambridge in the company of Adam Tooze and the end in Princeton in the company of Anne Hallward. I am indebted to my agent, Jonathan Conway; my editors, first Nick Reynolds and then Lucy Melville at Peter Lang, and Rob Tempio at Princeton University Press; Adam Freudenheim, Mary Fox, and Penguin Press for permission to quote throughout from the Sir Desmond Lee translation of Plato's *Republic* published by Penguin Classics; and my calmly indefatigable research assistant, Julie Rose. Above all I thank Diana Lipton, who is a friend nonpareil; my sister Diana Lane, and her family, for being a model of ecological commitment; my parents Norman and Sheila Lane, for their unstinting love and generosity; and Andrew Lovett, my husband, partner, friend, and life companion, for sharing his creative passion and, in every way possible, nurturing mine.

My first book was dedicated to my parents, elders, and teachers, and my second book was about 'Plato's progeny'. This one is dedicated to the progeny of friendship, family, and teaching: Jacob and Jonah Lipton; Maud Hasler, Zia Ratnasothy, and Eliza Brown; all my younger cousins, nieces, and nephews; and my students, including the remarkable students of Plato whom I was privileged to teach in the Philosophy Summer School in China in 2007 as well as my students in both Cambridge and Princeton.

PART I

INERTIA

Prologue to Chapter 1: Plato's Cave

[…] what do you think would happen, if [a released prisoner] went back to sit in his old seat in the cave? Wouldn't his eyes be blinded by the darkness, because he had come in suddenly out of the sunlight? … And if he had to discriminate between the shadows, in competition with the other prisoners, while he was still blinded and before his eyes got used to the darkness – a process that would take some time – wouldn't he be likely to make a fool of himself? And they would say that his visit to the upper world had ruined his sight, and that the ascent was not worth even attempting.

(The character of Socrates speaking in Plato, *Republic*, Book 7, 516e–517a)[1]

'Crazy!' 'Lunatic!' 'What is he talking about?' 'How dare he challenge our way of life?', people call out angrily to one another, hostile to a person newly arrived in their midst. The newcomer has challenged the fundaments of their social order. According to his presumptuous proclamation, what they call success is actually failure. Their career paths to power and prestige lead to public damage, not to public service. What they take to be solid facts are dangerous illusions. The technologies and infrastructure and assumptions in which they have invested their time and money and belief are fraudulent; the glare of reality would expose these as wishful delusions. The newcomer is likely to be shunned at best, stoned at worst. How could anyone be expected to tolerate such arrogant insults to their whole way of life?

Pull back the camera on this scene, however, and it appears in a new light. The busy self-righteousness of this political order is indeed, in reality, built on foundations of sand. The prizes they strive for are made of smoke and mirrors; success in their competitions is self-undermining. In fact, powerful figures, invested in the maintenance of this existing delusional social order, parade the objects and languages in which the people believe, denying that any external challenge to them could be valid. Denial of the external perspective looks from this higher vantage point like keeping one's head in the sand, refusing to face what is obvious and valid.

A passive citizen body, a conniving and self-interested set of sophistic opinion-formers and demagogic political leaders, a systematically misleading and damaging order of political structures and common beliefs and appetites: this is how Plato portrays the effects of his contemporaries' system of education – by which he means, very broadly, the effects of their system of values and practices. He describes the cities of his day as no more than caves. Trapped inside, people box at shadows, elbowing each other to achieve advantage and pre-eminence, while being all the time unknowing captives of a delusional state. The artificial firelight inside is but a feeble and perverse imitation of the light of the Sun which stands outside and above every given cave.

I have taught Plato's image of the Cave – for that is what I have been describing, from Book 7 of Plato's *Republic* – to hundreds of people, old and young, students and senior citizens, corporate executives and public officials. Several years before beginning this book, it began to nag at me. In clinging to the comforts and familiarities of our current way of life and its fossil-fuel infrastructure, despite a mounting consensus of scientific studies documenting the damage which this is doing, are we trapping ourselves in Plato's cave? What would it mean for our conceptions of our cities and our selves if we were to dare to leave the cave, facing the challenge of making our conveniences and competitions conform to the implacable demands of external reality?

This book is an attempt to answer that question. It does so by taking seriously the challenge which Plato poses, while developing a more positive answer than he offered to the question of whether a democratic society could conceivably generate such change from within. Plato portrays the democratic society of his day (or rather of his teacher Socrates' day, in fifth-century B.C. Athens, Greece) as a cave from which only one or two exceptional people may be able to escape. In fact he envisions only forced escape, as if someone would have to be plucked out of captivity by powers on the outside, and he depicts the Sun as an image for a single fixed and given truth, rather than a truth attained by the progress of human science and debate.

Today, our understanding of the way that science and knowledge-formation takes place in liberal democratic societies is very different from that of the *Republic*. Rather than seeing one or two people as possessed of a unique and given truth, the rest as benighted and deluded, we understand that knowledge is broadly produced and shared, with even specialized science being a debate among specialists that has public resonance, rather than an esoteric matter for a chosen few. Yet these differences do not obliterate an important commonality. Plato's image of knowers (in our case, scientists) having something to tell us that violates our most cherished assumptions, that makes people so angry as to deny and attack them as the messengers, has powerful resonance with our current predicament. The idea of man-made global warming has been such an idea, greeted with as much hostility and ridicule as Plato's cave denizens mustered for their unwelcome messengers from the outside world. (So too was the idea of passive smoking.) Now, ideas of the near-term, absolute, and wrenching changes that may be required of us appear as similar anathema to our cherished cave-like certainties. Denial and inertia in confronting the required changes are temptations that are very widely shared.

While ecological sustainability is by no means limited to the issues of climate or energy, I take those issues as my primary focus both as illustrative and as inherently important. The corresponding denial that interests me is not the straight-out denial of climate change, nor the undoubtedly significant role of the self-interested corporate deniers, but rather the everyday behavioural denial of those of us (almost all of us) who claim to accept the scientific case for the rising threat of climate change but who deny or evade the necessities of change which coping with that threat would impose. My starting point is the evolving International Panel on Climate Change (IPCC) position – representing international governmental as well as scientific consensus, albeit one which develops with recurrent need for self-criticism and correction – that climate change represents a real and present threat of disruption and damage to humans and to many aspects of the earth's ecosystems.[2] Those who reject that standpoint may still find aspects of this book of interest, insofar as it sketches out an ancient road map for social change, but will not share its primary purpose: to chart the psychosocial contours of what acting from such a standpoint will require.[3]

Strikingly, the term which Plato's character Socrates uses to describe what might force people out of the cave, or bring them to accept philosophers as rulers, is 'necessity' (*anankē*). Only necessity can force us to give up our most cherished illusions, to recognize with the aid of scientific enlightenment that our caves are no longer sustainable. Yet for Plato, necessity was not always or only something external to human action. It was not only a reference to flash floods or earthquakes. Rather, the same word could refer to the human *response* to natural or even political imperatives: 'necessity' could become operative through human action, including both political compulsion and individual initiative.

Insofar as unsustainability is unsustainable, something will sooner or later have to give.[4] So if necessity is the spur to getting people to give up the illusions in which they have deeply invested, that does not let us off the hook. There is a constructive role for human agency in channelling necessity, allowing it to be the mother of invention of a better world rather than a sheer and sudden force threatening to explode our cave. This book outlines what an intelligent response to ecological necessity in the domain of the political theory of the interplay between individual and society requires. Its focus is not on the politics of national or international negotiations, but on the associated and unfolding changes in individual and social outlook which may both prompt and be reinforced by such negotiations. An intuitive and imaginative model inspired by the ancients is what I seek to provide.

1

Introduction:
Inertia as Failure of the Political Imagination

The image of the Cave propounded in the prologue may seem too strong to be either palatable or plausible. How can one dare to say that dominant systems of values and practices and norms are fundamentally misguided? In fact we have just been through an eerily similar indictment of another dominant system of thought and action in the form of the global financial crisis. Consider the AAA-rated securities that were actually worthless; models of risk which ruled out of necessary consideration the very dangers which threatened to bring the system down; the promises to avoid moral hazard which were immediately broken. The topsy-turvy nature of reality, in which our cherished faith in house prices rising, the 'great moderation' of the financial markets, and the ending of the cycle of boom and bust were all exposed as delusions, show us to have been trapped in a precarious cave of our own making, wilfully hiding from the searching light which would reveal the cracks in its foundation.[1]

How can people trap themselves – how do we trap ourselves – in such caves of delusion? In Britain, the Queen posed this question on a visit to the scholars enrolled in the prestigious ranks of the British Academy: how was it that no one had noticed that the credit crunch was looming? (In fact, a few people *had* predicted such a crunch; the question was really why conventional wisdom wrote them off as fools and knaves, dismissing them as dangerous and deluded threats to the secure certainties of the cave.) The answer from the academicians was surprising. It was an appeal to the imagination.

So in summary, Your Majesty, the failure to foresee the timing, extent and severity of the [financial] crisis and to head it off, while it had many causes, was principally a failure of the collective imagination of many bright people, both in this country and internationally, to understand the risks to the system as a whole.[2]

This book proposes a parallel answer to the question of why – with mounting scientific evidence, and a plethora of available technologies – Western democracies by and large are still mired in inertia, unwilling to take the steps necessary to meet the looming challenge of climate change. Like the credit crunch, our failure to rise to – or in some cases even admit – the reality of the challenge is in large part a failure of the collective imagination.

In the financial realm, this collective imagination formed a limiting horizon, making some possibilities not so much literally unthinkable as outside the boundaries of 'normal' processes of reasoning and of 'normal' standards of the desirable and the admirable. The same phenomenon is at work in the looming ecological crisis. Even where rational solutions are available, such as zero-impact building or a ban on plastic bags, we see them neglected or evaded as inconsistent with the current imaginative horizon. One executive of a major British construction company has reflected ruefully on this phenomenon, observing that most builders do not build in zero-impact ways 'because they believe it isn't possible' – even though it demonstrably is.[3] When even an ardent inventor admits that the time-lag in adoption of the best and most useful new inventions tends to be fifteen years, because people are so resistant to change, an inquiry into the inertial drag of the imagination is a necessary complement to the multiple studies of the economic costs, technological possibilities, and normative ethical demands of climate change which dominate the field.[4]

Intimations of the need for an imaginative change

The need for a transformation of the ways in which we conceive the terms of political and economic life is increasingly felt, if inchoately expressed. One way it is sometimes spoken about is in the declaration, 'We need a new mythology.' In the space of six months, I heard that said – in almost exactly those words – by an equity funds manager, the head of an economics think-tank, and the former head of a national UK environmental NGO.[5] It's not a sentiment you would usually associate with any of them. It's not a sentiment that has been widely expressed in modern Western political life at all. In calling for a new mythology, what these leaders of business and NGOs meant is that we need a new vision of normality, of what fundamentally constitutes the relationships between public and private, the role of the individual, the values and costs and benefits which are socially acknowledged.[6] They mean that the technical, economic, and political debates have left something out: not that we need a literal 'mythology' in the sense of a made-up lie or fable or rationalization, but rather that we need to reconsider the basic units of value and meaning which we perceive and in light of which we reason.

I will interpret what these diverse social leaders meant by 'mythology' as referring to the more or less conscious assumptions, paradigms, and approaches that inform our perception and so structure the prevailing social 'ethos', the 'structure of response lodged in the motivations that inform everyday life', as one philosopher, G. A. Cohen of Oxford University, has described it.[7] Cohen argued that an egalitarian ethos was an indispensable conceptual element of social justice. My complementary claim is that transforming the way in which we imagine the social ethos is indispensable to the actual process of social change. If 'ethics' are rooted in 'ethos' (as indeed they were for the Greeks, being etymological kin), then both are rooted in turn in the way in which the faculty of imagination conceives them.

The Stern Review of the economics of climate change used more muted language to make a similar point. It called for public policy on climate change to 'seek to change notions of what responsible behaviour means': this is treated as a key lever for mitigating (limiting) the carbon emissions causing climate change.[8] The meaning of responsible behaviour is rooted in ideas about the meaning of harm which in turn connect to a wide range of beliefs, practices, emotions, and desires. The Stern Review assumed that it was the role of the state – public policy – to engage in changing such ideas. I will argue that while the state can play a role in this process, it is likely to start and to succeed in doing so only as part of a larger process in which individuals and groups throughout society can play an active part. Each of us can play a role in re-imagining the social ethos, even though doing so is a complex process which is beyond any one person's control.

Why worry about these fuzzy issues? Why not just focus on making markets work better by incorporating carbon emissions – climate change having been identified by the Stern Review as 'market failure on the greatest scale the world has seen'?[9] If we want to save capitalism while saving the planet, it might be objected, surely the urgent problems are technical and legal rather than psychosocial. Free markets constrained by law and regulation have been the preferred means of producing most private goods with a degree of collective harmony by most of the rich economies of the world over the last century. Markets work by incentivizing people to prioritize and economize on scarce resources, laws by expectations and sanctions making the law-abiding keep within permitted boundaries. On this view, the most important first step is regulatory, to establish a carbon price within a deep and liquid global carbon market or set of interlocking markets, either by cap-and-trade or by a carbon tax. Once this is done, coupled with a rationalization of the system of public subsidies in line with the goal of reducing emissions, we will be a large part of the way towards solving the problem by incentivizing the introduction of appropriate technologies. What can a discussion of fuzzy ideas about imagination and ethos and mythology add to such a practical, real-world approach?

Such a technical and legal approach is essential, and urgent. But we need to ask why it has not yet been implemented, and whether it will be able to do the job fast enough, all by itself. On both counts, my answer is that the psychosocial approach is a necessary complement. As to the first question, a large part of the reason for the delay is that real-world political change depends on there being enough individuals with the new vision and values to give politicians (especially, but not only, democratic politicians) courage, and political cover, to act. One leading environmentalist has recalled a moment early in the UK's New Labour government when Prime Minister Tony Blair was asking NGO leaders to suggest radical steps that would signal that New Labour was taking the climate change agenda seriously. One of those present piped up, why not ban incandescent lightbulbs? According to a recounting of this moment told to me on the condition that the source remain anonymous, Blair looked horrified and said, that's far too radical for government to do; it's your job to make the public happy with that first. Even so 'minor' a change as this very often requires widespread public change of attitudes *before* there is much chance of its being politically imposed. This is not to deny other reasons for delay, including significant vested interests and their lobbying power, but it is to emphasize one which is less tangible but yet also important in determining the space for political action.

The second question as to whether the technical-legal answer will necessarily act quickly and fully enough invites a negative answer. Given the constraints of the 'normality' mindset and the political pressures which it generates, even the initial international and national regulatory fixes are likely to be set at too low a bar. This means that mere compliance will not get us fast enough to the level of emissions reduction necessary.[10] Neither the law nor the market is a sufficient tool for this, though both are necessary. Laws can be captured by cunning lobbyists and can fail to be enforced by apathetic, corrupt, or simply straitened officials. Even the best-regulated markets offer unexpected loopholes which can be exploited for profit, rather than reliably funnelling investment in the publicly intended direction. So even if and when an effective global carbon market emerges, voluntary compliance and further action will remain important. The architecture of national and international regulation is vital to responding to the challenge of climate change. But, especially though not only in democratically governed countries, it is unlikely either to come about, or to succeed in all of its aims, without imaginative change leading to broader forms of public acceptance and participation.

This should not be a surprise. Voluntary obedience and action beyond what is required play a key role in human action generally. Consider the dramatic effects of 'work to rule' industrial action. When workers limit themselves to doing only what their job formally requires and nothing more, malfunctions and even chaos can ensue. Humans are social and communicative animals, and commitment in a communicative and collective endeavour feels very different from mere external compliance – with results that will, it seems likely, be very different as well.[11] Regulation which fails to engage with the habits, ideas, passions, and appetites of the people being regulated is unlikely to work very well.

Conversely, even if compliance imposed by regulation were achieved quickly enough, it is likely still to feel like sacrifice, like having to give up one's material comforts for reasons of an austere social goal. 'Mere compliance' with a carbon price could feel like wartime rationing, except with no end in sight. But this is not inevitable. It is possible that the real need is not so much for material sacrifice as for imaginative transformation. If we are willing to let go of the sunk costs that we have invested in imagining and living by the current system, we may find that we see the world so differently that at least some 'material sacrifices' will no longer look like sacrifices at all. Once our values and habits are recreated, new frameworks for judging harm and value, cost and benefit, will produce new evaluations of what is lost and what is gained.

Let me push this point one stage further. In some cases of sustainable action, material sacrifice may not even be necessary. Changing lightbulbs actually saves money as well as cutting emissions. Yet it still feels like a sacrifice, to the extent that Tony Blair was reportedly adamant (as just mentioned) that this would be a psychological bridge too far, and that the *Daily Mail* still in 2009 chose to ridicule and attack the idea of banning 'ordinary' bulbs; in the United States, a law passed in 2007 requiring higher efficiency of lightbulbs from 2012 onward – which in practice requires redesign if not abolition of the standard 100 watt incandescent bulb – is being subjected to a similar backlash in Congress and the media at the time of writing.[12] A similar conundrum has arisen in India about what *the Economist* calls 'the pestilence of plastic bags', which litter the landscape, clog drains, and harm the cattle which eat them. Yet the municipal imposition of penalties in Delhi has to be draconian, because 'the desire to pay the penalty is sometimes greater than the desire to change your mindset.'[13] Why should this be? Why shouldn't our supposed rational interest in saving money make it easy for us to change our lightbulbs or (facing even a small fine) stop using thin plastic bags, and welcome political pressure to do so? The answer is that our social imagination, our social mythology, frames this as a breach of normality. It is normal to have 'ordinary' lightbulbs, normal to be given plastic bags, therefore being asked or required to change these habits is unreasonable, and this sense of a violation of expectations actually trumps the urge to save money. Mythology is so powerful that it can trump material motivation.

My point here is in no way to imply that changing lightbulbs is doing enough, nor that most or all ecological measures are money-saving. It is that the case of lightbulbs – which would seem to be a best-case scenario for quick action – is an extreme illustration of how powerful is the inertial imaginative resistance to change. What one legal scholar has called the 'status quo bias' applies well beyond the making of law, in which new proposals are almost always at a rhetorical and argumentative disadvantage as opposed to the ensconced 'standard' of the status quo.[14] It is an important source of inertia: we are more attached to the status quo just because it is the status quo; this gives it a special edge over all alternatives, including those which are potentially far superior but which do not have the advantage of already being in place.[15] Attachment to the status quo also makes it difficult to establish a standard of assessment for imaginative and social change. Just because we have always drawn the boundaries of harm in one way, those boundaries appear natural and necessary to us, and benefit from our existing bias in favour of them.

The same point applies to individual motivation and action. The status quo is the standard against which we test, and on the basis of which we resist, proposals for change, even when the status quo is demonstrably dangerous.[16] To overcome such resistance requires a leap of initiative. The agents of change will be multiple, with varying differentiated roles in the process, so that while we don't all contribute in the same way, we may all take part if we so choose. This book will focus in particular on the role of the individual in contributing to such a transformation, not because individuals acting alone can do everything that is needed (there are major systemic factors that require political or commercial decision to change), but because the role of the individual has often been neglected.

Such a focus will both be informed by my appeal to Plato and also mark an important fault line where I break with Plato's assumptions. While Plato helps us by training a powerful lens on the mutually constitutive relation between the individual and the political community, his insistence that that relationship can only be positively shaped by a few people at and from the top hinders a full understanding of social change. Likewise, while Plato insisted that individuals should keep to their assigned social roles, with only one such role – that of the philosopher-ruler – being assigned to consider the good of the whole society, I will suggest that his notion of the good today must be incorporated into all social roles, not only that of the leaders. By asking how the individual at any level of society can contribute to imaginatively reshaping its ethos, and indeed must incorporate responsibility for doing so into whatever her social roles might be, we both learn from Plato and also move beyond him.

The skeleton of this book is therefore threefold: inertia, imagination, and initiative. Part I surveys the *inertia* of our current habits, and outlines a possible source for stimulating reform in the form of ancient ethics, and in particular in the work of Plato. Part II outlines elements which a new process of *imagination* of the constituents of the social ethos could reshape, doing so for purposes of illustration and stimulation rather than strict prescription: my interest is in exploring what it would mean to carry out social changes of the requisite kind, rather than prescribing in detail precisely what those changes should be. One central focus here is on the mutually constituting relation between the individual and her political society: individuals are shaped by the way in which they imaginatively conceive of political relations, but they can also play a role in reshaping this. Part III returns to the current roadblocks, suggesting ways in which a new ethos transformed by the acts of political imagination outlined in Part II could enable various actors to take the *initiative* in addressing the challenges of sustainability, and surveying how individual and social roles in society might have to change in order to do so. To prepare for these arguments, this chapter will now flesh out what I mean by ethos and imagination, how I define sustainability, and why I turn to Plato as a guide in this quest.

Defining ethos and the imagination

The terse definition of 'ethos' quoted earlier – defining it as the 'structure of response lodged in the motivations that inform everyday life' – was advanced by its proponent to argue that compliance with a set of basic rules and institutions in the absence of a reinforcing ethos can neither exhaust nor attain a basic social value. If people don't share and act upon the values animating the rules and institutions in their everyday choices, the society will fall short of attaining and exhibiting those values. But what is it that structures such responses and motivations? Here we must supplement the appeal to ethos with an acknowledgement of the background beliefs, images, and narratives which are more or less explicit and more or less common. Such beliefs, images, and narratives are in part the product of imaginative modes of perception, and they in turn structure habitual acts and practices, which may be individuated in terms of social norms. What interest me in particular are the elements of this ethos relevant to politics in a broad sense. These are not restricted to the imagination of particular political institutions, but range more widely to encompass the relationship between the individual and the political community and the units of value and meaning which are in play in that relationship.

We can imagine a different relationship between the individual and the polity, and instantiate this in a new set of habitual responses and motivations in everyday life as well as in engaging with specific political institutions. This axis has a long lineage: the ancient Greeks called it the relationship between *polis* and *psyche*, between city and soul. This re-imagining of the political even in a broad sense is only a subsection of the acts of collective imagination which might be relevant to the question of sustainability. The ways in which we imagine animals and the natural world – whether trees, for example, have legal standing, or whether we take wilderness to have value independent of human enjoyment or recognition of it – are of great importance to explore outside the confines of this book.[17] But those are not my subject here.[18] Supposing that we have at least a 'fiduciary responsibility' towards the earth,[19] I am primarily concerned with human-to-human interactions rather than with our relation to the natural world, asking how the demands of sustainability impinge on, and invite rethinking of, the relationship between city and soul.

While 'imagination' refers to a capacity for engaging in acts of imagining, it is sometimes used to refer to the set of mental contents created by such acts,[20] and I will sometimes follow suit. Such an elision is made by many appeals to the 'moral imagination', a phrase which goes back at least to statesman Edmund Burke's *Reflections on the Revolution in France*,[21] and which has been used by scholars of literature and politics for decades,[22] being given wider currency by the speeches of President Barack Obama in accepting the Nobel Peace Prize in 2009 and in mourning the victims of the violent attack in Tucson in 2011.[23] That phrase however in recent decades has been closely tied to a limited, albeit vitally important, content, that of cultivating the qualities of empathy and humanity. In contrast, the 'political imagination' as I use it is broader, encompassing a wider range (and not necessarily only a positive one) of values, visions, and qualities that inform the relationship between individual and political community: in the political theorist Sheldon Wolin's evocative and seminal discussion, 'vision and political imagination' are central processes of political theory.[24] The phrase 'political imagination' referring to a noun, the substantive contents produced by the imagination, has been employed by the political theorist Danielle Allen, who introduced one chapter of her book *Talking to Strangers*, for example, by remarking that

'A collective autobiography ought to explain how the landscape of the political imagination has come to have its political topography.'[25] It can also be found, without much elaboration, in a volume titled *Religion and the Political Imagination*, and in the context of a more fleshed-out account of the imagination and its political role in a book of essays on political theory called *Politics and the Imagination*.[26]

Consider as an example of divergent political imaginations, the Japanese and American forms of modern capitalism: both have broadly similar institutions and rules (though of course these vary in some vital particulars), but they embody very different assumptions and expectations about the treatment of workers, the responsibility of companies, and the role of the state.[27] Of course, the Japanese political imagination is constituted by a more or less coherent cluster of institutions, practices, norms, and beliefs, and its elements can't be plucked at random out of context. But there is nothing impossible in the thought that the Japanese could begin to shift their values, expectations, and assumptions, either deliberately or by necessity, towards others closer to the American ones, or vice versa.

Other examples of changes in imagining the ethos at the order of magnitude which interests me include the sea-changes in attitudes towards and practices of smoking in the last two decades; or empire in the post-World War II period; or big-game hunting since the Edwardian era. Or consider, over a longer historical time span, the perceived value of sun-bathing: we take for granted that this is an intelligible, or meaningful, thing to do (though now only when well protected by sunscreen), whereas such a way of spending time would have made no sense to an ancient Greek or a Victorian.

Of course, such general contrasts between of one society as a whole and that of another can be misleading: societies will typically include multiple, overlapping, and competing horizons of normality. (Plenty of people saw no point in sunbathing even in the halcyon days before knowledge of skin cancer and global warming.) And yet some aims are sufficiently widely shared, sufficiently little questioned in the media and public debate, to warrant a loose usage of the phrase in the singular. As one scholar remarks about the related notion of 'a system of values' (though this focuses primarily on norms and actions, without reference to metaphors and images), '[t]he vast areas of agreement [between individuals] often seem invisible because they are presupposed or assumed

without argument.'[28] Such an approach, focusing as I do on widespread
commonalities, contrasts with other academic approaches which explore
divergent imaginations among different groups in a given population:
the social psychology of 'mental frames', for example, which sees them
as varying between individuals, or the 'cultural theory of risk', which
distinguishes four broad types of orientation to groups and rules.[29] Such
approaches generate valuable insights into diversity and conflict, helping
to explain, as in the title of an important book by the former director of
the Tyndall Centre in Britain, 'why we disagree about climate change'.[30]
Yet, notwithstanding the obvious existence of such disagreements, my
interest lies in exploring the considerable extent of agreement which
comes into being in the course of defining and negotiating both formal
and informal political relationships. How we assume that harm must be
defined, for example, is a key issue about which people will disagree, but
on which society as a whole comes to some working resolution – and it
is that sort of resolution, which may no longer work as well as originally
thought, which I wish to interrogate.

One valuable analytical perspective on how broad shifts in attitudes
and practices to sunbathing or smoking or similar phenomena come about
derives from identifying and studying them as discrete norms. This is an
area of study which spans the gamut from anthropological accounts to a
growing discipline at the intersection of legal theory and rational choice.
Despite the fact that there is 'no common definition of social norms' either
within these disciplines or across them, certain subfields have crystallized
their own definitions in a productive way.[31] For some, 'norms are a system
of meaning', while for others, they are 'patterns of action', but more com-
monly, they are seen as statements that regulate behaviour, usually with
an 'ought' dimension.[32] Within the parameters of an agreed definition,
individuating and limiting the elements of the ethos as 'norms' has the
advantage of focusing inquiry on a seemingly limited and definable set
of expectations-cum-actions.

This perspective makes norm emergence and change seem a more
tractable phenomenon: scholars have explained how the practice of footbinding disappeared in China, and are now using that understanding to
inform local efforts to abolish the practice of female genital cutting in
parts of Africa.[33] The dynamics identified in such studies are illuminating
and I will draw on them further in Part III. Yet in considering the role of
the ethos and of the imagination in shaping it, we cannot limit the field

too neatly to individuated norms alone. Norms collectively comprise an ethos, which makes sense in turn only against a background of structured perceptions and assumptions derived from acts of imagination. Changes in individual norms do not necessarily amount to a systemic and integrated change of the kind which interests me, though they may be important contributions to such change.

Nevertheless, I share with the 'new norms' theorists a presumption that some if not all of these elements can in principle brought within our conscious control, and that individuals can act – taking on diverse roles in the process – to bring this about. Political and social initiatives can be taken by at least some individuals and can kickstart further changes. Not all elements of the ethos will change at once, but many are at least in principle subject to collective or semi-collective processes of change.

How do such processes begin? 'New norms scholars' have an answer to this: changes in norms are sparked off by individuals who act as 'norm entrepreneurs'.[34] A few individuals kickstart the process, embodying intrinsic commitment to a set of values and visions; others eventually join them for a range of reasons, whether being converted to the new values or simply jumping on the bandwagon of a successful social movement for more mundane reasons of seeking respect, recognition, or social advancement. Yet the 'new norms' literature tends to treat the original 'norm entrepreneurs' themselves as inexplicably arising out of the blue, due to a stroke of chance (Plato would call it divine fate). In contrast, my interest lies in what it is that can inspire an individual to set out on such a transformative path. Inspiration arises from new imaginative insights and then gives rise to broader imaginative – and eventually social and political – transformation. This process is not one-way only: each level of specificity and awareness – from the broad and partly submerged imaginative landscape which yields the more evident attitudes and actions that comprise a shared social ethos, to the specific and individuated norms of behaviour – is a possible node of change which can rebound upstream or downstream, reshaping the others in its wake. Or so I will argue.

One striking example of this process is the gradual emergence and legitimation of the notion of sustainability, as a result of the efforts of the green movement, Green parties, academics, and others over many decades. Sustainability as an idea has moved from the fringes to the centre of political debate; the challenge now is to integrate it into our perceptions and our practices. To understand what this would mean, a first step here is to flesh out how I understand this notion. My aim in this book is to focus on the ethics and ethos of sustainability, not to debate its scientific demands or implications, so my excursion into defining the concept will be brief.

Defining sustainability

The most widely used definition is probably that of the path-breaking 1987 United Nations report *Our Common Future*, also known – in honour of the chair of the World Commission on Environment and Development which produced it, Gro Harlem Brundtland – as the Brundtland Report: 'Sustainable development is development that meets the needs of the present without compromising the ability of future generations to meet their own needs.'[35] This focus on the future, however, risks downplaying and minimizing the nature of the standard with respect to the present. The appeal to 'needs' seeks a kind of philosophical bedrock. It is often thought that while we disagree about wants, human needs are self-evident: water, food, shelter, and so on. But in fact, philosophers and historians have long pointed out how even these most 'basic needs' are always interpreted within social contexts and conceptions of the good: it has been argued that early settlers in Greenland died because they would not recognize fish as 'food' even when starving.[36] Further, as political theorists have argued, the particular shape taken by our needs is socially dependent. I need mobility, but I don't necessarily need a car, unless I live in a city with no public transport or cycle lanes.[37] Conversely, to function in Kenya or China today as an entrepreneur on even the smallest scale, one needs a mobile phone: that is a legitimate need in the context of current practices of communication.

The Brundtland Report's reference to 'meeting the needs of the present' can only mean meeting those needs in relation to a certain understanding of value. A sustainable society will not be one which succeeds in doling out a set number of calories to imprisoned inmates just to keep them alive. It will be one which its members themselves recognize as thriving in a way which can be continued into the future, in relation to the interactive life-support systems of the earth.

This dynamic and imagination-structured approach is captured better in the definition of sustainable development offered by the charity Forum for the Future: 'a dynamic process which enables all people to realise their potential and improve their quality of life in ways which simultaneously protect and enhance the Earth's life support systems.'[38] As this definition shows, sustainability must be understood as a dynamic idea which will continue to change as contexts change. It relates to a broad condition for what I will call, in Platonic terms, a conception of the good – realizing potential and improving quality of life, protecting and enhancing the earth as an ecosystem. And it shows that we need not, and should not, take the status quo as the standard for sustainability. Sustainability is not about maintaining the status quo ad infinitum into the future. It is about reconfiguring society within the limits of the earth so that over time, society will be ever more able to realize and instantiate the good. What is unsustainable is what undermines the ability of society to develop in this way, or leads it to backslide in its ability to realize and instantiate what is valuable.

Sustainability, then, has ethics as much as science at its heart.[39] It makes sense to care about sustaining only something that we consider to be good, or at least to have the potential for good. Sustainability does not by itself answer the question of value, though it opens that question and invites debate as to how the values at its heart should be filled in.[40] What it does is to specify both that there should be a meaningful value at the heart of our endeavours – for why try to sustain something worthless? – and that those endeavours should only be carried out in ways consonant with protecting and enhancing the life-support systems of the earth.

Although sustainability is not the highest good itself, it is a necessary ingredient of and condition on the realization of the good. So one might pursue a career in publishing – sustainably; fight poverty – sustainably; raise children – sustainably. All of these only count as full goods when done in a sustainable manner. (This will rule out some aims which can't be pursued sustainably at all.) Strictly speaking, it doesn't make sense to make 'sustainability' itself into our principal goal; the goal is rather to achieve other independent goods in sustainable ways. The ultimate aim should be for 'sustainability' as a separate good to disappear, becoming wholly absorbed into the structure and nature of every other good that we pursue. In the meantime, however, significant attention and initiative are required to embed it as what philosophers call a side-constraint:

meaning roughly that any goal must be abandoned if it cannot be met while respecting the constraint.

It might be that at some time in the future, a technological revolution will make the immense potential of solar or wind or some other form of renewable energy available to us at very little cost of any kind. In that case, the sustainability of energy use, at least, would be a given for any and every possible goal – and so we would no longer have to worry about it as an organizing principle of psyche or polity. Yet so long as there are any scarcities in the human world – and it is hard to imagine that all of them could disappear – the issue of a psychologically and socially sustainable disposition in relation to them will remain.

Meanwhile, in order to incorporate the sustainability side-constraint – so long blithely ignored – into economic and environmental policy will require significant direct attention and consideration. Despite the fact that sustainability is to be incorporated into other goods that we pursue, in order to achieve that incorporation we need to focus on its specific requirements and demands. We need consciously to build it into our thinking and our institutions, in order for it to become an embedded and structuring part of our outlook. That task is supported by attention to our current conception of the social ethos and exploration of models for its reconfiguration.

Appealing to Plato: the reasons why

The terrain demarcated above could be explored from many points of view. As my earlier references to Plato's Cave and the Greek axis of the city and the soul already indicate, the vantage point chosen in this book is that of ancient Greek ethics and politics, and in particular, the work of Plato. In subsequent chapters I will say more to introduce Greek thought and its role in modern intellectual life, and the life and work of Plato himself. Here, I take a more personal approach to explain why I find Plato in particular so provocative and illuminating in thinking through the changes which sustainability requires.

Even if you are unfamiliar with Plato's writings, you are likely to have heard his name, and to know that he figures as arguably the most important and influential philosopher in the history of Western thought. What you may not have considered, even if you know his works, is that he can be read as having written a primer in the functioning of political possibility.[41] The *Republic* is a diagnosis of the ways in which city and soul were diseased in Greek societies, locked in some form of pathological embrace in which the dominant group imposed irrational goals on the society as a whole, and in which the satisfactions sought by the ambitious and competitive were consistently unsatisfying, leading to further degeneration as their children sought satisfaction elsewhere. It is at the same time an effort to transform the imaginative horizon of those societies, represented by the young Glaucon and Adeimantus, characters given the names of Plato's brothers, and by each reader who finds herself drawn in by the great reworkings of *polis* and *psyche* which the book proposes. The soul as healthy or diseased, and healthy only when it is balanced and orderly; the city as existing to serve its members rather than being a vehicle for their exploitation; the Sun as an image for the notion of absolute goodness; and the Cave as an image of delusory denial of the reality of the good: all these images have become staples of philosophical thought, without which the political thought of both the Latin West and the Islamic East would have been very different. It is Plato's images, as much as his appeal to reason, which have haunted readers over the centuries.

In speaking for over a decade to delegations and conferences about the ethics and politics of sustainability, primarily in forums convened by the Cambridge Programme for Sustainability Leadership (formerly the Cambridge Programme for Industry) in the United Kingdom, Europe, and the United States, for audiences drawn globally from the ranks of business, government, and academia, I found myself reaching for Plato in trying to explain the ways in which reason and desire might be re-envisioned, and the notion of a healthy society in which city and soul could be in harmony rather than in tension or mutual isolation. The richness and precision of Plato's imagery, its deployment targeted to particular audiences in order to challenge and reshape their assumptions and ideals, struck me as offering a structured account that models what transformative social change would look like and require. Plato himself stressed the need for *paradeigmata* or models (plural) in order to understand complex phenomena: Plato's work can now serve us as a *paradeigma* (singular) in its turn.[42]

Such a useful ingredient seemed to be neglected, however, in the cookbook of my main academic subject, political theory. There has been extensive and excellent work, of course, in the physics of climate change, in its biology, more recently in its economics, its domestic and international politics, and in applied ethics, exploring the terms of fairness of possible political solutions. But there has been less work drawing on the history of political thought – including the great books of the Western canon – either to situate and diagnose the challenges of sustainability or to sketch the outlines of possible solutions.

To turn to the history of political thought, however, is to encounter a further challenge to the relevance of the ancient Greeks, insofar as most modern political thinkers have marginalized them. Modern society is supposed to be built on a rejection of Spartan self-discipline and Athenian participatory democracy, in favour of the luxuries of commercial society and a capitalist economy in a representative state. Adam Smith, James Madison, and Max Weber are among the prophets of modernity who in key respects rejected aspects of ancient thought as irrelevant and misleading for modern politics, even while drawing on others. But the modern project so defined is built on certain flawed assumptions which put it at risk of running itself into the ecological sand.

These assumptions are ones which the ancient Greeks will in subsequent chapters help us to query and rethink. They include that of negligibility, to be discussed in chapter 3, together with a broader range of views about virtue, character, the good, and the relation between individual and society. Precisely in being free from advanced bureaucracy and capitalism, the ancient Greeks were aware of certain aspects of human development and potential which we have tended to forget. In appealing to them, we follow in the footsteps of many who have revived ideas that might seem untimely or anachronistic. As even an historian of ideas who stresses the importance of interpreting ideas within their context acknowledges, '[t]he history of political thought must consist, in significant measure, of actors doing things that historians of political thought insist that *they* should not do,' that is, appealing to ideas that would otherwise be anachronistic, and so giving them life within a fresh context once again.[43] This book is an exercise in such unabashed appropriation. While drawing extensively on study of and scholarship about Plato's writings, it does so in order to make use of them, and it rejects or reshapes the ideas they offer where necessary.

Why turn to Plato in particular, rather than some other ancient thinker, such as his younger Greek contemporary Aristotle or the later

Roman philosopher and statesman Cicero? It should be said that Plato is the leading but not only author on whom I will draw: his is the road map of social and political transformation which we will trace, but this will be augmented by other ancient as well as modern authors for specific points. I highlight Plato over other ancient authors for several reasons. While Aristotle is especially instructive on the rhetoric of political change, and can be read as offering deep insights into the mutual constitution of the individual and society,[44] he is less fertile in producing his own transformative images. He offers a deep understanding of the mutually shaping nature of individual and social practices on which I will draw but lacks any detailed model of a new society (the brief sketch at the end of the *Politics* is not comparable to the major works of Plato). The same is true of Cicero, despite his homage to Plato in writing his own *Republic* and *Laws* ostensibly modelled on works of the Athenian. Among thinkers of the ancient classical world, only Plato was fecund enough to give rise to a meditative philosophical system – known as Neoplatonism – which rivalled and inspired the monotheistic structure of Christianity as well as influencing the further development of Judaism and the later advent of Islam.

Is appealing to Plato, then, merely a substitute for religion today? After all, religions offer transformative images which mark the way to a blessed, saved, or prescribed form of life, and which are already deeply rooted in the minds of many people. The rethinking of stewardship and of the ethic of creation by many Jews, Christians, and Muslims, as well as other forms of ecological ethic in Buddhism and other Asian religions, may seem a more promising step than appealing to an esoteric and long-dead ancient author such as Plato. Some religious people may even be suspicious of Plato as an ersatz and so potentially misleading form of pseudo-religion. In the fourth century A.D., the Christian author St Augustine of Hippo passed through a Platonist phase on his journey to religious commitment. He later criticized Platonism as deluding itself about the possibility of self-sufficient human virtue, failing to attain the radical awareness of sin and dependence on God which only Christianity offered. The fear that an ethic modelled on Plato will be similarly flawed is one which many religious believers might share.

Augustine's criticism of ancient virtue ethics gave rise to another source of criticism about the relevance of Plato today. Such doubt can come from philosophers committed to modern versions of 'deontological' ethics, which treat impartial prescriptions for what is right as separate from – and more important than – individual conceptions of what is good. Such scholars reject an approach to ethics focused primarily on virtue and the good as opposed to duty and right. They are most likely to appeal to the ethics of Immanuel Kant, which offer categorical imperatives to govern the choice of maxims for human action.

Without entering the technical debates about whether virtue ethics and deontological ethics can be reconciled,[45] or about whether virtue has any real causal role in explaining human behaviour,[46] I suggest that raising the debate to a higher level – the level of the imaginative construction of the social ethos – offers a useful shift of attention. Here, virtue ethics enters the background assumptions and values of a society, whatever the particular ethical commitments of individuals may be.[47] My appeal to Plato is pitched at this more abstract level, treating his thought as a structural model rather than a substantive blueprint (though I do not dismiss the need for blueprints altogether, I do not offer one here).[48] Plato's ingredients are useful for us as a generic recipe to be modified and adapted, not in the specific cultural imagery which he chose to appeal to his long-ago contemporaries. He tells us, as it were, what sort of ingredients and methods are required to bake a loaf of bread, not what specific kind of bread we should bake. Some of those elements are ones which we tend today to overlook, to forget that we need – as if we were to forget that most kinds of bread require yeast – and that is what Plato can help remind us.

Some of Plato's ideas remain in the bloodstream of modern thought, but have been neglected or distorted; others need to be retrieved from their ancient context. In neither case do I suggest that we should adopt his metaphors or theories wholesale. Rather, my aim is to illuminate in Plato the structure of his effort at transforming the ethos of his own time, in order that we can appreciate the magnitude of the challenge and the terrain that any solution of our own will have to cover – as well as the junctures at which Plato's thinking misleads us or is no longer something that we can accept.

This means that religious believers and secularists alike should be able to find something of interest in this approach – and indeed, over several centuries, Plato and other strands of ancient ethics have played the role of an alternative moral resource to avoid dogmatic conflict.[49] The religious may turn to their own metaphors rather than those of Plato, but Plato can help remind them that such metaphors have to connect soul to city.

The secular may be less accustomed to seeing transformative visions as essential to political change than Plato makes clear that they must be. So too, Kantians may continue to hold that ethics must be categorically prescriptive of what is right, yet they can accept that it also matters what a society assumes the good to be. Plato won't settle any of these debates once and for all, but we can find in him something to offer to each side.

This book is called *Eco-Republic* because it displays Plato's ideal form of city and soul as a model for the greening of modern ethics and politics. The word 'republic' is a play on the English title of Plato's greatest and best-known work. But while the English title (following the Latin *respublica*) suggests a particular form of regime, the original Greek title, *Politeia*, means simply 'constitution' generally: what it means for a regime to be suitably ordered to count as a regime at all. For Plato, only the ideal form of city and soul arguably counted as a proper or real regime in this sense; perversions of that ideal could be regarded as pseudo-regimes, lacking the essential structure of unity.[50] So by *politeia*, he meant not so much a particular kind of government as the notion of good, and adequate, government altogether.[51] Likewise, by 'eco-republic' I do not mean a specifically 'republican' form of government, but rather any polity insofar as it is adequate to the demands of sustainability, which means among other things insofar as it is sustainable itself. How can we model a sustainable relation between what we may still call in archaic terms the city and the soul?

Before we can answer this question, we need to acknowledge a significant obstacle to it, for a deliberate reaction against ancient models of politics was promoted in the eighteenth-century development of a new ethic for commercial society. To see what was intended, gained, and lost by this development is the subject of the next chapter.

An Unconsciously Platonic Prologue to Chapter 2: Carbon Detox

A recent handbook for individual reduction in carbon emissions, *Carbon Detox*, is at pains to reject the most common justifications given for that aim. Don't reduce because you 'ought' to, the book surprisingly advises. Indeed, referring to the familiar argument that we must 'do our bit' to 'save the planet', author George Marshall says bluntly: 'forget this argument, because it doesn't work.'[1] Instead he counsels:

> The real reason you should reduce your own emissions is because you *want* to live differently. When you detox [from an addiction to all that causes high carbon emissions] you will do it as a statement of who you are – a smart and aware person living in the 21st century.[2]

The claim is that 'carbon detox' will not just help me live differently; it is also the 'smart' thing to do. Whereas 'people often do damaging things through ignorance', those in the know will want to do what is not only smart and savvy but also sexy and cool.

Without putting its case in these terms, *Carbon Detox* models an ancient Greek approach to ethics while rejecting the more familiar modern ought-centred ethics deriving from Christianity or from Immanuel Kant. Pursue your own flourishing – your own health and happiness – but do so in the most intelligent way; and that most intelligent way involves an ethics of self-discipline in a spirit of temperance and moderation in your own life, justice towards others, and the courage to make both happen.[3]

The author of *Carbon Detox* gives us the 'how', recommending and outlining this change in attitude. But he does not spend much time reflecting on the beliefs and habits and practices which have blocked such a transformation. Why have calls for carbon reduction so regularly fallen on deaf ears? That is a question we will seek to answer in the current chapter, while demonstrating also that the change *Carbon Detox* advocates has potentially deep roots in ancient ethics that can play a powerful role in clarifying it and demonstrating what is at stake. If ancient models of politics were largely abandoned for some good reasons in the transition to commercial society and capitalist economics, we now – as *Carbon Detox* unconsciously intimates – have newly salient reasons to adopt aspects of ancient ethics once again.

2

From Greed to Glory:
Ancient to Modern Ethics – and Back Again?

Introduction

'Hubris and greed and heedlessness': this is the way a *New York Times* columnist summed up two analyses of the cause of the financial crisis which peaked in 2008. She added one further diagnosis of the players in the financial game who provoked the meltdown: in some cases, at least, they were 'downright stupid'.[1] These condemnations epitomize some of the worst vices known to the ancient Greeks: hubris, or insolent arrogance towards one's fellows and towards the divine; greed, or rapacious and unlimited desires; heedlessness, the refusal to brook restraint, which the ancients would call intemperance; and stupidity, which in this case means not intellectual incapacity, but an inability to understand real consequences and to appreciate true value. If contemporary manuals such as *Carbon Detox* call for what are in fact – as we saw in the prologue to this chapter – Greek virtues, this commentator demonstrates that the need for them stems from the current prevalence of what the Greeks recognized as the paradigmatic vices. Seeing the relevance of these Greek failings makes it easier to appreciate what the Greeks understood by their opposites: the virtues. Justice, or fair play and mutual respect, in place of hubris; self-discipline, or intelligently directed and limited desire, in place of greed; a proper courage, which respects what is truly to be feared, in place of heedlessness and recklessness; and reason understood as wisdom, not mere calculating cunning, in place of stupidity: these constitute the four cardinal virtues of Plato's *Republic*.[2]

Successive waves of economic crisis have revealed the limitations of our current vocabulary (especially our 'official' political vocabularies) for speaking about them, limitations which mean that this lesson is repeatedly not fully learned. Remember Enron and WorldCom, and further back, Long-Term Capital Management, and further back … in each of these crises, commentators talked about the destructiveness of greed. Yet the economic and political systems did not fundamentally change. Instead, greed was portrayed as the failing of a few bad apples, who were unimportant for the evaluation of the system as a whole.

In fact, the lesson which we failed to learn from each of these crises is that the excessive greed of a few was merely the exaggeration of a system made broadly in their image: a system which was set up to allow people to push the limits for the purpose of material accumulation without any requirement to consider the bigger picture. The habits of the many were not negligible in the system: they both shaped it and were reinforced by it. And conversely: institutions are not immune to the qualities and aspirations and habits – in short, the virtues – of the individuals who operate in and by them. When Alistair Darling as British Chancellor of the Exchequer argued that bank boards of directors must exercise good individual judgement as 'the first line of defence' against financial failing, his argument made headlines – precisely because the institutional focus of modern politics, while extremely important, has tended to drive out such arguments altogether.[3] The same point was strikingly made about regulators by US Senator Christopher J. Dodd, in his reflections on the passage of the July 2010 financial reform bill: 'We can't legislate wisdom or passion. We can't legislate competency. All we can do is create the structures and hope that good people will be appointed who will attract other good people.'[4] Plato can help us to learn, and to find language to articulate, what so often otherwise escapes us: the inescapable importance of individual virtue and individual initiative. Without these, and the other imaginative insights associated with them, the most recent economic crisis will be merely one in a series, rather than decisive in reorienting the system towards a sustainable path.

If these virtues and vices are relevant to financial dangers, they are equally relevant to environmental ones. Many commentators have pointed out parallels between the two crises. Compare the mountain of heedlessly incurred, poorly understood financial debt, which eventually collapsed, to the looming pile of heedlessly incurred, poorly understood overdrafts on the carrying capacity and resilience of the planet which we are continuing to amass. In fact, as has been pointed out further by a more astute few, the two crises are not merely parallel but intertwined. Mispricing environmental goods (to the limit of zero) is not just a technical mistake, but rooted in the same outlook which mispriced financial risks: the same blinkers, the same division of labour to the point that responsibility for the system disappears. Most importantly for our purposes, the same Greek vices apply in both cases. In short, we've run up an ecological debt which on the current economic model we can't afford to pay.

The current reaching for Greek vices to diagnose the contemporary condition is a signal that we have more in common with the ancient Greeks than is often recognized. Indeed, it has recently been argued that 'our present habits, our enthusiasms, our preoccupations and our world view' have much in common with the colonies sent out by the ancient Greek city-states in their heyday (and with early imperial Rome): the issue is 'not how much we owe the Greeks and the Romans, but ... how much we are like them'.[5] Another astute student of the ancient world remarked similarly but more specifically on Greek ethical ideas, that while in some cases we could learn from them ('we shall make better sense of the ethical ideas we need if we look back to some ideas of the Greeks') in many others we rely on ideas like theirs but without acknowledging it: 'What is alive from the Greek world is already alive and is helping (often in hidden ways) to keep us alive.'[6]

These last remarks – by the late philosopher Bernard Williams – cannot be quoted uncritically for my purposes, insofar as Williams emphasized the pre-Platonic and tragic ideas and outlooks of the Greeks as most vital for us today, precisely because these reflected 'a consciousness that had not yet been touched by Plato's and Aristotle's attempts to make our ethical relations to the world fully intelligible.'[7] In other words, Williams's exploration of the Greeks sought, on the whole, to counter Plato and Platonic ideas rather than to build on them. His denial that the world is fully intelligible is an important point. Yet neither Plato nor Aristotle had ever held that the world *was* fully intelligible. For both, matter presented a limiting case, something brute which could be shaped ('informed') by meaning and purpose but which was recalcitrant, rebuffing our attempts to understand it fully. In appropriating Plato in this book, I reject the thought that he stood for full intelligibility of value and reality, while exploring the extent of intelligibility – and in particular of the soul–city relation – which he did posit. I hold that blindness to that form of (limited but real) intelligibility is debilitating. Seeking to understand the interplay between city and soul will offer empowerment, not delusion, even if its enlightenment is always incomplete.

The heart of Greek vices: pleonexia or overreaching greed

The desires and dynamics which threaten civic order came to be summed up by the ancient Greeks with a single primary concept: *pleonexia*, literally grasping-for-more, meaning an immoderate, overreaching desire for more than one's share. This was not the only Greek vice. Another was *hubris*, a form of arrogance directed especially against the gods, usurping their role with merely mortal powers and so doomed to fail. Yet it was *pleonexia* which embodied the tensions between the individual and the city. Indeed, despite full awareness of the power of ambition and *hubris*, the Greeks tended to see even tyrants as fundamentally pleonectic in their motivation. Power served greed, and so to tame power, one must tame greed.

In Plato's eyes, the Athenians in their individual and collective political capacities alike had been *pleonectic* above all in their imperial ambitions in the mid to late fifth century B.C., raking in treasure from their subordinated allies and from their conquered enemies alike. As one scholar writes:

> Destabilizing hitherto settled rules of engagement and categories of identification, including, especially, that of friend and foe, and in the absence of other principles of containment, the Peloponnesian War gave free rein to *pleonexia* in all its registers, psychic, domestic, and imperial.[8]

By contrast, the radical proposals made by Plato in the *Republic* for depriving the rulers of the ideal city of private property and private families were intended to curb such greed and its destructive effects. Without property or identifiable progeny, greed could have literally no purpose for the ideal city's rulers.

In his critique of *pleonexia*, Plato joined a broad current of Greek ethical thought. Before him, the epic and lyric poets had dramatized the dangers of excessive greed, although as has been noted, they did so without using the word *pleonexia*.[9] Homer's portrait of Achilles sulking in his tent because Agamemnon had taken a captive slave girl away from him for his own use indicted both chieftains as prey to greedy desires which threatened the survival of the entire Greek army besieging Troy. Hesiod's depiction of a quarrel between two brothers demonstrated the fatal rifts which greed could introduce into the social life of the family. Solon too, the revered sage and poet who had instituted a new legal code for Athens about a century before Socrates died, had made the abolition of debt-slavery the central plank of his reforms. Abolishing debt-slavery reined in the greedy desires of the wealthy and so prevented them from ripping apart the social fabric of the whole city.

The critique of *pleonexia* continued to shape currents in Greek ethics subsequent to Plato. His pupil Aristotle appealed to the legendary wisdom of the seven sages – 'Nothing in excess', inscribed over the entrance to the temple of Delphi along with the more famous 'Know thyself' – in building his own complex ethics around the idea of the mean: each virtue is a mean between two vices which represent complementary excesses. Moderation or self-discipline is a mean between *pleonexia* and stinginess: it is as wrong to fail to enjoy or give what is appropriate as to seek to enjoy or grasp too much. A more drastic critique of desire as such lay ahead in the hands of the Stoics (for whom the wise man wants nothing beyond virtue to make him happy) and the Sceptics (who invested as little as possible in their desires, since they could not know that anything was worth desiring). Yet while these later schools went beyond Plato and Aristotle in their critique of desire, they still agreed on the rejection of *pleonexia* itself and on its significance as a crux of individual–social relations.

The modern shift from greed to glory

Plato conceived of even the desire for power as a form of *pleonexia*, seeing ambition as a variation on the theme of grasping more than one's share. Yet he insisted that exercising power in order truly to benefit those ruled was something which those capable of doing so must undertake. While the philosophers might prefer to spend all their time in contemplation and study, they must out of necessity devote some of their time to serving the public benefit. Neither for Plato nor, *a fortiori*, for those of his contemporaries who lived for the honour they could reap in the political arena, could anyone claim a free pass to excuse himself from the concerns of the political realm.

That paradigm was challenged by the rise of Christianity, a development which can be sketched here only in the broadest of terms. Christian ambition to serve a God who transcended any particular civic allegiance (despite the complications introduced by the Christianization of the Roman Empire) threatened the comfortable links between individual and civic ambition. For many Christians, at least, the desire to secure individual salvation came into tension with the desire to serve the worldly interests of one's city, a fundamental tension which grand theories such as those of St Augustine could manage but not entirely resolve. While this led some down a quietist path of refusing to dirty their hands with worldly affairs, it led others down a newly dangerous path of religious fanaticism, in which desire was not for individual or even social gain, but rather for fundamentally remaking society in the image of one's faith. This latter path threatened civic peace while seeking glory for a particular version of religious faith, and to early modern thinkers troubled by the sixteenth-century wars of religion it would suggest the need for a wholesale rethinking of individual and public ethics.

We can trace, in other words, a broad shift from greed to glory and fanaticism as the passion conceived as most threatening to civic peace – and then a further shift, as one scholar of the subject has famously suggested, from 'the passions to the interests'.[10] Eighteenth-century thinkers offered the interest in making money and individual gain as a way to moderate the passions of glory and fanaticism which had fuelled the religious wars. From a Greek point of view, and exaggerating somewhat, we can almost say that the eighteenth-century revived *pleonexia* – but this time as a virtue, not a vice. They revived it as the lesser of two evils, encouraging people to pursue their interests in material accumulation as a safer path than pursuing their passions for heaven or for glory.

Let me clarify why it is an exaggeration to say that the eighteenth-century thinkers of commercial society treated *pleonexia* as a virtue, not a vice: this is because those thinkers – pre-eminent among them, Adam

Smith – were still imbued with Greek ethical ideals themselves. Indeed, such Greek ethical ideals were what offered them a viable alternative source of moral authority to Christianity. The individual would only live well, for Smith, if he or she resisted *pleonectic* temptation and moderated his or her behaviour according to a complex ethical code with Stoic inflections. Nevertheless, society as a whole could benefit from the greed for luxury of the rich, as their consumption would stimulate production and so provide employment for the poor. *Pleonexia* became in effect a social advantage, although not a full-blooded individual virtue. It was the commending of this social outcome which in subsequent generations would loom largest, not the seeming quibble of conscience about whether or not this represented a true individual ethical ideal.

Part of the commendation of a society built on unintended consequences – put most starkly, if controversially, by Bernard Mandeville, as we shall see – was the belief that a large society could function well only in this way. That is, if ancient ethics seemed to represent an outdated individual ideal, so ancient politics seemed to represent an outdated social possibility. The moderate revision of ancient ethics thus went hand in hand in the eighteenth and nineteenth centuries with a more wholesale, and undiscriminating, critique of ancient politics.

The context of the ancient polis

For Plato and Aristotle, the critique of *pleonexia* was advanced within the context of the city-state or *polis*. The virtues which restrained people from seeking more than their share were rewarded by participating in the *polis* in some form (even though Plato and Aristotle both challenged the terms of equal, universal citizenship for free men which democracies such as Athens had established; and even though Athens itself, like all contemporary Greek city-states, countenanced slavery). The most successful examples of the ancient *polis* prided themselves on similarly taming *pleonexia* and *hubris*. The Athenian self-praise expressed in Pericles' Funeral Oration as given by Thucydides, for example, focused on the freedom and equality which all citizens shared, which had the effect of warding off individual *pleonectic* desires and ambitions – though as critics such as Plato saw it, and as the Athenians themselves sometimes admitted, the city was liable to pursue greedy or ambitious aims in its own right.[11] Even more drastic was the Spartan model, in which the citizens did not personally pursue trade, farming, or manufacture, as did most of the Athenians whether rich or poor, but in which a small elite citizen body lived off the labours of an enslaved class which they dominated by their own military force. In Sparta, the ideal was that personal *pleonexia* was entirely tamed and subordinated to a passion for the good of the collective (although rumours of individual Spartan greed hidden behind the mask of common virtue abounded, at least in later antiquity).[12]

The making of Sparta into an icon of Greek politics as a whole – most influentially and fatefully by Jean-Jacques Rousseau – has long skewed comparisons of ancient and modern politics. Spartan virtue was almost exclusively military, its citizens living as a permanent armed guard against the possibility of revolts by their enslaved helots. The unity of the Spartan city was the unity of a tiny and embattled group, and the strict laws making ordinarily domestic activities public (such as eating in a common mess) were in turn a function of the need to maintain that drastic unity.[13] A generation after Rousseau and in the long shadow of the French Revolution, during which, '[f]or opposite exigencies, the Jacobins and the Thermidorians made all ancient Greece look Spartan', assumptions about Sparta still shaped views of ancient Greek politics more generally.[14] When in 1819, reflecting on the travails of the Revolution and its aftermath, Benjamin Constant cast the ancient model of liberty as based on public and collective warfare, in contrast to the modern one based on individual commerce,[15] his caveat that Athens was more the exception than the rule for his argument was easily overlooked.[16] An account more appropriate to Sparta has been carelessly taken by many of Constant's later readers to describe the ancient world as a whole.

Thus it was the story of Sparta which came to epitomize what would be called 'republicanism', in a line of interpretation which allied Sparta to Rome and applied this Roman label to it. (The Greeks themselves had trouble deciding what to call the Spartan model, which seemed to be a strange amalgam of monarchy and a democracy of oligarchs.) And the story which epitomized Sparta in turn, retold by Jean-Jacques Rousseau in his *Emile* of 1762, was this:

A Spartan woman had five sons in the army and was awaiting news of the
battle. A Helot [a worker enslaved by the city-state of Sparta] arrives; trem-
bling, she asks him for news. 'Your five sons were killed.' 'Base slave, did I
ask you that?' 'We won the victory.' The mother runs to the temple and gives
thanks to the gods. This is the female citizen.[17]

This Spartan mother's astonishing, almost superhuman valuing of the
welfare of her community over her own possible loss and sorrow became
an emblem of what was later considered the republican virtue of ancient
Greece. (Less heartrending but similar stories exist for ancient Rome,
above all, Cincinnatus returning to plough his humble fields after having
saved the republic.) The Spartan mother's model of austere self-denial and
dedication to the common good was viewed by many as the way to achieve
the highest form of polity: a republic sustained by the virtue of its citizens
in contrast to regimes dependent on coercion and subordination.

As Constant observed, the paradox of these regimes was that the
citizen was powerful in his civic capacity, but socially constrained as an
individual by that very common power in which he participated. As a
citizen, one wielded collective power; but as a private person, one was
at the mercy of that same power. It was against this model of the virtuous, self-denying, participatory citizen that much modern economic and
political thinking was directed.

Nevertheless, this moral did not ring as true for Athens as for Sparta,
as Constant himself acknowledged, even though in the former city, the
most liberal and in that respect atypical of the ancient Greek regimes,
the citizen body could from 508 B.C. ostracize and send into exile for
ten years whomever they collectively chose in a regular ritual. For while
Constant contrasted the ancient political economy of war and slavery
with the modern one of individual commerce, the Athenians were far
from lacking commerce (albeit that Athens also enriched herself significantly through war and slavery, above all the slave labour in the publicly
owned silver mines). The Athenian citizens, like the Romans after them,
combined their civic virtue with ardent, even avid, individual pursuit of
wealth. Most did not spend all day lounging in the Assembly: they had
businesses to run, things to do. The tension between minding one's own
business and engaging in public business was felt as a real one: it was the-
matized in speeches for the prosecution and the defence in many lawsuits,
and was a line that citizens had constantly to negotiate.

In other words, the Athenians recognized a line between the public and the private, but they drew its contours differently from the way that we do today. Instead of thinking in terms of fixed spheres, one of which (the private) is a castle shielded from public intervention, they thought in situational terms. In any given situation, an Athenian had to choose to act either as a citizen (*politēs*) or as a private individual (*idiōtēs*), concerning himself either with common concerns (*to koinon*) or with private ones (*to idion*). As one scholar observes, 'The Athenians distinguished between the individual as a private person and as a citizen rather than between the individual and the state'. *Idiōtēs* is the origin of our word 'idiot'.[18] And this is no accident. For while one did rightly sometimes pursue one's interests as an *idiōtēs*, one was truly an idiot if one did so in matters or moments when a more public-spirited engagement was required, or if one did so forgetting that one was also and always a citizen. We do inevitably have and pursue private concerns, but we can't indulge ourselves in the fantasy that there is a safe fixed line behind which we can retreat in doing so, indifferent to the effects of our actions on the public. On the contrary, it is incumbent upon us to reconsider where and how that line is to be drawn as circumstances change, and what is required of us even in respect of our private pursuits if we are to refrain from causing public harm – lest we qualify, truly, as idiots.

The modern model of commercial society as contrasted with the ancient republics

As much as he longed for the psychological simplicity of ancient Sparta, Rousseau took his predecessor Montesquieu's analysis of a republic of virtue one step further in arguing that such a simple and austere republic – based fundamentally on public-spirited virtue – was no longer possible in the modern age. The best that the moderns could do in advanced, populous societies such as France was to establish an analogue for that simplicity, in a modern republic which could accept a degree of private property (such as the smallholdings of the yeoman farmer idealized in republican Rome) while nevertheless uniting citizens through the general will and a spirited patriotism. This was only a halfway house to the modern, however, as this updating of the ancient republican ideal still demanded that citizens should eschew such amenities of modern life as luxury goods and the theatre. Luxury goods drove a concern with honour and status rather than civic equality. Attending the theatre, as Rousseau argued vehemently in relation to his native city of Geneva – a modern republic which he feared was falling from the necessary heights of virtue – encouraged people to be passive spectators, revelling in unnecessary emotional turmoil, rather than devoting their time and curbing their emotions to the service of the public good.[19]

Although Rousseau experimented with models of modern societies (political or familial or educational) which could achieve a sort of virtue similar to that of Sparta and republican Rome, many writers before and after him concluded that the Spartan model was wholly dead (a conclusion which its disastrous resurrection in the French Revolution eventually reinforced). It could not be made safe for the modern age. This was in part because modernity had replaced the civic religion of the Spartan priest-kings with the individualism of Christian salvation-seeking. Further, making public good depend on individual virtue had come to be seen as impossibly strenuous, as well as vulnerably risky. It was asking too much of individuals to stave off the corruption of self-interest forever. Instead, many eighteenth-century writers proclaimed that the public good might be brought about unintentionally, by the concatenation of actions of many different people each pursuing his or her own good. This idea took various and in some ways quite distinct forms, from the deliberate and extreme perversity of Bernard Mandeville's formula ('private vice' produces 'public virtue'), to Adam Smith's invisible hand operating in the market, and Jeremy Bentham's faith in the legislator's ability to bring such actions into harmony through law.[20]

For Smith and his friend and fellow-Scot David Hume, as well as their French correspondents Condorcet and Turgot, commercial society would truly spread enlightenment, cultivating sociability and urbanity, spreading literacy and respect for women. Theirs was a vision of empowerment and enlightenment, a class-divided but increasingly prosperous, educated, and civilized society.[21] Instead of seeking to educate self-denying Spartan mothers and fathers, their prescription was that the luxuries of the rich could stimulate the economy. As noted above, it was held that this would indirectly, and unintentionally on the part of the rich, benefit the poor, who would gain decency and dignity through employment and public education. Virtue was replaced by luxury as an organizing principle of civic prosperity, while the Greek fear that greed would lead to tyranny was to be tamed by separating economic wealth from political power (a separation never in fact fully achieved).

This optimistic vision was challenged as the first waves of industrialization decimated through disease, degradation, and early death the ranks of the poor workers sucked into their vortex. But eventually, the development of mass consumer goods, coupled with the stabilization and improvement of working conditions gained through industrial action and state regulation, allowed the fruits of commercial society to be enjoyed by most if not all. And indeed, much of the original vision has been achieved. The Western democracies are indeed, by any historical standards, prosperous, educated, and domestically civil. The most recent, and dramatic, experiment with (what is effectively) capitalism has moved in the same direction, lifting hundreds of millions of Chinese out of grinding poverty, bringing the disruption of urbanization but also its opportunities for self-reinvention.

These are not negligible achievements. And the ways in which they have scored modern hearts and minds, aspirations and appetites, should not be too readily despised. Individuality, education, aspiration, the empowerment of women, all of these are the fruits of the commercial society we have inherited. We should take care not to reject or overlook the real social gains which enlightenment and commercial society have brought.

Yet these achievements are bought at an increasingly high and increasingly unsustainable price. The applauding, or at least licensing, of *pleonexia*, which was at first done within remaining Greek ethical constraints for the individual, has long since broken those bounds. To schematize again very broadly, the nineteenth-century discovery of possible productivity gains in industry far beyond the relatively constant yields of agriculture, derived in great part from the harnessing of new forms of energy, abolished the final constraints on *pleonexia* which earlier Enlightenment appeals to Greek ethics had retained. If consumption stimulated greater productivity, then greed was not only permissible but even (albeit with concern) enjoined. *Pleonexia* went from being viewed as a signal vice, to a tolerated evil, to an accepted and sometimes even celebrated pathway from individual to social good – and now, with the erosion of any notion of voluntary moderation, it has come full circle to become a threat to social stability, health, and indeed sustainability once again. The complexity of our political world today is that, while religious fanaticism remains a threat, we can no longer afford to indulge in greed as the lesser evil.[22] To recover the language in which to explain greed as a vice, and articulate the social context of self-discipline as a virtue, it is natural to begin by exploring their original contours in the ancient Greek political imagination (as the *New York Times* columnist quoted at the beginning of this chapter seems unconsciously to have felt).

Putting the critique of consumerism in perspective

It is important to remember that criticism of commercial society, or what later came to be called 'capitalism', arose almost as soon as the great experiment itself began. Figures of the 'counter-Enlightenment' lambasted the original movement's laxity or abandonment of religion, its destruction of old organic communities of tradition (including the hierarchies of rank and sex). Romantics bewailed the alienation from nature and community wrought by urbanization and industrialization. Idealists lamented the sometimes crassly utilitarian forms of politics which failed to achieve national unity or civic harmony. Marx and Engels and their followers excoriated commodification, the alienation and exploitation of the worker, and the deceptive ideologies of nationalism and liberalism which hid that exploitation.

For the most vehement critics, the values of commercial society have been degraded, or exposed as a delusion in the first place. Luxury has become crass junk; individual dignity has become degradation; privacy has become alienation; and so on. In place of the dignified, sociable coffeehouse is the grossness and isolation of the TV dinner. In place of the development of individual powers and education is the stupefaction of consumption. In place of transcendence and community is the coarseness and insatiability of materialism. In place of dignitaries representing a distinct order of social aspiration are celebrities as avatars of popular consumption. Consumption and materialism rule the political and psychological roost.

Such harsh rejection of commercial society is increasingly expressed by some wings of the green movement. But this is not a new rejection: the criticism of materialism and consumption as corroding social bonds and eroding individual virtues is longstanding. Indeed, it has historically been one of those peculiar points on which the far Left and the far Right meet. In the 1920s and 1930s, condemnation of the lax, selfish individualism, of the hollow liberal parliamentarism, displayed by the capitalist mass democracies was advanced by communists and by proto-fascists alike. Today, some of the extreme forms of the green condemnation of capitalism can sound disturbingly like Sayyid Qutb's Islamic fundamentalist condemnation of the West. Western societies as morally lax, succumbing to physical appetites, deluded this-worldly materialists who are blind to the transcendent values of community, nature, or God: none of this is new, and we should be wary of wholesale condemnations which merely echo those of such diverse and sometimes dubious patrimony.

Further, some of what is condemned in modernity is only a particular development of widespread human characteristics. The desire for adornment, for example, is as widespread a feature of human society as one will ever see. So is the desire for mobility. And the fact that consumption has become so visible a feature of capitalist societies – because capitalism has brought it within reach of so many people – does not mean that capitalist societies are uniquely or evilly consumerist. As one economist remarks, 'Vulgar devotion to consumption alone is more characteristic of pre- and anticapitalist than of late capitalist societies.'[23] Critiques of capitalism which overly idealize the alternatives have been legion.

Some of those who point out certain commonalities between earlier reactionary (or radical) critiques of capitalism and the green movement do so in order to discredit calls for sustainability altogether. Critics such as Frank Furedi complain that green activists are self-satisfied zealots, motivated not by external realities but by the impulse to don their hairshirts and to deny the pleasures of air travel to the poor.[24] That is not the message of this book. Together with most governments and scientists in the world today, I take it as sufficiently scientifically well established that the need for action on climate change – and on a broad range of associated ecological and social challenges, from rainforest destruction to desertification and pressure on water supplies – is urgent and unequivocal.

The present purpose is rather to argue that the current Western social model can be saved from itself, by moderating it with a set of ideas against which it was forged but in light of which it can be reinvigorated. (Compare the way that Aristotle argues, in *Politics*, Book 5, 1309b–1310a, that each kind of distorted regime can be improved and saved by infusion of principles from an opposite kind.)[25] Capitalism has much that is valuable about it, and it is far from true that its denizens are hopelessly deluded, infantilized, and addicted to consumerism without any trace of higher values or social concern. Many of the satisfactions of modernity are real: being freed from the backbreaking labour and limitations of subsistence farming; being given the opportunity to develop one's individual talents and potential, rather than remaining restricted by class or caste. Outside very constrained and peculiar ecological and political spaces, pure altruism and austerity have never survived very well. There is a good reason why human history moved beyond that, and the Enlightenment was right to recognize this. The loosening of the reins of austerity is something that humans will tend, all other things being equal, to seek. What the Greeks would counsel is that they are loosed in moderation, with self-discipline, rather than with abandon.

So a better way to look at the present failings of capitalism is this. It is true that commercial societies have developed bad habits, as aspects of the original vision have been lost, and self-undermining tendencies have developed along certain undoubted fault lines in that vision. This means that many of the habits and assumptions of business-as-usual cannot continue. Expectations of what is normal and possible, what is reasonable and admirable, have to be changed, on pain of the unaffordability of the ecological debt they engender. These have to be tempered and reshaped. Rather than condemning our desires for consumption altogether – which will probably be fruitless – the question is whether we can be smarter about how we control them, limit them, and satisfy them.

Ancient ethics can re-enlighten the Enlightenment values of capitalism. They can help us act more intelligently: virtue as making appetites smarter and more self-disciplined, self-interest as genuinely enlightened, leading to a transformation of one's understanding of one's self and one's interest, rather than simply as a callow slogan. In particular, the Platonic insistence that the virtue of moderation be married to intelligence – that we be smarter about how we think about our happiness and health, in the terms of *Carbon Detox* – offers a model for how to do so. By seeing ourselves as citizens of eco-republics, who share a common good and need to take responsibility for producing it in common, as (e)co-producers, we can begin to make capitalism work sustainably.[26]

The message of this book falls therefore in the middle of the spectrum of possible responses to ecological crisis. On one extreme are those who look to technological fixes. Seed the oceans with enough iron filings and the whole problem of climate change can be solved. This approach alone is dangerous and implausible, though if conditions worsen dramatically, it may turn out to be a risk worth taking. Yet history is replete with examples of unintended consequences from such experiments, the cane toad infestation of Australia being but one example. Moreover, techno-fixes which do not stem the further production of the problem will easily be overwhelmed. It is implausible to believe that any techno-fix will be able to get us out of crisis with any measure of confidence or safety.[27]

On the other extreme is the call for a wholesale rejection of materialism, trade, and movement of peoples, in favour of localism, community, spirituality, or transcendence. This is the path which would reject the Enlightenment achievement of commercial society as fundamentally mistaken. But this too, as I have begun to argue above, is wrongheaded. To denigrate and reject capitalism outright is to ignore the value of the opportunities it has created. It is also to fail to connect with the billions of people in China, India, Southeast Asia, Latin America, and sub-Saharan Africa for whom capitalism of some kind – while needing substantial political restraint, regulation, and liberty, to be sure – remains the most practical path to a better future.

That leaves the paths in the middle. There are many admirable people and organizations who have blazed valuable trails here: from Jonathon Porritt's book *Capitalism as if the World Matters* to the New Economics Foundation to the Earth Charter.[28] Many important policy ideas have emerged in this space. What this book seeks to contribute is a map of how to rethink the social and psychological vision so as to restrain the excesses of capitalism while still reaping its real benefits. It is not consumption per se, but unbridled, *pleonectic* consumption that loses sight of the unity of the good and the value of health, which threatens the sustainability and even the stability of our societies. There is no way back from 'Sex in the City' woman to Spartan mother. Yet the ancient Athenians, together with their son and critic Plato, can help us to learn how to produce collective prosperity by incorporating an alertness to the civic good into our self-enrichment, and recognizing in each of our individual roles that we can't afford to be wholly indifferent to that good.

Indeed Plato's *Republic* itself points to the fact that justice and the virtues arise only when consumption and even some luxuries are already in play. No justice is to be found in a 'city of pigs' (372d, Lee translation altered), which is Glaucon's scornful term for a primitive agricultural society without developed arts of architecture, cooking, music, theatre, or other such accoutrements of civilization, because none is needed there. Justice and the other virtues arise to tame the 'fever' (372e) which inflames societies that have developed such arts and sciences. It is true that Socrates calls the 'city of pigs' actually a healthy city (372e) – and we shall see in Part II that health is the underlying requirement in the *Republic*'s framework for achieving happiness. Yet this does not imply that there is only a single path to health. One can be healthy before ever contracting a fever, but one can also recover health after a fever – albeit with one's constitution permanently altered by the experience of the illness. That is the *Republic*'s attitude to the health of the city. We don't have to give up all our luxuries – but we do have to think seriously about how they can be kept from destroying our individual and social health, incorporating them instead into an equilibrium informed by the virtues.

Sources of indifference and 'idiocy'

This chapter has traced how the modern idea of reliance on unintended consequences has come to replace and marginalize the virtues as a path to social benefit. Reliance on such a mechanism of indirection licenses indifference on the part of the individual to the overall social good: she thinks herself entitled to ignore it, even perhaps sees herself as obligated to ignore it, if the social mechanism of indirection is to work its wonders. In the next chapter, we will explore a kindred source of false confidence licensing the individual to ignore the social good, and indeed the social effects of her actions. This is the idea of negligibility: that the effects of individual action are negligible with respect to social outcomes, so it simply doesn't matter how she acts (irrespective of whether she can also confidently invoke the invisible hand as a reason for acting to pursue a narrow definition of her own advantage only). This cluster of ideas and assumptions as a whole produces a kind of indifference on the part of the individual to the effects of her actions, whether in a spirit of entitlement or, for some, in a spirit of despair about being unable to make a real positive difference. Before being able to appreciate the Platonic insistence on the mutual constituting of individual and city, we need therefore to clear away this further obstacle to accepting it. Chapter 3 therefore tackles the idea of negligibility and its implications directly.

Prologue to Chapter 3: Plato's Ring of Gyges

[…] men practise it [justice] against their will and only because they are unable to do wrong. This we can most easily see if we imagine that a just man and an unjust man have each been given liberty to do what they like, and then follow them and see where their inclinations lead them. We shall catch the just man red-handed in exactly the same pursuits as the unjust, led on by self-interest, the motive which all men naturally follow if they are not forcibly restrained by the law and made to respect each other's claims.

(The character of Glaucon speaking in Plato's *Republic*, Book 2, 359b–c)

Plato's brothers are dissatisfied with a display of argument by Socrates in which he had sought to persuade another character that 'injustice never pays better than justice' (354a). One of them, the dashing Glaucon, argues that justice is only a second-best compromise which people make when they think they can't get away with more profitable injustice. To illustrate that claim, Glaucon invokes a story about an ancestor of Gyges, a barbarian king (the story is usually referred to as the 'ring of Gyges'). This ancestor was a humble shepherd in the service of his own king at the time of an earthquake which revealed a buried corpse wearing a gold ring, which the shepherd appropriated and put on.

He was wearing this ring when he attended the usual meeting of shepherds which reported monthly to the king on the state of his flocks; and as he was sitting there with the others he happened to twist the bezel of the ring towards the inside of his hand. Thereupon he became invisible to his companions, and they began to refer to him as if he had left them. He was astonished, and began fingering the ring again, and turned the bezel outwards; where-upon he became visible again. When he saw this he started experimenting with the ring to see if it really had this power, and found that every time he turned the bezel inwards he became invisible, and when he turned it outwards he became visible. Having made his discovery he managed to get himself included in the party that was to report to the king, and when he arrived seduced the queen, and with her help attacked and murdered the king and seized the throne. (359e–360b)

Anyone finding such a ring would act similarly, indulging in injustice with impunity, Glaucon avers. If we think we can get away with satisfying our lust and greed, we'll do so – and if we don't, everyone knowing of our foregone opportunity would think us 'a most miserable idiot' for having foregone it (360d). This is proof that despite their public protestations of the value of justice – made in order to preserve the second-best norm of justice 'for fear of being wronged' (360d) – people don't actually hold justice to be a true intrinsic good. Rather, Glaucon endorses one aspect of the claim made by the earlier and unsuccessful challenger of Socrates (Thrasymachus), rephrasing it as the claim that 'no man thinks justice pays him personally' (360c).

For Glaucon, the ring of Gyges is a thought-experiment only. No one can in real life actually know himself to be secure in possessing the kind of impunity that such a magic ring would provide. Yet there is a modern version of the ring of Gyges which has exercised a pernicious effect on contemporary thought. This is the idea that the effect of individual action is negligible in its effect on many social outcomes, and, in particular, on many actions designed to achieve sustainability, for example by reducing greenhouse gas emissions. By negligible here is meant not that the actions are those of a ghost, completely causally inert, but rather that they are so minimal with respect to bringing about a specified effect that they can be ignored. Their ignorability makes them analogous to the invisibility of the actions taken by someone using the ring of Gyges. In both cases, although for different reasons, such reasons can and will be systemati-cally overlooked by anyone studying the specified effects.

Social scientists and popular culture have combined to tell people today that their actions are negligible and irrelevant, so that they may as well indulge in their chosen vices since their actions make no difference. If the ring of Gyges story was told as a challenge to Socrates to prove why being just is advantageous to the individual, the modern idea of negligibility is often told – or at least heard – as a licence to those hearing it not to bother being just or virtuous at all, because doing so will cost them more than its minimal effect on the outcome is worth. For his purposes of defending justice, Plato had to rebut the ring of Gyges challenge over the course of the *Republic*. For our purposes of sketching a sustainable ethic, we have to rebut the premise of negligibility and its implications. This is the purpose of Chapter 3.

3

Underpinning Inertia: The Idea of Negligibility

Glaucon was troubled by the thought that if people could act with assured impunity, they would pursue their lust and greed irrespective of the demands of justice. Modern writers and thinkers are too often untroubled by a parallel thought. Rather than worrying that if people could act with assured impunity, they would act unjustly, they assert that it is entirely possible in many important domains for people to assume that their actions will be negligible in their effects on particular social outcomes. Whether or not this assertion is intended to encourage or simply to describe, it can have the effect of licensing people to indulge in lust, greed, or other vices irrespective of the demands of justice or (I will argue) the social good.

Negligibility is a well-established and precise term in economics and political science: it is the assumption that each agent is so small a player that what he or she individually does in such pursuit doesn't materially affect the social outcome. It has been formulated as a technical point in economic theory, treating each firm as a price-taker in a competitive market, in which (barring monopolies and other distortions of market power) no one firm's actions can alter the price which emerges at equilibrium.[1] That technical point however has generated a broader perspective of negligibility for individual agents of any kind in relation to social phenomena. To put the point colloquially: negligibility implies that as an individual, much of what I do is irrelevant to social outcomes – and so, as an implication, I can do whatever I want without concerning myself with its social effects, but at the same time, I am powerless to effect significant social change through my own actions. Negligibility purchases impunity with powerlessness. Hence it blocks individual action to effect social change. While it does not exhaust the current social ethos, it unifies and structures a wide range of its elements, as an underlying assumption which may not be conscious but which expresses itself in tacit or explicit expectations about appropriate action. Tackling it directly is therefore a prerequisite to the imaginative restructuring of that ethos for which Plato will provide a model in Part II.

My concern to rebut the presumption of negligibility does not derive from the belief that individual action is the only path to the political and social changes that are required. Political negotiation, new incentives, and infrastructural investment are crucial paths to follow. Yet even these require individual initiative to be launched, as well as the support of constituencies ultimately composed of individuals. It is a fallacy to see the need for individual action and the need for social or political action as opposed, as if by attending to one, one is ignoring the other. In fact the opposite is true. Individual action – of a variety of kinds, to be explored below – is a key constituent of bringing about social and political change. This is a lesson which appeal to Plato will reinforce in Part II: in his terms, an interest in the mutually shaping link between the city and the soul is not a substitute for politics, but an essential element of it. For the moment, however, we need to reinforce it by dispelling the illusion of negligibility. For if we remain prey to that illusion, we will be fatalistic about the value of attempting any kind of individual action for social change at all. Inertia, not initiative, will reign.

An introduction to negligibility

> [...] probably all the great sea fisheries are inexhaustible; that is to say that nothing we do seriously affects the number of fish.
> (T. H. Huxley, speech at the International Fisheries Exhibition, 1883)

Negligibility holds that the actions of any one individual in such societies are insignificant with respect to certain specified overall outcomes. T. H.

Huxley's remark quoted above illustrates the confidence in negligibility which humans have long felt with respect to natural systems.[2] Surely the earth is so large, its species so numerous, that individual human actions are irrelevant to its ongoing life. We know that in the case of the Mauritian dodo, such reasoning had tragic consequences. The net effect of myriad individual acts of hunting was to extinguish those species. But we are reluctant to draw the same conclusion in respect of many other forms of individual action. In particular, we are reluctant to apply it to our individual contributions to carbon accumulation in the atmosphere, and we are reluctant to apply it to other aspects of our individual contributions to social life. We have developed certain habits of expecting that our actions will be negligible and so imagining that we can be indifferent to their effects. I will explore the intuitive modern shape of this assumption, before looking at a specific proposal to diagnose and solve it.

Mass society

The idea that the modern person is a negligible part of his or her polity can already be found in the early nineteenth century, in Benjamin Constant's reflections on the difference between the modern politics of representative government and the ancient politics of collective sovereign decision which we met in Chapter 2. Whereas '[t]he most obscure republican [citizen] of Sparta or Rome had power', he remarked, in the same speech given in 1819 from which we quoted earlier, '[t]he same is not true of the simple citizen of Britain or the United States. His personal influence is an imperceptible part of the social will which impresses on the government its direction.'[3] And he went on to stress the theme of imperceptibility: 'Lost in the multitude, the [modern] individual can almost never perceive the influence he exercises. Never does his will impress itself upon the whole; nothing confirms in his eyes his own cooperation.'[4]

This comment on modern politics and the negligibility of the individual within it was reinforced by analyses of politics, economics, and society later in the nineteenth century and in the early twentieth century. To sum up these analyses in a single image, modern politics is based on the idea of a faceless mass society and the imagery of the industrial machine, in which we are all mere cogs and so broadly irrelevant to the outcome of the whole. From the lumpenproletariat of Marx and Engels, to the crowd psychology of Gustave le Bon, to the theorists of mass advertising (Freud's brother-in-law among the first, followed by Vance Packard), mass media (the disillusioned Walter Lippmann), and the large corporation (Adolf Berle and Gardiner Means), the transition from the nineteenth to the twentieth century brought with it a politics of the masses. To the jaundiced eye of Joseph Schumpeter, for example, democracy came to mean merely the right of people to choose one leader from a handful of the self-advancing elite, and doing so beset by propaganda and irrationality.[5]

The political fear of the masses, the attempt to cow, or at least to mould, and contain them through some sort of leadership principle, was matched in the same and other quarters by cultural contempt for them. From Matthew Arnold's sneer at philistinism, to the Frankfurt School's equal disdain for the masses who had chosen Nazism and those who had chosen American capitalism, the view that most people are merely fodder for mass culture matched the view that they are fodder for political manipulation. The idea that any one ordinary person could cultivate sufficient virtue to contribute to social growth, rather than being merely the object of social manipulation and historical forces beyond her ken, became suspect. The very thought that individual virtue matters was squeezed out of the framework of a society imagined in mass terms. Never mind that the failure of a single 'cog' can cause disaster, as in the endangerment of the Apollo 13 mission or the Challenger space shuttle tragedy; the politics of the masses, whether positive or negative, insists on the irrelevance of a single individual.

The result of these historically shaped attitudes is a widespread scepticism and cynicism, viewing individual effort in relation to many social problems as negligible. Roughly, the complaint goes as follows: whatever I might do is too insignificant to make a difference, so as a single person in a mass society, why should I bother acting at all? In fact, corporations and countries have been quick to pick up an analogue of this point, to argue that they too are only tiny players in the national or global picture and so should be let off the hook of culpability for climate change.

Industries excuse themselves from acting by pointing out the relatively minor contribution which they make to national or global greenhouse gas emissions. The most recent estimate by the Intergovernmental Panel on Climate Change (IPCC),[6] for example, put the global contribution of aviation to man-made greenhouse gas emissions at 2 percent (the UK ministry DEFRA in 2007 estimated it to constitute 6 percent of total UK emissions). Campaigners and scientists contest those figures: the phenomenon of radioactive forcing, which makes aircraft emissions more dangerous to the climate because of the high atmospheric level at which they are emitted, means that the total global effect even now may be closer to 4 percent as the International Institute for Sustainable Development (IISD) has argued.[7] But for our purposes here this controversy, though crucial in itself, is irrelevant. Grant for the sake of argument that the current level of equivalent emissions is already 4 percent today, as the IISD critics urge. Even so, the current level seems small. We are easily inclined to think that to tackle something which is only 4 percent, or 2 percent, of a problem, is not worth doing; it appears to be a distraction from tackling the big problem as a whole.

The same argument is repeated at the regional and sectoral level. The former UK environment minister, Phil Woolas, asked about a proposal to include regionally dominant aircraft and shipping industries in the EU carbon trading scheme from which they were previously exempt, said, 'Why should Merseyside pay?'[8] I take him to have been claiming that Merseyside is only a relatively tiny proportion of UK emissions, and so it makes no sense to include its emissions in a cap when doing so will have tiny benefits compared to great disproportionate harm on its key industries.

And so too at country level. I take the example of the United Kingdom here, but it is important to note that similar questions have begun to be raised about the United States: even its clearly significant contribution is now exceeded in absolute (though not per capita) terms by that of China. But consider the more extreme case of the United Kingdom, a country responsible on one estimate for only 1.7 percent of total global emissions from the consumption of energy.[9] Its absolute contribution is dwarfed by that of the United States, and its per capita contribution is cast into the shade by the rapid growth in emissions from countries like India and China.[10] In such contexts, it can seem pointless for the United Kingdom to act; pointless for the individual industry to act; and by analogy pointless for the individual citizen (of almost any country) to act. In seeing ourselves as members of a global mass, we easily see ourselves as powerless and ineffectual. We see ourselves as impotent (nothing we do makes a real difference) and therefore innocent (our emissions, in fact all our actions, are irrelevant to the real problem). In this light, the moral division of labour seems to be clear: those making the big impact (whoever they are) should be responsible, but the rest of us are off the hook, exonerated by our anonymous negligibility.

Is this view of our own impotence, irrelevance, and innocence a mistake? I will argue that it is. We need to distinguish four claims which might be inferred from this broad phenomenon. The first (1) is that it is *irrational on a cost-benefit analysis* to take action A, because the social benefits of doing A are so small as to be outweighed by the costs of doing A. The second (2) is a stronger version of that irrationality claim: it is *irrational as an analytic claim* to take action A, because doing A makes no difference to objective O, so it is irrational to do A in order to bring about O. The third (3) is an assertion of *imperceptibility*: doing A makes a difference to O which cannot be perceived, and so you should not do A to bring about O.[11] The fourth (4) is the straight claim of *negligibility*: doing A makes only a very small difference to bringing about O, and there is no evident threshold such that it could be known to contribute to bringing about O on its own, so you should not do A to bring about O. Each of these is a distinct normative thesis, although they are in some cases interdependent: (1) may rest on (4), for example. The case which interests me is (4), which I take to be the emitting or refraining from emitting of some unit of greenhouse gases: where we admit and can perceive that doing A makes *some* difference, albeit a very small one, to bringing about O, but there is no evident threshold (as there is in the case of voting) by which it is possible or likely to be known to bring about O on its own.

Why should we act when our action is expected to be negligible with respect to some outcome, so defined? The first point is that the definition of the outcome which rationally and morally concerns us is both crucial and not to be taken for granted. One possible such outcome is the total global aggregate of greenhouse gases. But it is also rational to define my goal, and so the relevant outcome, in terms of the emissions of my country, my city, my family, or even myself over time. We may have independent moral reasons or even obligations to care about each of these outcomes, not simply about the global aggregate; on the same basis, the moral good that we do in donating money to save the life of one child is not defeated by the fact that other children will still die from diseases that could have been prevented had we ourselves or others donated more.[12] Huxley's assertion, as quoted above, implied that if all we cared about were extinction, our action in catching any one fish will be negligible to bringing about that outcome and so can be taken with impunity. But we might decide to frame the problem in terms of reliable fish supplies for our sake, or a sustainable fish population for the sake of the ecosystem as a whole, or of our own contribution to these goods, in each of which cases the threshold would be far different. It may be psychologically useful and even morally required to choose reference points which will make one's contribution appear even more significant. Rather than considering the emissions of one's country or the world as the reference point, one may instead choose to consider the carbon emissions of one's city. An example of success in such a strategy is the way that the mayor of Bogotá, Colombia, worked to reduce municipal water consumption by reporting it in the newspaper daily, so that citizens could feel that doing their part made it go up or down.[13]

Nor is the choice of more individualized and localized reference points necessarily arbitrary. Recent research in healthcare, for example, documents the dramatic effects which a few high users of health services have on the cost of the system for their insurance or civic cohort: to whatever insurance pool these people are assigned, they are likely to drive up the costs drastically, if they do not receive an equally drastic form of individualized medical and social attention.[14] Part of the value of recognizing the contributions of individuals to social outcomes is that it also helps us to recognize the value of treating individuals as such, rather than in mass terms. Plato in another dialogue, the *Statesman*, emphasized the ideal but impossible political arrangement of individualized attention, having his protagonist the Eleatic Visitor ask rhetorically, 'how would anyone ever be capable ... of sitting beside each individual perpetually throughout his life and accurately prescribing what is appropriate to him' (295a–b).[15] Although it is impossible to go this far, moves to assign individual health coaches and hold individualized conferences of care in order to drive down excessive costs one by one begin to approximate such attention, and so to defeat both the prescription of mass care and the presumption of individual irrelevance to mass outcomes.

The second point is that even if our contribution is very small in relation to our chosen threshold, there may be both instrumental and intrinsic reasons to care about it: instrumental, insofar as the structure of the problem may be such that there is no big emitter out there whose contribution dwarfs ours; intrinsic, insofar as we often have reasons to do things which cannot themselves be decisive in bringing about some desired overall outcome. We have moral reasons to give a small donation to a cancer charity even if it does not in itself help to attain any salient threshold (I leave aside the question of whether we have reasons to act where doing so could not make any difference at all in relation to any salient threshold, since this is not the case with carbon emissions). This is a logical point. As one philosopher puts it, 'It can be rational to do something that makes an actual positive difference to a good thing … even if the precise contribution that one makes is not of large enough grain by itself to bring about the good thing.'[16] Reasons for acting are not automatically defeated by apparent negligibility.[17]

Finally, having chosen a threshold by which to assess the negligibility or otherwise of our contribution, we need to recognize that our actions can have indirect as well as direct effects in bringing that outcome about. Those indirect effects may include acting as an example that influences others, or helping to generate market demand which acts as an incentive for others, or contributing to a critical mass which will act as data for others who have to take political decisions, for example. Once multiplied by these indirect effects, our actions may cease to count as negligible at all. And given that these indirect effects are very often uncertain, unpredictable, and hard to measure, there is a case for erring on the side of their possibility by taking action A rather than foreclose them from the outset by deciding not to take it.[18] In what follows we explore direct and indirect effects in more detail, focusing on the political case of companies, sectors, and companies which claim negligibility on analogy with the individual case.

Direct effects: really negligible?

The central argument of the *Republic* is launched at 368e–369a, when Socrates suggests that justice in the individual soul can be discovered by looking first at justice 'on a larger scale' in the city, comparing this to looking first at large letters in order then to be able to decipher the same letters writ small. Following this model, we consider in this section the case of contributions by various industries, sectors, and even

countries to greenhouse gas emissions, in order to assess the remark-
ably common assertion that these are so small as to be negligible (the
question of negligible with respect to what being often elided). So, is it
reasonable for any industry or country to let itself off the hook by pointing out what a relatively small percentage contribution it makes to total
global emissions?

Emphatically not. This move relies on a background assumption that
because climate change is a big problem, it must have a single big cause,
and that it makes sense to tackle that big cause – responsible for say 70
percent of the problem – rather than tinkering around the edges with the
small stuff. But this is simply not true.

First, every single emission contributes to the composite problem,
which is made of trillions of tiny emissions. Thus there is no threshold for
making a literal difference to the problem: every single atom of greenhouse
gas emission saved is a literal improvement. There might be thresholds
for certain feedback effects, such that beyond them, saving a given unit
of emission is unable to make a difference in stopping the effect. But the
science is so complex that it is difficult to be certain that we know what
those thresholds are. The more plausible objection comes from another
angle: that most emissions come in bunches, and that it makes practical sense to tackle the biggest bunches first, rather than worrying about
small ones. That might be true if there were a 70-percent-(or more)-of-
the-problem-sized bunch, and if it were the case that focusing on smaller
bunches simply distracts from focusing on that very large bunch. In the
case of CFC emissions in the 1970s, for example, the emissions could
be easily traced to a limited set of industries and companies (refrigera-
tor and deodorant manufacturers among them) and so it made sense to
focus directly on them. But the claim is false on both counts in the context of climate change. Emissions are spread throughout the economy,
in a vast number of sectors and industries, indeed in all of them, as even
manufacture of windmills itself takes some CO_2 emission (though the
net emissions per unit of energy generation will be far less than with
fossil fuels), and anyone using a computer or heating a building will be
generating emissions. So to try to reduce emissions requires tackling a
wide range of sources, each of which will only be making a relatively low
contribution to the whole problem, and no one of which distracts from
a more vital solution to another.[19] Every possible solution is a relatively
small percentage of the solution, while no possible solution is more than

a relatively small percentage. In these circumstances it is illogical to take refuge in being oneself only a small percentage of the problem, because there is no other comparable body whose contribution is of a dramatically different order of magnitude and who therefore has significantly more reason to act than oneself.

There is one further wrinkle here, which is that the very assignment of percentages of the problem depends on what else one chooses to hold constant. The aviation industry has made much of the fact that not only did the IPCC estimate aviation's contribution to total emissions as 2 percent in 1999 in its *Special Report on Aviation and the Global Atmosphere*, but they also in that report predicted that it would be only 3 percent of total emissions in 2050. But that is based on an expectation of a roughly business-as-usual course leading to total global emissions doubling in that period. It is a prediction in other words of a bad scenario, not of one which the IPCC recommends the world actually follow. And within the United Kingdom, the Department of Transport predicted in 2007 that aviation's share of UK emissions could rise to 21 percent by 2050. But the real crunch comes when one considers not what emissions are *likely to be* on current trends by 2050, but rather what the UK national carbon budget *should be* by that date. A 2006 working paper by the Tyndall Centre for Climate Change Research, 'Growth scenarios for EU & UK aviation: contradictions with climate policy', predicted that aviation emissions would (on rates of growth even lower than those current at that time) rise to 50 to 100 percent of what the total UK carbon budget should be by that date. Apparent smallness at one time and in one frame becomes something very different in the context of another.

The indirect effects of individual action

Let's grant however that while my individual emissions do add up and fractionally weigh on the scale, nevertheless with respect to a global threshold – which for the sake of argument I will now consider to be the relevant one – they seem unlikely to make a difference. That argument doesn't prove however that my action in cutting my own emissions, let alone political actions I might take to lobby for emissions regulation, is equally negligible in its indirect effects. Let's consider each of those points in turn.

First, to elaborate on the structure of the problem assuming a global threshold. If there is a tipping point to solving the global problem, and we don't expect that our action will serve to reach it, then it can seem unimportant to contribute our mite. It may weigh on the scales but be inadequate to solving the problem. If so, then while it might not be strictly irrational to cut back ourselves, perhaps it is not a good place to invest individual effort; in a world of scarce time and human energy, perhaps we should just focus on something else.[20]

This sort of view is widespread in psychological and sociological research. As one focus group respondent put it:

> Yeah, I feel the same way like what am I gonna do. America isn't even sign-ing up to the Kyoto Agreement and you think it's such a big country and if it's not doing that and their petrol is so cheap, then what difference am I going to make? I care about the environment but don't see that I'll make a difference.[21]

And even environmental campaigners themselves sometimes assert the negligibility of individual emission reductions, as a way of trying to pri-oritize state action: one debate on the BBC Radio 4 *Today* programme featured an environmental campaigner dismissing the relative merits of the rival 'eco-cars' being driven by various politicians by asserting that the benefit gained from an individual driving such a car was like: '... far-ting in a hurricane, when compared to a plane load of tourists heading off to Tenerife on a 757'.[22]

Is my contribution really irrelevant? One question here is what it is that I take myself to be trying to achieve in making my small instru-mental contribution to reducing the problem. If it is aimed at tipping the balance here and now in relation to the global threshold, it is probably not adequate to getting over any threshold of significance in making a difference, and so may feel psychologically irrelevant even though it is not strictly instrumentally so. But if it is aimed at advancing the cause,[23] so that it can be seen as increasing the evidence for the growing concern and commitment of the populace, and so can play a role in changing others' perception, including that of politicians, about the utility of further action, then it cannot be known to be inadequate in advance, and so should and need not feel, or be, irrelevant.

This explanation is modelled on an argument in a related debate: why people vote. Voting has long been thought to exhibit the same sort of negligibility problem that we have been exploring: if my one vote is unlikely to make a difference, why should I bother to cast it, when I could be using my time and energy in more effective ways? Interestingly, whereas some social scientists argue that on the assumption of negligibility people should (rationally) not vote, others argue that people should (rationally) vote – but may permissibly vote irrationally, indulging their pet fantasies or fears on the grounds that they won't do any harm.[24]

Despite certain disanalogies (the thresholds are clearer in voting, for example), it is instructive to analyse the debate over voting in parallel stages to the arguments I have been making above. First, one can argue that no single vote can be known to be negligible or irrelevant in advance: more than one election has indeed been decided by a single vote.[25] Yet still, even though we know that there is a chance of being decisive in a given election, we may think this is very unlikely and so think about investing our energy elsewhere – just as we think that the small chance of being decisive in getting over a climate threshold (and given that these are inherently less clear and knowable than the voting threshold) may mean it's more worth our while to worry about something other than cutting our own individual emissions.

The second step however is to think harder about what it is that one might achieve by voting, or in the parallel case, by reducing one's own emissions. Here again, social scientists and political theorists offer a range of theories. One view is that what I'm trying to achieve in voting is to play my part in electing my candidate – if I think she has a reasonable chance of winning; if I don't think she does, then I'm trying to signal that at least I support her to encourage the scattered few who might do so also.[26] Another view, however, has the advantage of uniting these two cases (where I think my candidate has a reasonable chance, and where I think she doesn't) under a single explanation. What I want to do is to advance my cause, and so I vote not to be decisive (though I may be) but because I care about how many votes my candidate gets, whatever the chances of her winning might turn out to be.

Indeed, I might not know what her chances of winning are. I may not always be able to tell whether I am a mainstream voter voting for

a mainstream and plausible candidate, or a lone wolf voting for someone who hasn't a hope of winning. What if my candidates have always
in the past lost, but it is just possible that others are willing to act this
time, though I can't know that for sure? This can happen in the context
of voting when upsets are possible but seem antecedently unlikely: consider the 2010 upset of Massachusetts voters electing Scott Brown as their
first Republican senator in decades. It is even more likely to be the case
with climate change, where we lack the established habits and history
of voting, and where the boundaries of normality are in the process of
shifting fast.

Is a person's installation of solar panels more like her voting in an
election in which she is reasonably certain that many others will vote
for her candidate, so that she is aiming to contribute to a sufficiency of
energy saved (votes cast) even though her own panels will not be strictly
necessary? Or is it more like her being a lone wolf, in which case her
solar panels are a symbolic affirmation of her identity even though so
few others are likely to install them that they will make only a tiny (but
not, as argued above, strictly negligible) contribution to saving power?
On the cusp of social change, she may not know which situation she is
in, and indeed the situation may be in the process of changing, without
her knowing that a tipping point has been reached.

In other words, the concern with advancing one's cause is a common
motivation shared by both the mainstream voter and the lone wolf, and,
indeed, irrespective of whether I know or can guess which of these I am.
If I care about advancing my cause, I won't consider my vote negligible,
whatever I think the outcome is likely to be – and all the more so, knowing
that my best guess about that may turn out to be wrong. By supporting
my candidate, I encourage her other potential supporters in the future
(and if I support her in ways besides voting, I encourage her other potential supporters in this very election). And this is the common experience
of social change. Social change is precisely the project in which one is
working from negligibility now to mainstream in the future: to join it is
to advance a cause, and one way to do that is by incorporating a new set
of values into the political imagination. Part III will consider in more
detail how this might be done. Here, our concern is to show that one
need not and should not be hamstrung by fears of negligibility, whether
in taking individual instrumental action or in engaging in movements
of politics or social change.

How to choose where to invest one's energies? In particular, if one is more likely to have an impact on others through advocacy, should one bother cutting one's own emissions in the meantime?[27] On the one hand, many routes to cutting individual emissions themselves require concerted social action: bicycling to work is easier and safer with designated cycle lanes, or at least a critical mass of other cyclists. On the other hand, there is power in deciding not to wait for others to change, but, as Mahatma Gandhi exhorted, to 'be the change that one wants to see in the world'. A Platonic picture, too, starts with the possibility of individual reorientation: the person pulled more by love of learning than by greed for money; the person who turns, albeit compelled by necessity, around in the cave to face the light. Part II will argue that the Platonic portrait of the virtues – uniting intelligence, courage, moderation, and justice – fleshes out the thought that the smart thing to do is to act well oneself, whatever others decide to do. This is not to deny the importance of politics, but to say that it begins in part with the personal. The person who embodies a new outlook becomes in virtue of that very fact a node in a new political imagination, the first step to creating a new social ethos.

Recognizing this helps us to respond to a final objection: the protest that it is unfair to expect me to act when others do not. Fairness itself, in the shape of reciprocity ('I will if you will'), is a powerful motivation for norm-compliance.[28] So breaches of reciprocity readily invite the objection, 'why should I, if you won't?' I do not at all disparage the value of reciprocity; it is a powerful motivator, and should be harnessed as such in organizing social relations in relation to desired social aims. Yet if it is absent, is that in itself a reason to shirk contributing one's mite to those aims? Asking that question requires us to clarify exactly what is at stake in such an objection.[29] Its usual home is in relation to compulsory regulation rather than voluntary action: people naturally resist unfair coercion ('why should I have to, if you don't?'). In the context of individual voluntary action however, unfairness seems to reduce to a core of fearing to be taken advantage of. It is as much a cognitive objection as a moral one. While in the compulsory context I resist being unfairly coerced (treated: that is, being the passive recipient of an unfair action), in the voluntary context I resist being a patsy (that is, being the agent of my own undoing, by choosing to worsen my own situation relative to that of others).

So the objection only bites if I evaluate taking the action in question as worsening my situation relative to that of others. Because of this, showing that it can be sensible for me to choose to act plays an important role in defusing the unfairness objection. The more we find inherent reasons to act, reasons that become meaningful against the background of a changed imaginative context, the less the unfairness objection is likely to worry us. If I decide that it is not pointless for me to reduce or to advocate, I have at least some reason to do so irrespective of what you choose to do. Thus individual action is not irrational or pointless even in the face of widespread social inertia. On the contrary, such initiative – and in particular initiatives to reshape the social imagination – constitute an important path for moving forward.

If negligibility is defeated, what follows?

By this point I hope to have persuaded you, the reader, that it is a mistake to take for granted that your actions are negligible in shaping social outcomes, an assumption which is a key plank in sustaining the current inertia. What then, you may wonder, should you do? The remainder of this chapter will sketch out the claim that non-negligibility requires us to assess not only existing legal rules, but also the choices that we make within them, in light of a broader social ethos, in particular, in the case that concerns us, an ethos of sustainability. Here I join forces with the argument reported in Chapter 1 about the indispensability of an ethos of justice to achieving a just society, on the grounds that even just rules leave open individual choices which then have important consequences in shaping the level of justice attained overall. Likewise, an ethos of sustainability is indispensable in achieving a sustainable society, on the grounds that even sustainable social arrangements (which we are far from yet achieving) leave open individual choices when then have important consequences in shaping the level of sustainability achieved overall. While, as was stressed by G. A. Cohen in the case of justice, this does not close down all 'personal prerogative' to 'pursue self-interest to some reasonable extent',[30] it does give each person a responsibility for orienting his or her choices in light of an ethos of sustainability. In comparison to Cohen's justice argument, however, we have to go one step further. Whereas that presentation analysed static societies in which an ethos of justice had either been achieved or not, our concern is with how a new ethos can be introduced and with the interlocking roles of political imagination and the individual in doing so. So rather than simply being able to play one's part in an existing ethos, the question is what responsibility each of us bears for helping to bring a new ethos into being by changing the ways in which we imagine its basic elements.

I will examine three central elements (far from exhaustive) in what a new ethos of sustainability (or sustainable ethos) would look like and how an individual might help to bring it about, each progressively more demanding. The first stays within the limits of the existing legal framework (broadly defined by Mill's harm principle) but observes the implications of redefining harm. The second broadens this out to a redefinition of costs and benefits more broadly. And the third tackles the question, is obeying the law – even a law which takes account of these new understandings of harms, costs, and benefits – enough to achieve sustainability? Or is an ethos reshaped by new imaginative perspectives and informing individual actions – not every action necessarily, but also not no action – essential to bringing about a sustainable society?

Step 1: the harm principle

A free society rests on the freedom of the individual to pursue whatever goals she chooses, so long as her doing so does not cause harm to others. That maxim of John Stuart Mill's mid-nineteenth-century classic *On Liberty* remains a benchmark of liberal political philosophy, even though it is not exceptionless and specifies only a necessary condition rather than a sufficient one for state coercion: 'the only purpose for which power can be rightfully exercised over any member of a civilized community, against his will, is to prevent harm to others.'[31] It can be linked to the contrast between the 'liberty of the ancients' and the 'liberty of the moderns' drawn by Mill's older Swiss contemporary, Benjamin Constant, which we met earlier.[32] According to Constant, the 'liberty of the ancients' (in particular, the ancient Greeks) consisted in the freedom of citizens to participate in democratic decision-making about collective aims which might make profound interventions in their own lives and choices, while the 'liberty of the moderns' consists in the freedom of citizens to be left alone to choose and pursue their own goals and values. As he wrote, 'The aim of the ancients was the sharing of social power among the citizens of the same fatherland: this is what they called liberty. The aim of the moderns is the enjoyment of security in private pleasures; and they call liberty the guarantees accorded by institutions to these pleasures.'[33] Mill's 'harm principle' entitles the state to consider limiting the freedom of the moderns only where the exercise of that freedom would cause harm (and not merely, for example, offence) to others. Otherwise, on this view, people should be free to choose whatever goals and values make sense to them, even if these are repugnant or senseless from the standpoint of others.

A first step in rethinking our responsibility for remaking society in a sustainable direction is to recognize that the harm principle may, in the circumstances of climate change and other environmental threats, entail very different limits on action than have hitherto been considered normal. Whereas current readings of the harm principle have tended to assume that harm must be relatively direct and immediate, and its legal instantiation until very recently was made on the basis that carbon emissions did not constitute harm, getting to grips with climate change will alter those assumptions. Harm which is indirect and slow, which accumulates on an ongoing basis rather than being expressed in a single discrete act, leads to very different results when fed into the 'harm principle' than the harms with which the liberal paradigm has classically engaged. Our actions must now be constrained not only by traditional prohibitions on familiar forms of harm (the classic examples are shouting 'fire' in a crowded theatre, or stretching out my arm in such a way that it connects strongly with your face), but also requirements to avoid or, where unavoidable, minimize the infliction of indirect and slowly gestating harm, and to take account of the complex science which demonstrates pathways by which rising concentrations of greenhouse gases in the atmosphere can cause harm to human interests as well as more general forms of disruption.[34]

If the harm principle is reinterpreted in this way, by a redefinition of the nature of harm itself together with the incorporation of knowledge about the action of greenhouse gases, it follows that the sustainability condition on choice and pursuit of personal goals and values may be much more demanding than has been usually thought. This implies that the space within which I am entitled to a free choice of interests, goals, and values may be narrower than I have until now believed. The point here is about the limits of law: if my free choice is limited by the harm principle, and the harm principle provides grounds to support new laws preventing me from carrying out newly recognized forms of harm, then the domain of my free choice will be correspondingly reshaped.

Counting carbon emission as a 'harm' is of course not a straightforward task, given that no one can live without emitting carbon in their exhalations, and so zero emissions is neither a possible nor a desirable aim. But such emissions constitute a closed loop within the biosphere. The real locus of harm is that burning fossil fuels, in particular, releases carbon which had been stored in the earth into the atmosphere, which is not part of such a closed system. It is on these grounds that the United States Environmental Protection Administration (EPA) has determined that excessive carbon emissions can be conceived and regulated as pollutants.[35] One need not aim to bring down pollution levels to zero to make it possible to regulate pollution. Legislators and regulators will have to set standards for what counts as 'excessive' emissions and so as actionable harm, and what counts as a legal defence against charges of causing this newly identified kind of harm.

While it is not the aim of this book to specify such standards, they might for example involve showing that a company's harmful emissions are limited to the lowest amount possible as measured by best practice for a given sector. Production methods which are less efficient than the best-practice norm could be fined or even shut down. Of course, the law will have to weigh whether regulation of a given harm is appropriate in relation to existing legal rights, or whether the scope or implication of those rights is limited by such harm. It will also want to take into account sociological studies of the efficacy of increasing levels of regulation from an initially low level of penalty. That initial penalty alters the way that people see the practice and its violation (beyond the alteration allowing the law to have been passed to begin with), enabling a new perception to take hold. Penalties can be later increased as attitudes to the norm change further, in a cycle of bootstrapping in which both public and private initiative play a part.[36] Voluntary compliance still plays a crucial role in this dynamic, as those who choose to comply and to adopt the new outlook have an important role in encouraging others, initially resistant or indifferent, to do so as well. This is because such people will typically measure 'injunctive norms' prescribing certain forms of action against the 'descriptive norms' according to which they see people around them actually living.[37] To the extent that more people model voluntary compliance, the change in law will be more likely to have the desired effect (especially in cases where compliance is difficult to observe or sanction), and so to play a role in encouraging further change.

Such policies of setting best practice standards for emissions, or banning certain methods of production altogether, might seem draconian. In fact, it is the logical result of admitting new types of harm into the traditional formula of liberalism: with new scientific accounts of harm, new social understandings will emerge, meaning that old legal principles will start to give new results. Lawsuits in tort for harms aggravated by human contributions to climate change are already being discussed and some, indeed, so far successful.[38] So even on impeccable liberal principles, changes in our understanding of science may compel the setting of drastically different boundaries of harm. Such compulsion results from new scientific and policy questions while in turn further shaping the broader public ethos in this space.

Step 2: broadening out to (other) costs and benefits

The argument just made about the harm principle has important implications for a wider range of cost and benefit calculations, in relation to individual and social choices, even where the imposition of a legal sanction is not in question. Just as sustainability implies a redefinition of harm and so a new line to be drawn in the application of the harm principle, so too it implies a redefinition of costs and benefits more generally. This may be less clear-cut than the seemingly more measurable case of harm. What counts as a cost and what counts as a benefit may in the transition to an ecologically sustainable world have to be radically rethought.[39]

A graphic illustration of this is the following dialogue, sketched on the basis of a real conversation described to me by an environmentalist and scientist friend. I have named the characters to evoke Socrates and Thrasymachus (the combative and sceptical opponent to Socrates on the question of whether it is advantageous to be just, in Book I of Plato's *Republic*). Sara is overseeing the installation of solar panels on her roof when she is ridiculed by her neighbour Tom:

TOM: 'Those solar panel thingies will never pay for themselves.'
SARA: 'Didn't you recently buy an expensive new sofa?'
TOM: 'Absolutely – got a bargain in the Christmas sales.'
SARA: 'But the sofa will never pay for itself either.'

How do we read this story? You may be moved to defend Tom, on the grounds that sofas are useful for sitting and cost much less than solar panels, whereas very expensive solar panels that don't save money are useless. But to say this is to remain in the grip of a non-sustainable mindset. First, it is not necessarily true that expensive sofas are better for sitting on than cheaper ones. Second, even if the more expensive sofa were indeed better for sitting on, the point is that sitting on a sofa is not something that we normally think should pay its way in our household economy. Sitting on a sofa, and having an expensive sofa, is taken to be an intrinsic good, the sort of thing that is obviously to be classed as a benefit which will for many people justify its not inconsiderable cost.

Of course, we don't want to defend solar panels solely in terms of display, though we shouldn't underestimate the social value of making them a high-status good to display. Virtue is not the only mechanism leading to social change: other motivations, including reputation and esteem, are also powerful sources of initiative to harness. (Even a story told by one consultant about a friend who was so keen to install solar panels as a matter of display that she installed them on the less sunny side of her roof, has a silver lining: making such panels a matter of status consumption may still be contributing to a valuable social good.)[40] But so long as they work to save any carbon emissions at all – even if not enough to pay for their installation financially – they do have a discrete and real value. In the eco-republic, assessing costs and benefits must be done in terms not only of the metric of money but also more broadly in terms of the measure of sustainability. This is more complex than any single metric, and our reasoning, our very identification of costs and benefits, will have to become correspondingly more complex.

Some of these redefinitions will become embodied in law over time: laws requiring companies to take responsibility for recycling their products, for example, internalizing the cost of recycling to the original production process. Others will not. Yet if individuals carry on oblivious to sustainable ways of looking at costs and benefits, all the laws in the world are unlikely to be able to make social arrangements sustainable overall.

Conversely, someone who cares about sustainability has reasons to show that in her private actions, and to contribute via those actions to the emergence and sustenance of a new ethos. Her reasons may include the value of being part of the solution, not part of the problem; the value of cutting down on emissions as both intrinsically worth doing and as part of contributing to a social reorientation of value, to a social campaign to make sustainability the *sine qua non* of public and private decisions alike, rather than to subject it to death by a thousand short-term financial calculations. By seeing solar panels as something we might value in themselves, as we would a new sofa, rather than a wholly fungible source of energy to be sought at the lowest possible price, we contribute to embedding them in the public imagination as non-optional, inherent goods.

I am treating solar panels here simply as an example. The example does not mean to imply that solar panels are always the most cost-effective choice within renewable energy options: within that set of options, it makes sense to use price as a measure to drive social and individual investment. But to assess renewable energy options as a whole against current forms of fossil fuel use simply on the basis of cost – even a cost setting a price on carbon – is to miss out on the need for a sustainable ethos to evaluate costs and benefits differently in themselves. Sustainability may be operationalized in institutions through new forms of regulated pricing. But to hold it hostage to getting that pricing just right – without any other inherent benefits on its side – is to leave it prey to possible failure. An ethos of sustainability would encourage individual and social choices to be made beyond the sole measure of the financial bottom line.

Step 3: is obeying the law enough?

As the previous paragraph began to suggest, the answer to the question posed in the title of this section is 'No'. One reason is that while the existence of laws against harming others will deter many people from so doing,[41] nothing stops others from breaching those laws and then paying any penalty after the fact. Indeed this attitude to law and regulation, in the form of a doctrine of 'efficient breach' of contract for example, has even been recommended by some adherents of the 'law and economics' movement, for whom the greatest good is overall economic efficiency. As some advocates of this view have argued, 'Managers not only may but also should violate the [legal] rules when it is profitable to do so.'[42]

The 'efficient breach' approach makes heroic assumptions. Among them are positing that the framers of the law were able to calculate precisely the exact social cost of its breach; that all such breaches are fully reparable by after-the-fact compensation (which is not the case where avoiding the social cost of bankruptcy limits the state's ability to impose fines, for example); and that all penalties due will in fact be identified and collected by tax agencies or police. Where these assumptions are unwarranted, a principled indifference allowing people or firms to commit whatever social damage they are willing to pay for is potentially destructive.[43]

All of the heroic assumptions involved in principled indifference to lawbreaking are likely to be violated in cases of environmental damage. Given the imperfect and evolving nature of the systemic repercussions of any one environmental harm, it is unlikely that laws will get the cost of committing such harm exactly right; there may also be on-balance reasons for not making certain actions illegal, even though we consider them immoral, wrong, and to be discouraged. Even if something has been made illegal, after-the-fact compensation can seldom fully repair any damage caused. And enforcement is, in the real world, always imperfect, while making something illegal and then policing it involves considerable costs in itself. For all these reasons, if people don't start to expect themselves and each other to take sustainability into account in formulating their ends, it may be impossible to respect it as a constraint at all.

Thus it is crucial to deter environmental harms from being committed, and not just to rest content with being able to sanction them after the fact. Laws and regulations certainly play a role in effecting such deterrence: many people and corporations choose to be law-abiding. But a fuller and wider compliance, complying with the spirit as well as the letter of the law, rests on adoption of an ethical outlook, embedded in an ethos of sustainability. In such an outlook, the free choice of options to follow is not constrained only by the threat of legal sanctions. It is informed from within by an orientation towards the value of sustainability in one's personal choices, even those which the law leaves open.[44]

The idea that one option with relation to energy use is no better than the rest, that it is a matter of principled indifference for society which options individuals choose to pursue, is an excessive and illusory luxury that can no longer be maintained. If people pursue frivolous or self-destructive courses of action chosen without reference to the condition of sustainability, this threatens to do harm which cannot be compensated for in time, and meanwhile wastes valuable social resources and energy. A society in which people pursue evanescent entertainment while the planet collapses around them (not unlike the later days of the Roman Empire, when it was the political structure rather than the planet which was crumbling) is unlikely to flourish – and arguably does not deserve to do so. A society in which no one chooses their personal projects with any interest in their sustainability is unlikely to be a sustainable society. Indifference to sustainability is corrosive of its being achieved, as compensation after the fact is unlikely to be fully effective, and chances will be missed to pursue it directly.

What would this mean in real life? Consider one of the most difficult problems in this area, the problem of population reduction. Pending transformative technological changes (which may come, but possibly not for decades), there is an indisputable relation between increased population and increased pressure on natural resources and the carbon emissions storage capacity of the earth. Even highly efficient lifestyles still make individual humans, like other animals, net carbon emitters. One solution would be to say that having children imposes a serious harm on others, because it creates a new source of carbon emissions (as well as other potential burdens, for example for the care for such children should the parents fail), which in the case of well-off children in the rich world will also be disproportionately larger than the footprint of the contemporary children who are poor. Mill himself held a parallel position in relation to the effects of over-population on wages: he wrote that '... in a country either over-peopled, or threatened with being so, to produce children, beyond a very small number, with the effect of reducing the reward of labour by their competition, is a serious offence against all who live by the remuneration of their labour.' Hence regulations requiring proof of economic ability to support children in such circumstances would be 'not objectionable as violations of liberty'.[45] The case of carbon emissions reverses the burden of proof which Mill envisaged on the rich and the poor. In his day, over-population involved the poor burdening the rich. Today rich parents are the ones threatening to burden others, including the global poor, by raising their offspring in a high-carbon lifestyle. So there is a prima facie case for governments to impose policies to curb population growth.

However, that case is more complex than it first appears. Children are also the source of potential technological advances, the promise of future wage-earning to fund the pensions of their parents' and grandparents' generations, and the bearers of an intrinsic value which a simple carbon calculation cannot capture. Moreover, a case for concern is not automatically a case for coercion. The coercive one-child (with some exceptions) policy imposed by China restricts basic liberties and imposes significant individual and social costs, whereas the human capability-fostering policies of the Indian state of Kerala have brought down fertility even more dramatically without the inherent social bad of compulsion.[46]

The implication of this analysis is that while there are important reasons to protect the freedom to bear children, the exercise of this freedom cannot be entirely insulated from legitimate social concerns. Having children is a fundamental liberty and creates a benefit for future society, but also creates a harm or cost. Governments can legitimately call people's attention to the ecological cost which a rising population imposes, and can require trade-offs, so that those who have more children might have to pay higher family carbon taxes, for example. Further, rich-sector people[47] who do have more than one child have an ethical duty to consider how they can bring down their total family emissions and the future emissions which their child will go on to make. Choosing to have children is not a cost-free or insulated option. It carries with it ethical duties and may legitimately invite persuasive pressure while remaining a legally protected free choice.[48] If we exercise that choice without regard to sustainability at all, we undermine the achievement of a sustainable society.

To sum up: a free society rightly leaves much up to the option, or prerogative, of the individual to decide, and does so because of the value of individual liberty. But the space of that prerogative has first to be circumscribed by harm to others, an understanding of which is not naturally pre-given, but depends on both scientific knowledge and the political attempt to come to grips with that knowledge: that was the first point made in this section. Where harm occurs, society has to make a further determination of whether or not, on balance, it is best to regulate the action that would cause that harm by means of law, or whether to leave such constraint to the informal sphere of social pressure. Further, it was argued that within an optional choice space, what people actually choose to do will depend on how they see costs and benefits – not only how they weigh and measure them, but also what they take even to count as such. And finally, it was argued that optional choices matter because laws and regulations (being imperfect political products) cannot always fully or sustainably achieve the social outcome at which they aim, or cannot do so quickly enough, or may not come about at all without a change in the social ethos, or may be all-things-considered undesirable for reasons of the value of liberty or the disvalue of coercion despite the damage done by the harm going unregulated. For all these reasons, a concern with sustainability cannot be limited to a narrow focus on law and regulation alone, though it certainly must embrace those methods.

If the first and third points comprise the oft-announced bad news that we may have fewer options (even on impeccable liberal principles) than we have previously thought, the middle point is the potentially good news that we may have more options depending precisely on how we think. If we can come to conceive of leisure or living within our ecological means as a positive benefit, a condition to be cherished and prized, then achieving sustainability will not so much constrain our freedom as it will simply newly demarcate it. This is the promise of a new process of imagination.

Conclusion: from negligibility to negligence

Insofar as individual negligibility is a broadly ingrained assumption, it is an obstacle to thinking about what individuals might do, because it blocks any thought that individuals should bother doing it. If I choose to do something that undermines the achievement of a social goal, negligibility seems to promise that the system will be immune to my actions anyway, and so to reinforce my sense of indifference to the social good. Conversely, if I recognize the role which my actions play in shaping both the social ethos and the social outcome, I cannot afford any more to be indifferent to the question of what is good. This is why, before turning to the Platonic account of ethics, value, and virtue sketching an intimate relation between city and soul, I have sought to re-establish the case for holding that the individual has significant scope for shaping society through her actions, attitudes, and decisions: she is not simply an anonymous, negligible, and irrelevant cog in the machine.

Seeing the individual as negligible in relation to the mass has made it easy to downplay or dismiss the importance of individual virtues and actions in relation to the common good, and so has contributed (along with other causes which we will examine) to the evacuation of self-control or self-discipline as an admired virtue of the individual character. This mass outlook has severed the link between the virtues of individual psychology and those of the social structure, the link between the soul and the city which the ancients had known, and created a one-sided model of virtue and the social ethos in its place.[49]

It is against such indifference that Plato argues for the importance of individual intentions and actions, first by investigating the relationship between individual and city, and then by arguing for the importance of direct attention to what is good. These two points will occupy us in Part II, in Chapter 5 and Chapter 6 respectively, once we have introduced Plato and his *Republic* as a model in more detail in Chapter 4. Having challenged some disabling modern assumptions, we are now ready to explore what the ancient Greek imagination might have to offer.

PART II

IMAGINATION

Prologue to Chapter 4:
Post-Platonic Perspectives on the Republic

The first model for a totalitarian state, laying down the template for Hitler? Or the first model for radical communism, threatening the traditional family? The 'beautiful city' (*Kalli-polis* in ancient Greek) of the *Republic* has been read as everything from a prescription for universal poverty ruled by universal dictatorship,[1] to a destructive fantasy which is intended as satire, to a utopian dream which can't possibly be realized. We have to confront this plethora of interpretations in order to understand both how they can be so diverse, and the grounds for appropriating the *Republic* in this book in yet another way: as an abstract model of questions that need to be asked rather than a blueprint of answers to be applied.

As I wrote in an earlier study, *Plato's Progeny*, the *Republic* has been appropriated by both Left and Right, by nineteenth-century communists as well as by twentieth-century partisans of fascism. The reason, I think, is as I stated there: the 'radical means' which it proposes for its ideal city – including depriving its rulers, both women and men, of private property and free choice of procreation – has appealed to the Left, while 'the holistic goal of a citizenry shaped to be cohesive has appealed to the Right'.[2] Some of those in the middle, animated by liberal values, have condemned the *Republic* as the original recipe for political totalitarianism. This was the burden of Karl Popper's attack on Plato in the first volume of *The Open Society and Its Enemies*, dedicated in the midst of World War II to debunking *The Myth of Plato* (the title of the first volume) as the template for the subsequent destructive myths of Hegel and Marx, and the kindred totalitarian aspirations of fascism. And indeed it was true that Popper, and the British scholar and politician R. A. Crossman, who had attacked Plato a few years earlier, were aware of a real and disturbing trend in German thought of the interwar and wartime years: Plato used as a model for a programme of state-controlled dictatorship and eugenics. (We will consider Popper's charges further, focusing on a particular issue at stake between totalitarian and liberal readings – the 'noble lie' – in Chapter 4.)

The blatant appropriation of Plato for fascism had been nourished by a more ambiguous interest in his imperatives of founding, legislating, and educating the body as well as the mind, an interest animating various intellectual circles in early twentieth-century Germany. While some members of the circle around the poet Stefan George became avid Nazis, others fled or resisted, including most famously the failed assassin of Hitler, Claus von Stauffenberg.[3] The political split in this circle echoes the fact that liberals too have found inspiration in the *Republic* over the centuries, interpreting its emphasis on character and social harmony as part of an ideal of voluntary rather than forced virtue. To defuse the charges of exploitation and tyranny, liberals such as Benjamin Jowett and Richard Nettleship, teaching at Oxford in the mid-nineteenth century, emphasized the fact that the ideal city is based on consensus and the common good: all must accept the rule of the philosophers in order for the city to achieve moderation and justice, and that rule must help its subjects to acquire and maintain virtue.

Such a wide range of readings of the *Republic* leaves open the field for its appropriation once again. In doing so we must be conscious of the elements within it that have nourished totalitarian uses and interpretations: the eugenics, the procreation directed entirely from above for one group of people, the injunction that state legislation should 'leave the unhealthy to die, and those whose psychological constitution is incurably corrupt it will put to death' (410a). Starting from a democratic and liberal perspective, these provisions must be rejected, yet the goal to which they are directed, that of individual virtue and social harmony, cannot be wholly abandoned. The task then becomes how to conceive of the means to achieve it. In particular, the question of whether the changes the *Republic* envisions can only be instituted and maintained by force, or at best by a manipulated consensus, poses a challenge for the project of this book. If achieving a sustainable society is a fundamental imperative, how far should we be prepared to allow government to go in imposing or even simply facilitating this? Is the use of the *Republic* as a model an implicit invitation to government to impose its own vision of sustainability on the rest of us?

My answer is a challenge in return. The *Republic* models aspects of the psychosocial dimensions of sustainability that, I propose, do need to be achieved. Incorporating them into a liberal society, using liberal means, is the challenge that we face, and which a voluntary change of ethos can help to achieve. If we fail, it is possible that the environmental and social stressors which climate change will bring about will undermine not only the sustainability but also the liberalism of our society. If unsustainability is indeed unsustainable, something will have to give: let that something be our attachment to unnecessary and debilitating assumptions, rather than either our liberal values or our social survival.

4

Meet Plato's *Republic*

Plato's *Republic*: stability and sustainability

As arguably the first and greatest work of Western political philosophy, the *Republic* portrays the designing of an ideal city which is stable and unified. This stability and unity emerge from the mutually supportive fit between the psychology of its imagined citizens and the principles governing its imagined city. That fit, in turn, emerges from cultural beliefs, or civic mythology, which reflect and embody a rational understanding of what is and is not valuable. Plato of course was not interested in ecological sustainability as a civic goal.[1] But his idea of stability serves a parallel purpose: to establish a homeostatic self-regulation of the ethos of the city in relation to the ethos of the individuals whom it educates and who in turn come to govern or be governed within it. If city and soul fit together stably, the city can sustain its own character across time even as individuals are born, educated, and die, and its citizens in turn can sustain their own characters while living within it.

Stability – which modern liberals such as John Rawls also acknowledge as an important social value when achieved by means of the right reasons[2] – is only worth sustaining if the character being sustained is valuable (this is a version of a point made in Chapter 1). Plato recognized this, as we will see, and he went further: he held that stability *can* only be sustained by individual and civic characters which are independently valuable. In other words, those who are aiming at short-sighted or destructive purposes are less likely to maintain and reproduce their purposes over time. Corrupt people may manage to shape the social fabric of their own day in their own image, but their children's generation is likely to rebel against the parents' corrupt values. Only an internal, intrinsic tempering can avoid this downward slide.

It is this notion of tempering the values and appetites of ordinary people, rather than radically transforming or suppressing them, in order to achieve a society that homeostatically maintains its own balance between the values and aims of its citizens, which can inform the course of a path towards sustainability today. By drawing on reason, the model society of the *Republic* tames and reshapes the material desires of its citizens so that they are compatible with the psychological and material sustainability of the society. In its respect for reason, the *Republic* honours the drive for enlightenment. In its acknowledgement of the role of appetite and desire, it accepts, rather than simply tries to repress, these key drivers of human behaviour, active both in classical Athens and today. And in its attempt to reshape the interrelated maps of psyche and polity, the *Republic* charts the importance of the political imagination and suggests models according to which a new eco-republic might be configured. The *Republic* offers parables which resonate in manifold respects with the challenges we face. How we choose to address those challenges, how far the model can serve us in doing so, and how we choose to appropriate it, remains up to us.

Plato's life and work

Plato lived four centuries before the birth of Christ, from (on one good estimate) 424/3 to 348/7 B.C.[3] During his youth, his native city of Athens was one of the most powerful political entities in the Greek world, which had led the Greeks in their defeat of the mighty Persian Empire decades earlier. Athens was a democracy, in which all (male) citizens had equal rights of speaking and voting in the Assembly which made decisions about how to act, and equal opportunities to put themselves forward for selection by lottery or election for serving on juries, on the Council, and in most of the other offices of the regime.

As a young man, Plato lived through two crises: a political crisis which also precipitated a personal one. The political crisis was the ruinous generation-long series of wars between Athens and the Greek rival city-state of Sparta. In a desperate bid for victory, urged on by the dazzling young politician Alcibiades, the Athenian Assembly decided to stake the city's survival on a naval expedition to capture the island of Sicily. But the expedition, with Alcibiades one of the generals at its head, failed disastrously. Alcibiades fled into exile to avoid accountability and even joined the enemy side for a time. Having won the war, Sparta backed a bloody oligarchic coup which briefly overturned the Athenian democratic regime; democracy was restored by the efforts of its partisans in 403 B.C.

Four years later, the reverberations of that short-lived oligarchic coup caused Plato a personal crisis. He had as a very young man become a pupil of the philosopher Socrates. Socrates was, as the Roman statesman Cicero later described him, the first person to bring philosophy down from the heavens to the earth (*Tusculan Disputations* 5.4.10), meaning that he reoriented its concerns from cosmos to ethos, from what there is to how to live. He did not seek political influence by trying to influence his fellow citizens in the Assembly or law courts, which were the usual paths to fame and power for ambitious Athenians. Instead, while he agreed to stand for selection by lottery to serve on the Council and performed required service in the military, he spent most of his time questioning his contemporaries about what they knew about how to live well (how to display excellence, or succeed, which are connotations of the Greek word *aretē* often translated as 'virtue'). Unlike other well-known teachers of the day, who were paid privately by their pupils' families, Socrates did not take money for teaching. He claimed to be asking questions so that he himself could learn from anyone claiming to have knowledge. But the force of his questioning, rejecting easy or self-indulgent answers, exercised a powerful effect on the young people who were drawn to him.

Socrates left no writings. All that we know about him we know from others, and indeed much of it from Plato. For although Plato seems to have spent about a dozen years away from Athens in the aftermath of Socrates' death, at some point when he was aged around forty, he returned to set up his own school there, the first Greek institution of higher learning, named the 'Academy'. At some point also, like many fellow Socratics, he began to write dialogues with (in almost all of them) Socrates as a leading character. Most of these works written by others are lost, though we have names and excerpts or summaries from a number of them, enough to assure us that this became a recognizable literary genre in the generation after Socrates' death. Plato's are among the only surviving accounts of Socrates of this kind (the others are primarily by Xenophon, an Athenian general and friend of Socrates, who reported a number of shorter conversations in his *Memorabilia* as well as leaving his own versions of Socrates' *Apology* or defence-speech at his trial, and of a *Symposium* in which Socrates is depicted as participating). While Xenophon's are of interest, it is the Socratic dialogues by Plato which do most to develop the themes on which this book dwells.

It is in these dialogues that we find Plato portraying Socrates in conversations with actual and fictional characters who include Athenian and foreign men of affairs, famous generals, travelling intellectuals, prizewinning playwrights, leading politicians (including Alcibiades, in the days that he was Athens' darling), and ambitious young men like Glaucon and Adeimantus in the *Republic*. Other notable depictions of Socrates include the *Symposium*, which recounts a banquet where Socrates and his friends challenge each other to make speeches in praise of *eros* (the driving force of passionate love), and the *Apology*, *Crito*, and *Phaedo*, which portray the moving and dramatic scenes of Socrates' trial, imprisonment, and execution.

Those scenes constituted the personal crisis for Plato mentioned above. In 399 B.C., Socrates was indicted, convicted, and executed on charges which included corrupting the values of the young men with whom he conversed philosophically. (Some contemporaries seem to have thought that these charges were pretexts for the real grievance, which was that some of Socrates' closest associates had become traitors to the cause of the Athenian democracy.) Already shaken by the misgovernment which had precipitated Athens' military destruction, and now by a democratic jury's fatal misjudgement of Socrates, Plato seems to have come to doubt the cogency of public opinion. In his dialogues, he lambasts the demos for being too easily captured by cunning politicians, too susceptible to the sway of base desires, and incapable of bringing knowledge or judgement to bear on crucial political decisions. As a result, he began to explore the fundamental questions of truth, purpose, and authenticity that came to constitute his mature vision.

He expressed this vision by writing dialogues in almost all of which Socrates is made the leading character (this is why sometimes we refer to

'Socrates' and sometimes to 'Plato' when discussing Plato's writings: Plato's ideas drew on those of Socrates, while he makes his teacher a leading character in the dialogues which explore these ideas). Socrates cross-examines his self-important or youthful contemporaries about the knowledge or excellence that they claim to have, exposing contradictions in their thinking and so challenging their claims to social authority and respect. They are unable when pressed to answer the question of how one should live and what one should do. Without being able to answer that question, their claim to exercise authority of any kind is fatally undermined. One way to see the *Republic* is as a sketch of the kind of authority that could sustain such cross-examination: the authority of philosophy.[4]

Plato's *Republic*: a summary

The *Republic* itself is in ten books, significantly longer than any of Plato's other dialogues except the *Laws*. It is rich in detail, characterization, imagery, and language steeped in Greek myth and poetry, especially in the works of Homer and Hesiod. As such, any summary can only be a bare outline intended to orient those who are unfamiliar with it, rather than to replace a reading of the work in its own right. It is told by Socrates as narrator, purporting to recount an experience in which he found himself (in about 420 B.C., at the age of about 50) at a gathering in the Athenian port of Piraeus at the home of a prominent group of metics (a category of privileged aliens resident in the city), along with Plato's brothers Glaucon and Adeimantus, the foreign orator and political practitioner Thrasymachus, and several others. Socrates begins by asking his elderly host, Cephalus, about why he values his wealth, and this leads into a conversation about the value of justice, first with Cephalus, then with Cephalus' son and heir Polemarchus, and then with the mordant and rude Thrasymachus, who argues that justice is good for the rulers who define it but not for their subjects who are exploited by it.

The Book I debate with Thrasymachus is resolved by arguments which the latter visitor seems to accept reluctantly, unable to find flaw in Socrates' logic, but unconvinced at a deeper level by the direction of his argument. That debate is succeeded by a second challenge raised by

Glaucon and Adeimantus in Book 2, who accept that justice may be the second-best option for those who can't get away with breaking the law, but who challenge Socrates to deny that the best life involves reaping the fruits of unjust action whenever one can be sure of doing so without detection or punishment (a denial made more difficult by the frequent and insouciant violations of justice committed by the gods and heroes in Greek myth). This is the occasion for the famous 'ring of Gyges' story recounted earlier in this book in the prologue to Chapter 3, in which Glaucon tells the tale of someone with an invisibility ring who used it to get all the sex, money, and eventually power that he could, breaking all the most sacred norms that stood in his way of doing so.

It is to respond to both challenges (Thrasymachus: justice is political exploitation of subjects by rulers; Glaucon and Adeimantus: justice is only expediently, not inherently, valuable for the just person) that Socrates looks into the origin of justice. He proposes that they 'look at a community coming into existence in speech' (369a),[5] saying that they should 'start our inquiry with the community, and then proceed to the individual and see if we can find in the conformation of the smaller entity anything similar to what we have found in the larger' (368e–369a). First the city, then the individual, is divided into three parts (rational, spirited, and appetitive), and four virtues – wisdom, courage, self-discipline, and justice – are then identified in relation to the city and individual respectively. This discussion seems to have been concluded at the end of Book 4 with the identification of justice and self-discipline in the internal harmonious structures without which both soul and city will be plunged into division and civil war, and so with the identification of justice as an intrinsic good (hence also a non-exploitative one). But the brothers challenge Socrates to say more about the peculiar life required of the rulers of the city if they are not to turn into vicious exploiters of their public. This leads to the 'digression' in Books 5 to 7 in which Socrates reveals that this fine city ('Kallipolis') will be possible only if women who are capable of ruling do so alongside the men; if the guardian-rulers have no private property or family, instead breeding on the city's command children who will be brought up in common; and if the guardian-rulers are in fact philosopher-kings and -queens, who rule in virtue of their knowledge of something called 'the Form of the Good'. The 'digression' includes the images of the Sun, the Line,[6] and the Cave, the last already met in the opening prologue in this book, the first to be discussed below.

In Book 8, Socrates resumes the project on which he had been about to embark at the end of Book 4, of describing the imperfect cities which would come about due to a progressive decline of the virtues of the ideal city: timocracy (or the rule of an honour-loving elite); oligarchy (or the rule of the wealth-loving few); democracy (or the rule of the pleasure-, freedom-, and equality-loving many); and tyranny (or the rule of the power-, lust-, and greed-crazed single man). The tyrant is judged in Book 9 to be both the most unjust and the unhappiest of these men, and so the proof of the answer to the original challenges is complete: being unjust is a path to unhappiness, being just is a path to happiness (although full happiness is not guaranteed, at least the just person will have the psychically well-ordered and healthy soul without which it is impossible). The soul is compared here in another famous image to a person with three parts inside: a tiny person who is the reason; a lion who is the spirited part; and a many-headed beast who is the appetitive part (echoing too an equally famous image earlier in which democratic politicians are compared to beast-tamers who know how to manage the democratic beast). Finally, after a resumption of the discussion of the dangers of imitation from Books 2 to 3, Book 10 concludes with the 'myth of Er' in which the rewards of justice in this life (a well-ordered soul) are finally linked back to the rewards of justice in the next life, in which the reward will be not direct, but come (on the assumption of reincarnation) in the form of choosing one's next life well or badly.

A brief mention was made of the 'Form of the Good', and so of the 'Forms' or 'Ideas', above. In writing his dialogues, the *Republic* among them, Plato was reflecting on the big philosophical questions: How should one live? Is there knowledge relevant to living well, and if so, what is it? Can we have access to the truth, and if so, how? What is the ultimate structure of reality? In sketching out the structure of these questions, Plato explored some very large claims: that ultimate reality is not what we see around us, but a structure of Ideas; that the highest such Idea is the Idea of the Good; that the world is intelligible insofar as it is understood in light of the Good; and that these Ideas are universally valid. These claims entered into certain versions of Judaism, Christianity, and Islam, and have shaped philosophy in each of these traditions and in certain secularized forms to this very day.

In the nineteenth and twentieth centuries especially, some thinkers have tried to overturn the role of the Ideas, arguing for example that the world of universal Ideas is an illusion, a sickly ideal invented only to smother the real world of competitive striving for power in which we each proclaim the values that best suit our own pursuits. This case was made perhaps most powerfully by Friedrich Nietzsche, who averred, 'I should prefer to describe the entire phenomenon "Plato" by the harsh term "higher swindle" or, if you prefer, "idealism", than by any other.'[7] The best defence against such criticism is to remember that Plato always presented the Ideas not as facts but as visions or images. As a philosopher (in Greek *philo-sophos*), he was literally a lover-of-wisdom, not someone who had already attained full wisdom. Like the Socrates he portrayed, he knew what direction to pursue, and sketched out possibilities of what one might find there: most importantly, the need to question what is real and what is merely apparent, and to seek comprehensive and integrated understanding As visions, these possibilities can serve to orient our thinking and action, even if we cannot prove whether or not they are ultimately true. Absolute wisdom may forever elude us. But the visions provided by the greatest lover of wisdom in the Western tradition – Plato – are still signposts to enlightenment. These visions can provide us with context and imbue us with passion. Before considering them, however, we need to consider what Plato himself was doing in amassing and offering them. What was his purpose in writing the *Republic*?

Plato's *Republic*: its purposes

Plato's *Republic* seems to have been written to escape the antithesis of its own day, the choice between Sparta and Athens, the latter a trading and entrepreneurial society despite its reliance on slave labour in certain parts of the economy. Contrasting Spartan oligarchy with Athenian democracy, Spartan militarism with Athenian intellectualism, Spartan closedness with Athenian openness, Plato drew up a model of a novel alternative, a city which would be constituted by enlightened reason working to create a new political imagination. As one scholar puts it, placing the dialogue in the context of Athenian democratic and theatrical practices,

I believe that Plato writes the *Republic* as an offering to his fellow Athenians that is meant as a cure (*pharmakon*) to purge (*kathairein*) and transform what he takes to be problematic in their specific worldview and in the ways this worldview had been constructed and contested by the poets, sophists, and citizens in their aesthetico-psychological and political capacities as poet, actor, and spectator. He introduces not only a brand new meaning of justice into their conceptual schema, but also a new poetic-philosophic activity that fashions new symbols and revises concepts central to their worldviews 'to force them to conceive of what had been to them inconceivable,' [n.41] and he does this while simultaneously interrogating the aesthetic and psychological mechanisms by which such an activity is done.[8]

That city was not left to languish on his pages, irrelevant to political life if not actually achieved. Instead, Plato has recently been shown to have been effecting a new imagination in his readers by means of his writing itself. Rather than waiting for the millennial creation of a new city to do the work, Plato as writer dramatized a transformation in the imagination of his characters and sought thereby to effect the same in his readers.

Advancing this argument, another scholar, Danielle Allen, puts her claim thus: 'Plato was the world's first systematic political philosopher, but he was also, it appears, the western world's first think-tank activist and its first message man. He wrote to change Athenian culture and thereby transform Athenian politics.'[9] According to Allen's analysis, Plato's writing not only achieved this, but also offered a theory of its own achievement, spelling out how linguistic and imaginative change constitutes cultural and so political change.[10] Without recapitulating her full account of his theory here, I will be drawing on its insights to develop my parallel story of what cultural and political change today will involve.

If this is Plato's conception of how to bring about political change, it alters the way we should approach the hoary but powerful accusation, made most dramatically by the liberal Viennese philosopher Karl Popper in New Zealand exile during World War II as we saw in the prologue to the present chapter: that the *Republic* is a recipe for totalitarianism.[11] I have argued elsewhere that this accusation missed the fact that the aim of the ideal society depicted is paternalist rather than exploitative: the ideal city of the *Republic* is built for the sake of those who need political help in governing their own desires and emotions, not for the sake of the ruling philosophers, who are qualified to provide that help but do not need it for their own sake.[12] Allen's argument further modifies the force of Popper's accusation. If Plato's fundamental project is not actually to offer a blueprint for building such a society, but rather to transform his readers' and so his society's (and later societies') imagination by means of writing and reading, then the charge of totalitarianism cannot apply directly. Plato may have projected paternalist models, but he did not use totalitarian means to instil them.[13]

Plato's *Republic*: a licence for political deception?

Or did he, or would he have done so? Popper charged that Plato countenanced lying as a means of ruling within his ideal city. Allen makes a similar charge within the domain of her revised conception of Platonic writing as Platonic politics: that Plato countenanced lying within his writing, justifying the use of untrue images and models so long as they were means to a putatively good transformative end.[14] The central case for both charges is the 'noble lie' (the usual translation of *gennaios pseudos*, though one editor notes that this could also mean 'a true-blue lie', in the sense of 'a massive, no-doubt-about-it lie')[15] at the end of *Republic* Book 3. The substance of this lie is a justificatory image for two civic beliefs and functions, one unifying, the other differentiating. On the one hand, the citizens need a powerful shared civic identity; on the other hand, the city needs to distribute them into one of three functional social classes: producers, soldiers, or rulers (the latter at this point in the dialogue conceived as generically or conventionally wise, not yet revealed as full-blown philosophers). The lie operates to persuade them on both fronts, telling them first that they are all born from a particular place in the earth (an actual traditional belief of the Athenians) and so uniquely bonded in natural brotherhood; but second that their assignment to classes is manifest in a natural hierarchy of metals contained in their souls, the rulers gold, the soldiers silver, and the producers bronze.

The 'noble lie' operates to naturalize political purposes. It draws on an account of lying given by Socrates earlier in the dialogue: that lying which works to achieve good and knowledgeably defined ends is morally permissible. In the case of the 'noble lie', Socrates takes it to be both valuable and true that some are intellectually and morally capable of ruling, others of soldiering, and others of neither, hence being relegated to producing; while it is valuable, though arguably not true, that all citizens are brothers, naturally bound into civic identity and patriotism.[16] The lie dramatizes these valuable beliefs and makes them effective for those who might not grasp or be motivated by them if stated baldly. In these terms, the lie does not change what otherwise needs to be done politically: the same people will rule, guard, and produce on the basis of the lie as would do so on the basis of the (putative) truth alone. Nevertheless, such a rehabilitation only goes so far. Allen still charges Plato with licensing deception, and distances herself from this as a means which she cannot accept. As she writes in her own voice: 'in advocating deception, Plato pushed a pragmatist understanding of the work of philosophy well beyond any limits that I … would endorse.'[17] Like Popper's, this view follows a standard liberal rejection of deception as a means inconsistent with equal citizenship.

The text of the *Republic*, however, does more to complicate its message than such a view acknowledges. For starters, it is not the *rulers* in the projected city who are to tell the lie to their subjects. Rather, they too are ideally to be among the audience for the lie, brought up to believe it as if it were true. Instead, it is the self-proclaimed legislators and founders of this ideal city – Socrates, Glaucon, and Adeimantus, the three characters participating in this part of the discussion – who imagine themselves telling the lie to the rulers of the city they are founding 'in speech'.[18] In other words, the lie is to come from outside the whole body of citizens, rulers and ruled alike. It is to shape their imaginations from the outset, not purveyed by the rulers as a weapon of rule, but rather serving as a precondition for the very establishment of that rule. The twin images of natural bonds and differentiations are the basis on which the terms of political rule are initially established, not images to be manipulated either benignly (Allen) or oppressively (Popper) by actual rulers themselves. (The text does not speculate on the duties of rulers who come to learn that it is strictly speaking a lie, yet go on telling it to their fellow citizens.)

What difference does this make to our reading of the *Republic*, and more importantly, what difference does it make to the prospect of using the *Republic* as a model for mapping an imaginative transformation towards a sustainable society? In putting the 'noble lie' in the mouths of the founder-legislators but specifically not the internal rulers of Kallipolis, I take Plato to be insisting that some images are beyond the direct and immediate control of politicians. Whereas Allen highlights the deliberate alterability in Plato's approach to the political imagination, my reading of this point highlights a wider ingrainedness and recalcitrance, the extent to which such landscapes change in mysterious and yet pervasive ways, shifting unexpectedly and uncontrollably under the feet of the rulers themselves. Popper and Allen see Plato as a master of manipulation, confident in its prospects for success, while I see him as aware of the limits of direct manipulation and yet of the importance of the shared beliefs and images that outstrip its reach. The aspiration for the rulers themselves to believe the noble lie is in our terms an acceptance that politicians too must find themselves operating in a new mental landscape, one which is being transformed in ways not wholly within their control.[19]

If what is wrong with lying is that it undermines and disrespects the value of the individual, this represents a broader attack by Popper on Plato: that the Greek did not value the individual as such. As Popper put it, Plato was a 'holist' who valued the society as a whole and considered the individual at best a means to achieving that end, at worst utterly dispensable, if failing to be such a means.[20] It is true that the *Republic* takes an holistic view of the social good and advocates a strictly hierarchical form of politics, in contrast to the individual good ('the pursuit of happiness') and the egalitarian basis which characterize modern liberal politics. Yet, without defending the rigid hierarchy of the Platonic approach, there is a sense in which it is Plato who takes the individual more seriously than do most modern liberals. This is the question of negligibility met in Chapter 2: whether the individual's habits, choices, values, and preferences actually make a difference to the society as a whole. Although many of the Enlightenment thinkers who helped to shape liberalism were certain that they did, this thought had tended to become lost in the modern insistence on the separation between public law and private morality as a political axiom – no matter what the consequences of that which unfolds in the private realm. Insofar as moderns tend to insist that people should be left free to do what they like (within the limits of the harm principle), and fail to consider the consequences if what people like to do undermines the survival of the polity or society itself, it is actually the modern pundit – not Plato – who is manifesting a belief that the individual does not matter. Somehow, the modern society is supposed to be immune to the habits and characters of individuals. Or to put it another way, indifference to individuals' choices is underwritten by the belief that those individuals are negligible from the standpoint of society. What they do, don't do, care about, desire, and believe is negligible to the career of society and can be safely neglected and left alone.

Of course, few if any actual thinkers or politicians would go so far as to betray no interest in social mores. But with some important and honourable exceptions,[21] there is little vocabulary in current liberal doctrines to articulate why they should care about such mores, or what they should do about them. The assumption that personal character is a private matter, that people should be left to get on with their lives, and that what they do in that space is indifferent or negligible from the standpoint of political decision-making, runs deep, if inchoate. In contrast, it is Plato who, in caring so much about how people are to be educated and live, demonstrates a much deeper belief in the significance of the individual. If people care about the wrong things, or are not habituated to virtuous action, the structure of society will disintegrate. 'By maintaining a sound system of education and upbringing you produce citizens of good character; and citizens of sound character, with the advantage of a good education, produce in turn children better than themselves ...', as Socrates says (424a).

Admittedly, Socrates focuses especially on the habits and characters of the guardian elite, while saying less about those of the lower classes. But while his discussion of education is framed in terms of training the guardians, since there is to be meritocratic selection from all social classes into the guardian ranks, the early childhood education at least must pervade all of the society. It is this which is in view when Socrates goes on to insist that 'those in charge of our state must stick to the system of education and see that no deterioration creeps in' (424b). Moreover, in the hierarchical conception of the Platonic ideal society, if people's self-discipline breaks down and leads them to seek to fill roles for which they are not suited, this too would destroy the society. We need not accept the hierarchical and eugenics-based picture here in order to take the point that individual virtues matter profoundly to the well-being and stability of a just society.

That basic insight can and will be illustrated by the details of the *Republic*'s account in the chapter that follows. Yet those details also risk obscuring the value of the insight itself. For the way in which Socrates fleshes out the analogy is peculiar and controversial – and in certain respects at odds with key values of modern politics. Specifically, he divides

both city and soul into three parts: each has a rational part which is naturally fit to rule the other two; a spirited part which is naturally fit to support reason with appropriate attitudes of anger, honour, and pride; and a
desiring part animated by the bodily appetites and associated secondary
desires such as the desire for money.

In the individual soul, the exact nature of these parts is a matter for
scholarly debate: are they each like tiny agents, or are they merely styliza-
tions of different sources of motivation for the overall individual agent?
Similarly, the manoeuvres which Socrates goes through to identify three,
and just three, such parts are open to question. Yet the fundamental idea
that the individual is subject to different kinds of motivation, and that
these need to be integrated into a functional hierarchy on pain of ceas-
ing to be a rational agent at all, remains a good starting point even for
modern psychological theories.

In the city, by contrast, the idea that there are three distinct social
classes, ideally composed of those and only those naturally suited to
belong to that class, and governed in a strict hierarchy by the class whose
natural suitability is to rule, is immediately disturbing. It reads like a
schema of the feudal or theocratic politics of the '*ancien régime*' which
modern liberal democracies were designed to reject. A class of wise
rulers – later in Book 5 revealed to be ideally philosopher-kings and
-queens – governing a military caste and a lowly, subordinated group of
artisans and farmers: surely this is a parody of antiquated politics with
nothing of value to offer the modern world. Indeed, one might object
to the 'basic insight' that I claimed to identify above by contending that
the *Republic* argues exactly the opposite: not that any and every citizen
can have a shaping impact on social values and attitudes, but rather that
the ruling or dominant group are the only ones whose shaping impact
matters (or at least, are those whose impact most matters, to a far greater
degree than that of any other group). 'If', says Socrates of the guardian-
rulers, 'they don't quarrel among themselves, there will be no danger of
rebellion or of faction in the rest of the community', to which Glaucon
emphatically agrees (465b).

My reply is to concede that the details of the *Republic*'s model of
the city are antiquated beyond repair, and that even the way in which it
presents its basic insight is flawed by that antiquated outlook – but to
insist nevertheless that the insight is there to be found and worth rescuing from the flaw in its presentation. To take that flaw first: the *Republic*

asserts that it is above all the dominant group in a society – those who will sooner or later become its rulers – who shape that society's values. So Socrates worries in great detail about the educational and living arrangements for the dominant group of wise rulers whom he proposes, while having very little to say about such arrangements for the lower social groups: he assumes that the rulers are those with the power either to save or to destroy the society. The justification for their paternalistic rule is that the rulers, when well educated and prevented from becoming corrupt, can rule society well, whereas if any other group were to take the reins it would destroy it through incompetence or greed. The corresponding hope is that the rulers will redesign the culture as a whole in the image of the good, saving their future successors – as well as the rest of the society – from the perverse and destructive images and stories that an unregulated democratic culture had previously produced.

The flaw in this vision is its assumption that the only way to achieve healthy change is for a small group of rulers to wholly control all forms of culture and communication, relying on the further assumption that such control can be entirely exercised from the top down. Call this composite the asymmetrical assumption. If this assumption is not true – if bards in Plato's day, bloggers in our own, inevitably escape such control to some extent, and can be sources of constructive change from below – then Plato's story needs to be rethought if it is to be of any modern use. My reading of the *Republic*'s basic insight is such a reappropriation, rejecting the asymmetrical assumption. Instead, I offer an appropriation which generalizes the fateful city–soul interaction among the ruling elite in Plato's account to a universal city–soul interaction in my own.

It is true that the idea of a city with functional groups fixed by merit (a merit to which education contributes but which depends initially on nature) is a non-starter for a liberal and democratic, let alone capitalist, regime. Yet the thought that the virtues need some social embodiment, some group to articulate and defend them, remains valid. If we don't trust self-appointed philosopher-kings, how do we mean to think instead about ensuring that rational judgement has social and political advocates? If we don't want our collective values and achievements to be driven wholly by short-term material desires, how and where do we envisage advocacy for longer-term values finding a social space and political voice? The *Republic* puts these questions squarely on the table. If we don't like its answers, it becomes incumbent on us to develop our own.

Thus we find the opposite of this aspect of Popper's denunciation to be true. We moderns tend to think that however people choose to live privately will have no bearing on the maintenance of the polity. Plato, on the other hand, thinks that how people live privately has massive significance for whether or not the polity can be maintained. From this vantage point, it is the moderns who consider the individual to be negligible, in that they consider the effects of her character and choices to be politically negligible, whereas it is Plato who considers the individual to be vitally significant, in that he considers the effects of her character and choices to be politically paramount.

At issue between Popper and Plato is the question of agency in bringing about political change. Plato is usually read as holding that such transformation must be top-down: the rulers who know the truth must impose it on everyone else through political means (Popper) or the writer who knows the truth must impose it on everyone else through linguistic means (Allen). On my reading, however, by assigning the telling of the 'noble lie' to the founder-legislators who stand outside the membership and roles in the imagined city. Plato is dramatizing not a further level of top-down control but rather its opposite: the thought that our imaginative topography escapes anyone's full control and ramifies in unpredictable and not wholly manipulable ways. Plato dramatized that by imagining a set of persons outside the order of the society they were creating; in Part III I will explore what it means for societies which lack such imaginary founder-legislator figures. What matters is that the two alternatives which Plato is usually depicted as posing – either elite political control, or a democratic lack of overall control which is tantamount to anarchy – are not exhaustive. The further alternative, the one which I think he also envisaged, is that imaginative order and so political order are at once more pervasively rooted and more unpredictably changeable.

What that alternative means for a transformation of modern society into a more sustainable one will be the subject of Part III. Before that, we will explore the imaginative changes which Plato modelled in this light.

Prologue to Chapter 5:
Plato on Why Virtue Matters

For the children in the good society outlined in the *Republic*, both body and character are to be trained from the earliest age (even prenatally, according to the *Laws*, another Platonic dialogue) in modes and rhythms of music which habituate them to be receptive to the virtues. The stories they are told, and the manner in which they are told, are to represent the virtues. Socrates calls for songs which 'represent appropriately the voice and accent of a brave man on military service or any dangerous undertaking, who faces misfortune, be it injury or death, or any other calamity, with the same steadfast endurance', and which:

> represent him in the voluntary non-violent occupations of peacetime: for instance, persuading someone grant a request, praying to God or instructing or admonishing his neighbour, or again submitting himself to the requests or instruction or persuasion of others and acting as he decides, and in all showing no conceit, but moderation and common sense and willingness to accept the outcome …

In sum, he recommends those musical modes 'which will best represent sound courage and moderation in good fortune or in bad' (all quotations immediately above, 399a–c). This can sound strange to modern ears, though it should not sound quite so strange if we consider our own uses of music to drill, to enthuse, to instil different ways of life, whether in the military or the punk underworld or the peace movement. One scholar has gone further, likening ancient Greek music and poetry to modern television, cinema, and advertising.[1] The Greeks drew on a relatively limited fund of myth, and, in a culture which was still largely oral in the fifth century B.C. when Socrates lived, these mythical motifs and characters pervaded the recitations and memorizations of poetry by which children were educated, the publicly commissioned comic and tragic dramas, and the religious festivals of which these plays formed part. While the sources and stories of modern media are more complex, the insinuations of advertising, the endless replays of television which still, for many children, form a larger part of their childhood education than does formal schooling, and the larger-than-life status of film and television stars is comparable to the deep and pervasive role that music and poetry about the gods and heroes played for the Greeks.

We too periodically concern ourselves about the pervasiveness of these media and their content. Recurrent debates about whether to regulate sex and violence on television, or pornography in shops and now on the internet, testify to that. Plato started a similar debate in his society, coming down hard on the side of a thoroughgoing regulation for the same reason as today's proponents of crackdowns on TV violence: for the sake of the lasting effects they have on the minds and characters of children. He was so concerned about this that he was willing to censor all available media, not simply to try to target that aimed at children. Plato's solution was a strongly paternalistic and controlling one. As has been pointed out, his challenge is nevertheless one which applies as much to modern democratic societies as to the society of his own time (and of his ideal city), and if we do not wish to impose such strong coercive censorship, then we need to come up with a more liberal solution which can do the job. That is the task for Part III. Before that, we need to explore the location of the virtues in the interrelationships between city and soul in greater depth.

5

The City and the Soul

In Chapter 4, I compared social sustainability to Plato's goal of social stability: a sustainable society must be sustainably stable, and a stable society will – in light of ecological constraints that Plato did not recognize – only be sustainably stable if it is in fact ecologically sustainable (otherwise ecological damage will inflict harms that risk undermining social stability). Now I will explain in more detail the basic parallels and points of intersection between soul and city, psychological stability and social stability. We will see that stability itself is only possible on the basis of an underlying value of health. It is health, as essential for happiness, which emerges as the key value of the *Republic* for both individual and city – and one which is resonant with implications for our understanding of what an ecologically sustainable society would mean.

Health – underlying happiness

A healthy life: in this section, I will argue that Plato treats health as a social and individual value which is more fundamental than (because a precondition for) happiness, and that we have much to learn from his approach. This is an unusual claim to make.[1] The usual claim is that the principal aim of all schools of ancient Greek ethics is happiness.[2] While this is not wrong as a generalization, and while happiness (the happiness of the just person, the unhappiness of the tyrant) is key to the overall argument of the *Republic*, I will argue that Plato there makes a distinctive move in relation to it. By taking happiness to depend on health, and so emphasizing the latter as a precondition, Plato is better able to speak to wide audiences in his own time and in ours.

First, some remarks on the ancient and modern understandings of happiness. 'Happiness' or 'flourishing' have become the preferred English translations of the Greek *eudaimonia*, which literally means 'favoured by the gods'. Deriving from this sense of divine favour, the Greeks emphasized the objective condition and standing of the *eudaimon* person. Whether or not someone is *eudaimon* is best judged not by themselves, but by a spectator, as it were the spectator-judge of a Greek tragedy, who will vote for whether to award the play a prize at the end of the festival, and who can see the mark of divine disfavour in a figure like Oedipus or Medea earlier than those characters would be aware of it themselves. Aristotle would go so far as to say that one cannot judge whether someone's life has been *eudaimon* until after that person dies, for only after death can a life be judged as a rounded whole. This brings out that it is one's life as a whole which is to be judged as *eudaimon* or not, not some transient mood or subset of activities.

While united in taking happiness to be the objective of life, the later Hellenistic schools diverged in their teaching as to what the true path to happiness might be. For some, like the Epicureans, happiness would come about from pleasure rightly understood, supreme in which was the pleasure of friendship; others treated pleasure as a secondary attribute of virtue, so that the virtuous life would be pleasant, but disagreed further about whether virtue was sufficient for happiness (roughly, the Stoics) or whether, while virtue was necessary and primary, other external goods were also needed for happiness (roughly, the Peripatetics, following Aristotle). Among those external goods valued by the Aristotelian Peripatetics but treated as a 'preferred indifferent' by the Stoics was health, together with not being in prison, having one's family survive, and other such goods. So health, by the time of the later Hellenistic debates, had become at best a subordinate element in happiness.

Despite these differences, for most Greeks happiness remained above all an individual aim (the *Republic* is radical in its Book 4 suggestion that the happiness of the city should take precedence over the happiness even of its rulers). The city might help individuals to cultivate and display the qualities which could make them candidates for *eudaimonia* (though divine favour, or what we would call luck, could also interfere). Recently, however, economists and psychologists have rediscovered happiness as a possible goal for the society as a whole.[3] This is an ironic turn in a long historical story. One strand in the Enlightenment reorientation of modern society had rejected hoary theories of duty and precedent in favour of a revisionist political philosophy of utilitarianism: positing a stripped-down version of happiness, in the form of the aggregate of individual pains and pleasures, as the social goal. But individual pains and pleasures are hard to measure and to compare (the problem of 'interpersonal comparisons of well-being').[4] So the social goal turned into the maximization, or at least optimization, of individual preferences, which could (it was thought) be taken to be revealed in behaviour, in what people actually choose. That became the basis of welfare economics, which has largely played the role of public philosophy for liberal democratic capitalism in the twentieth century and into the twenty-first.[5] But are preferences really a good measure of welfare? What if people have self-defeating, or racist, preferences? What if their preferences over time are incoherent, or short-termist, so that satisfying preferences now forecloses on the possibility of a better future which the people themselves would then (and perhaps even now) prefer?

These and similar considerations are part of what has led to the revival of happiness as an alternative goal for public policy, a happiness not denatured into trivial preferences, but rather restored to something like the rich and objective fabric of flourishing which concerned the Greeks. Psychologists are beginning to stress the difference between transitory satisfactions and life-satisfaction over time; economists are asking whether economies built around consumption, which inherently promote frustration and inequality, should be reassessed against a more complex standard of the social good. (A further aspect of this revival is the critique of GDP and of the notion of growth, to be considered in Chapter 6.)

I am in sympathy with the motivations of these approaches. But there are a number of problems in taking 'happiness' to be the standard, not least the ingrained English-language tendency to consider it to be a subjective matter, as well as its aspirational and so potentially controversial content. One can imagine a public reaction against government promotion of happiness, as people claim the right to be unhappy in their own way, insisting that government should limit itself to providing less controversial and demanding goods such as safety and basic welfare.

Strikingly, I think that this sort of wariness about happiness as a full-blown aim is anticipated in Plato's *Republic*. While happiness remains the overall goal which structures the argument, showing that the just man will be happy and the unjust man unhappy, that overarching claim is undergirded by an appeal to health. This I think is because it is hard for anyone to deny that health is valuable, if not a *sine qua non*, for both social and individual goals. If Plato succeeds in making the happiness of the just person appear obvious, he does so largely by making that happiness a matter of the person's psychic health. Such health at the level of the individual as well as of the society is expressed in terms of an order of concord or harmony, using imagery drawn from music.

As is typical of Plato, however, while the notion of health as a form of order is a valuable insight, the specific form in which he expressed that insight – a form of strict and purportedly natural hierarchy – is more problematic. The definition which Socrates offers of health, as an account first of justice and then of virtue in general, is this:

> SOCRATES: '[H]ealth is produced by establishing a natural relation of control and subordination among the constituents of the body, disease by establishing an unnatural relation.'
>
> GLAUCON: 'True.'
>
> SOCRATES: 'So justice is produced by establishing in the mind a similar natural relation of control and subordination among its constituents, and injustice by establishing an unnatural one.'
>
> GLAUCON: 'Certainly.'
>
> SOCRATES: 'It seems, then, that excellence is a kind of mental health or beauty or fitness, and defect a kind of illness or deformity or weakness.'
> (444d–e)

True, the particular quality of 'rule' and 'control' and 'subordination' here is difficult to swallow, pervaded as it is by the naturalized hierarchies which we acknowledged earlier. But again, we can identify an underlying point which remains valuable even if and when we reject the specific formulation in which Plato expressed it. That underlying point is that order is necessary for health, and more generally, that health is a kind of order, in which each part of the body is doing what it should do and nothing is doing more or other than its own task (cancer, for example, being an excellent example of *polupragmosunē* or cells running amok, doing far more than they should normally do and interfering with the work of others). This Platonic idea of virtue as health, meaning that the virtuous dispositions are those which help to maintain and express this order, is a less abstract and outrageous notion than it might first seem (though that is not to say that it is devoid of all ideological content).[6]

Socrates goes on to describe the way in which the just man functions, which again can be taken as a synecdoche for the functioning of the person who is virtuous overall.

> SOCRATES: 'The just man will not allow the three elements which make up his inward self to trespass on each other's functions or interfere with each other, but, by keeping all three in tune, like the notes of a scale (high, medium, and low, and any others there be), will in the truest sense set his house to rights, attain self-mastery and order, and live on good terms with himself. When he has bound these elements into a disciplined and harmonious whole, and so become fully one instead of many, he will be ready for action of any kind, whether it concerns his personal or financial welfare, whether it is political or private.' (443d–e)

Notice the benefits that virtue is said to provide. The virtuous man will 'live on good terms with himself' and will be 'ready for action of any kind … whether … political or private'. Virtue as health is the precondition both for happiness and for agency. Without sufficient rational self-governance, and the courage, self-control, and justice which this requires and facilitates, we will not be the sort of agents which the public realm requires, and neither will we be best placed to achieve our own ends or to pursue happiness. Virtue is not an optional perfectionist pursuit. In this light, it is the basic parameter of health, without which soul and city risk crumbling into disorder, at worst dissolving into civil war. Health itself is the basis of agency, again not an optional perfectionist pursuit as one might take happiness to be, but rather the order without which one cannot coherently intend or act at all. So internal justice makes both for health and for treating others justly; both arise from the same root. There is no conflict between them, and the best way to see why we should be just is not to appeal to duty or law but to explain that only if we are just do we enjoy the psychic health necessary to achieve any other set of goods.

Physical health is a good image for agency precisely because health is a complex relationship of changing processes which have to be maintained in a dynamic balance. It is not reducible to any simpler metric, such as the metric of pains and pleasures, which we will see that Plato's character Callicles believes dictates a life of consumption, of as much food, sex, and wine as possible. (Later Epicurean philosophers, despite the way in which their name has been misappropriated to stand for luxurious self-indulgence, maintained that the most pleasurable life would actually be a moderately ascetic one.) Instead, any decision about food or exercise has to be taken in light of a whole picture of how to live one's life, so that one neither over-exercises or over-diets (anorexia is as much a danger as obesity), while balancing nutrients and enjoying health-giving foods (such as red wine and chocolate) in moderation. Any attempt to reduce health decision-making to a simple rule – and worse, a monetary rule, such as saving money by eating only at fast food restaurants, with the consequences graphically displayed in the film *Supersize Me!* – will fail.

This truth about the complex measure of health is one which modern societies are being driven to acknowledge in relation to obesity, for example, but which we still too often lack the vocabulary and sophistication to register in full even on the level of bodily health. What can only be called an epidemic of obesity, arising in large part from the endemic patterns of commuting and child-rearing which privilege sedentary travel and television, raises an acute need for such a complex redefinition of health. But the current models of financial cost-benefit assessment make this almost impossible to do. School sports playing fields are sold off to make money for hard-pressed school districts (in the US) or local authorities (in the UK); school 'lunches' (US) or 'dinners' (UK) are contracted out to the lowest bidder. The difficulty is the assumption that the financial cost-benefit metric is both appropriately neutral and appropriately straightforward to maximize ('operationalize'). In fact, the measure of health that we need is neither neutral nor simply given to maximization. It requires local authorities and other public bodies to consider a wide range of goods, some of them of intrinsic but not financially realizable value, and to consider the intimate connection between the body and the mental and emotional capacities of which Plato was well aware. In the same way, staying healthy requires us to consider a wide range of goods, some of them valuable only insofar as they are limited rather than maximized. The idea that some goods are valuable only when limited, not when consumed to excess, is a crucial complication of any simple metric of value.[7]

As a standard for psychological as well as biological welfare, health is a complex and multidimensional state which cannot be achieved without virtuous agency. Yet it is also a state whose value is evident. One may choose to compromise or sacrifice one's health for other goals (political or personal), but it is hard not to acknowledge that something of value is being lost in doing so. This, I conjecture, is why Plato had recourse to health, rather than to happiness, as the fundamental measure of the soul.

An objection: Socrates versus Job

Many readers will ask whether the relationship between interpersonal justice and health, let alone the further relationship of justice to happiness, is still being claimed on the basis of a sleight of hand. How can Plato justify the claim that (as I put it above), the pleasures won by unjust actions 'turn out to be destructive to the person himself by destroying his social relationships'? We all know stories of people who break the law, or treat others badly within the law, and yet seem to flourish. Ancient authors from Plato to the Bible struggled with this problem: the flourishing of the wicked disturbs Job and Jonah as much as it does Socrates. The biblical texts solve the problem by appealing to the inscrutability of God's ways. Socrates solves it by showing us the experience of the wicked in a different light. They only appear to be flourishing when flourishing is defined in terms of insatiable consumption; when the focus is broadened to a range of other human goods, such as friendship and relationship, we see that the wicked are inherently self-destructive.

Socrates argues this most clearly later in the *Republic*, in the course of giving the final proof that the life of the insatiable person with total power – the tyrant, as he was thought of in Greece – would be most miserable rather than most happy. He shows this first by considering the nature of the tyrant's psychology, in which rather than appetite being governed by reason, the reason and spirit are instead made slaves to the appetites. Socrates demands:

can it possibly pay anyone to make money by doing wrong, if the result of his so doing is to enslave the best part of himself to the worst? No one would say it paid to sell his son or daughter as a slave to harsh and wicked masters, however high the price; if one ruthlessly enslaves the divinest part of oneself to the most godless and abominable, is it not a miserable piece of bribery ...? (589e–590a)

This (albeit couched again in the Greek understanding of the divine) is an appeal to common sense. Enslaving oneself or one's beloved child to harsh external masters is obviously not in one's interest; neither then is enslaving oneself to one's appetites. The person who does this with most abandon – the tyrant – is never able to satisfy his desires. And worse, being untrustworthy himself (because he will sacrifice anything to the satisfaction of a moment's pleasure), he is not able to trust others, because they will not trust him. Thus – indeed like tyrants through the centuries – he is dependent on his bodyguards of whom he must also be eternally suspicious. He has no friends because no one can trust him, nor, therefore, he them. (Stalin was on the verge of death for hours before any of his entourage dared to approach him, for fear of his murderous wrath.)[8] Whatever power he gains (whether the full political power of the tyrant proper, the limiting case which Socrates considers, or the power of the playboy billionaire), he cannot buy or command the good of peace of mind.

> SOCRATES: 'He can never satisfy his desires, and behind his multitudinous wants you can see, if you know how to survey it as a whole, the real impoverishment of his character; his life is haunted by fear and ... torn by suffering and misery ...'
>
> [GLAUCON agrees]: '... Add to that ... that his power will make him still more envious, untrustworthy, unjust, friendless, and godless, a refuge and home for every iniquity, and you can see that he's a source of misery above all to himself, but also to his neighbors.' (579e–580a)

This is obviously the extreme case. But Socrates uses it to make a more general point: far from there being a linear relation between power or money and the achievement of welfare, in fact indulgence in pleasures tends to undermine and ultimately destroy the goods of social relationship and self-control.[9] Welfare is not all of a kind, and the superficial, easy kind will not only distract from the achievement of deeper and more lasting happiness, but actively destroy it as a possibility. If such indulgence undermines our health as agents, we will be unable to pursue any meaningful goals at all.

This is a thought which modern society is able to recognize in its most pathological applications. The psychology of the drug addict is one which most people agree to be debasing and destructive of happiness, precisely for the reasons which Socrates gives: in pursuing temporary highs at any price, the addict becomes untrustworthy – she steals and lies to feed her habit – and so destroys the possibility of stable relationships on which human happiness really depends. But what we acknowledge in the case of the drug addict we are chary of admitting in the case of those addicted to money, fame, or power. We need to learn to recognize this structure in the less pathological cases of apparent success as well as in the abject examples of total failure.

The *Republic*'s images of soul and city

In order to understand the role of the virtues in achieving health in Plato's model, we need to step back to consider the way in which the *Republic* (at least in Books 1 to 4 and 8 to 9)[10] defines the nature of the city and the soul in more detail. Doing so helps both to motivate a concern with virtue and to illustrate what that means and why it might arise. This can help to complement philosophical accounts of virtue ethics by providing a concrete set of images and exemplars through which the interconnections of the virtues are refracted. While some theories of virtue ethics focus on locating virtue in a comprehensive theory of value, others on defending a meta-ethical position for virtue ethics against consequentialism or deontology, my aim is more limited: to articulate the psychological and social implications of a core set of Greek virtues.[11]

Famously, Socrates develops over the course of Books 2 to 4 a model of the city and then a parallel model of the soul. In each case, he begins with a simpler two-part distinction. His model of the city begins as a simple economy which, as soon as it begins to produce and purchase luxury goods, has need of a separate group of armed guards to defend it. That claim is made to look commonsensical, though in fact it would have been controversial among many of Plato's Athenian readers, who lived with a democratic ideology and practice in which all male citizens played a role in the city's military functions. Socrates then slips in a further qualification, that the true 'guards' who rule the city will be those older men who most reliably know best and love it best, while the fighters per se will serve as their younger auxiliaries, using their military training to support the guardians' convictions (412bff.) Only later, in Book 5, does Socrates reveal a further demand on the 'guards': their knowledge cannot be mere aged wisdom, it must in fact be exhaustive knowledge of philosophy, culminating in the recognition of the Form of the Good (to be discussed in Chapter 6).

The result is a strict separation of functional classes. This is not however a rigid caste system. Children born to parents of one class may turn out to be properly suited themselves to the function of a different class, to which the guardians will duly transfer them. Functions are defined by birth in the sense of one's individual nature (though nurture and experience are needed to develop that nature correctly, or can conversely corrupt it and so disqualify a child from playing a role to which he or she was originally naturally suited). But they are not defined by birth in the sense of inherited status. The regime is to be a rigid meritocracy.

Much of this is alien to modern sensibilities. To our ears, it is repugnant to divide society into a class of natural rulers (supported by a class of soldiers), ruling over the lowest of the three classes who are relegated to artisanry and farming, without any active political role to play. The repugnance is at least double. First, the thought of rigidly divided social functions, in which one function is that of ruling, which will be monopolized by a single group rather than being open to contestation and rotation, appals many a modern democrat almost as much, though perhaps less viscerally, as it would have repelled an ancient Athenian one. Second, that membership of that monopoly group of rulers should be self-selected by a purportedly natural standard of merit is further repulsive to both modern and ancient democrats. (For all the important differences between ancient and modern democracy, it is instructive that such negative reactions should be shared.[12]) So why am I bothering to rehearse this archaic account?

The reason is that while the detailed natural determinism of Plato's account cannot be rescued today, his underlying thought that political formations are shaped by the characters of the citizens, and shape them in turn, remains fundamental to an intelligent political sociology.[13] Not that character is the only force shaping political outcomes, not by a long shot: sociology today has documented the importance of internal bureaucratic pathways, path dependence, economist interests, and other factors. But it a force which we tend to overlook at our peril. Overcoming our repugnance and rejection of Plato's detailed picture, we have still something to learn from it at a higher level of abstraction. If his model of how city and soul interact is not to our liking, we still have need of such a model, and the task of constructing a better one will be made easier if we understand the inside workings of his.

Such an understanding begins from the fact that Plato presents his model as counter-intuitive even for his own characters, the youthful Glaucon and Adeimantus who are enrolled as Socrates' conversation partners to construct it. In fact, the young men do not demur at the construction of the civic part of the model, even though it would have been contrary to democratic ideology in the ways described above. Their aristocratic leanings, their inclination to think of themselves as superior to the democratic fray (as documented in the way they ask Socrates to explain why it would not be advantageous to oneself to act unjustly so long as one could get away with it or square it afterwards with both gods and men), seem to lead them to accept the notion of a defined class first of military guards, and then of natural rulers, far more readily than an ordinary Athenian democrat might have done.

Interestingly, however, given the brothers' spirited willingness to imagine what it would be to be a secretly unjust man, superior to others in the fruits of one's injustice while protected against suffering its ordinary consequences of punishment or reputational loss, the point at which they baulk, Glaucon nevertheless is initially inclined to posit only two, rather than three, parts of the soul. In particular, having accepted that reason is different from bodily appetites and desires (the Athenians would be accustomed to separating reason from desire, though Socrates unusually makes the bodily appetites rather than a more general passionate love the focus of the latter), Glaucon shows himself inclined to assimilate spiritedness and anger to the bodily appetites and desires (439e). That is, the ordinary Athenian conception, which he thinks he accepts, has no place or way to account for the tendencies of his own character, as if spiritedness and the desire for honour were just another desire alongside hunger or thirst. Ordinary Athenian psychology was self-deceiving in this way about the nature of aristocratic spiritedness, and Socrates' model is designed to bring this out, making Glaucon aware of the nature of his own inclinations.

Socrates offers an 'image' (*eidolon*) in the form of a story, to dramatize the existence of a spirited part of the soul, and in so doing, as has been argued, to 'shift the landscape of [Glaucon's] imagination'[14] so as to alter his perception of other values.

> Leontius, the son of Aglaion, who was on his way up from the Piraeus, under the outer side of the north wall, when he noticed some corpses lying on the ground with the executioner standing by them. He wanted to go and look at them, and yet at the same time held himself back in disgust. For a time he struggled with himself and covered his eyes, but at last his desire got the better of him and he ran up to the corpses, opening his eyes wide and saying to them, 'There you are, curse you – a lovely sight! Have a real good look!' (439e–440a)

The details of the story are too complex to recount here. The important point for our purposes is the further image that Socrates draws, depicting individuals as often suffering from an internal 'civil war' between the various parts of the soul, one in which spirit only ever allies itself voluntarily with reason against the appetites: 'don't we often see other instances of a man whose desires are trying to force him to do something his reason disapproves of, cursing himself and getting indignant at their violence? It's like a struggle between political factions, with indignation [the spirited part] fighting on the side of reason' (440a–b).

Agreeing with this, and with further examples of how people often get angry at what they suffer when they believe they have been unjustly treated (but not when they know it is they themselves who have acted unjustly), Glaucon is able to accept that spiritedness and anger are a different class of motivation from the bodily appetites, so becoming aware also of the true meaning of his own spirited nature. In dividing the soul into three parts – reason, spirit, and bodily appetite – the *Republic* aims to elicit self-knowledge in its readers. The model seeks to persuade us of the ways in which our own souls are at risk of domination by desire, ego, anger, honour, greed, and to demonstrate the costs of our failure to live up to an informed commitment to the rational good.

Virtues of soul and city in the *Republic*

Given the models of soul and city outlined above, what sort of virtues and vices might one expect to find? A first stab at an answer to this might take each of the three parts to have a characteristic virtue and corresponding vice: for reason, the virtuous disposition is to act wisely, the vicious one ignorantly; for spirit, acting courageously and in a cowardly way respectively; for appetite, acting moderately or excessively. The first two of these are exactly what Socrates describes. In the case of the third, however, he denies that there is a virtue or vice characteristic of appetite alone. Instead, the virtue of self-discipline (also translatable as moderation) and the vice of excess or corruption pertain to the relations *among* the parts. Self-discipline arises when the appetites are disposed (and agree) to be ruled by reason assisted by spirit; corruption, when the appetites rebel against such rule, seeking their own satisfactions rather than following the limits and aims which reason prescribes they should pursue.[15] Socrates, it seems, is loath to allow any independent scope to the appetites to recognize or abide by suitable limits. That must be the job of reason to prescribe. Having defined the appetites very strictly, so that the desire for drink, for example, is not a desire for a good drink but merely for drink as such (439a), he now reinforces that privation by insisting that even the virtue to which they might be disposed cannot arise inherently or naturally within appetite alone, but must reflect its being firmly governed by reason.

So far we have identified three virtues and their corresponding vices, indeed three of the four which Plato took to be the cardinal virtues (though many Greeks would have added piety as a fifth virtue). But the paradox is that the virtue we have so far failed to mention is that of justice – which had been presented in Books 1 to 2 as the primary topic of the *Republic* (first in terms of the question 'why be just?', and then in terms of the underlying definition of justice itself). That failure repeats one dramatized in the text of the *Republic*, when having identified wisdom, courage, and self-discipline in the city, Socrates professes justice to be hidden in a thicket from which it must be hunted out (433bff). What it amounts to, he proposes, is that 'each individual ... get on with his own job' (433d). This would have been instantly understandable to a Greek reader as the opposite of 'meddling in other people's business', or *polupragmosunē*.

Keeping oneself to oneself, as the opposite of busybody meddling, was for a certain strain of conservative Greek ethics the very essence of justice (and for many, a reason to be sceptical of radical democracy, since that seemed to represent precisely the meddling of the poor in the business of the city and often in the affairs of the rich).

Justice and self-discipline, then, are mirror images of one another. Justice is each part of the city and soul doing its own work, self-discipline the agreement by the lower parts that the higher parts should do their own work in ruling. Again, while acknowledging the offensiveness of Plato's strict hierarchy, we can find something valuable here. Both justice and self-discipline depend inherently on the notion of limit and restraint. Justice is the specific form of self-restraint which prevents one from busybody interfering; self-discipline or moderation, *sōphrosunē*, is in Plato's hands a form of self-restraint from pursuing goals other than those reason dictates, but it is in general Greek usage a more general and pervasive commitment to self-restraint (indeed, it can also be translated as self-control). Without such moderating self-discipline, none of the other virtues is possible; if greed or anger get the better of us, we won't be able to live up to our best ambitions or our most truthful acknowledgements.[16] This is why I have argued elsewhere that moderation is the virtue, or initially the proto-virtue, at the psychic core of all the others.[17]

Here is Socrates explaining this position:

> SOCRATES: '... the reason ought to rule, having the wisdom and foresight
>   to act for the whole, and the spirit ought to obey and support it.'
> GLAUCON: 'Certainly.'
> SOCRATES: 'When these two elements have been so brought up, and trained
>   and educated to their proper function, they must be put in charge of
>   appetite, which forms the greater part of each man's make-up and is
>   naturally insatiable. They must prevent it taking its fill of the so-called
>   physical pleasures, or otherwise it will get too large and strong to mind
>   its own business and will try to subject and control the other elements,
>   which it has no right to do, and so wreck the life of all of them. [...] And
>   we call an individual brave because of this part of him ... when he has
>   a spirit which holds fast to the orders of reason about what he ought or
>   ought not to fear, in spite of pleasure and pain?'
> GLAUCON: 'That is quite right.'

SOCRATES: 'And we call him wise in virtue of that small part of him which is in control and issues the orders, knowing as it does what is best for each of the three elements and for the whole made up of them.'

GLAUCON: 'Yes, I agree.'

SOCRATES: 'Then don't we call him self-disciplined when all these three elements are in friendly and harmonious agreement, when reason and its subordinates are all agreed that reason should rule and there is no civil war among them?'

GLAUCON: 'That is exactly what we mean by self-control or discipline in a city or in an individual.'

SOCRATES: 'And a man will be just by following the principle [doing one's own] we have stated so often.' (441e–442d)

By internalizing justice, defining it as a matter of psychological configuration, Plato has been accused of performing a bait and switch in his answer to the question of whether the just person will be happy. That question invokes the conventional view of justice as a relation between persons, as a matter of how a person treats her fellows, whereas Plato's answer treats justice as an internal psychological state. But in fact Socrates goes on to show that the way someone internally just will characteristically, and reliably, treat others deserves the name of justice for exactly the same reasons of interpersonal treatment as the conventional account would give. The achievement of internal justice entails the exhibition of interpersonal justice. (Crucially, however, as the reflection on the invisibility ring story earlier in the *Republic* had demonstrated, the reverse is not true: someone may exhibit interpersonal justice out of fear of punishment, without having internal justice; but in that case her interpersonal justice will be vulnerable to changes in the external climate – she may act unjustly if she thinks she can get away with it – and will not bring her the happiness which internal justice as an integrated part of virtue can bring.) As Socrates and Glaucon agree in describing the reliable behaviour of the internally just person, alternating as usual:

SOCRATES: 'suppose for instance we were asked whether … [the internally just person] would embezzle money deposited with him. Do you think we should reckon him more likely to do it than other people?'

GLAUCON: 'He would be the last person to do such a thing.'

SOCRATES: 'And wouldn't it be out of the question for him to commit sac-
rilege or theft, or to betray his friends or his country?'

GLAUCON: 'Out of the question.'

SOCRATES: 'And he would never break a solemn promise or any other
agreement.'

GLAUCON: 'Certainly not.'

SOCRATES: 'And he would be the last man to commit adultery, dishonour
his parents, or be irreligious.'

GLAUCON: 'The last man.'

SOCRATES: 'And is not the reason for all this that each element within
him is performing its proper function, whether it is giving or obeying
orders?'

GLAUCON: 'Yes, that is the reason.' (442e–443a)

One way to put Socrates' point is that, insofar as reason governs the
just and self-disciplined person's appetites, those appetites will neither
get out of control, nor will they fixate on pleasures which turn out to be
destructive to the person himself by destroying his social relationships.
The just person does not experience the out-of-control lust or greed
which would tempt him to embezzle, steal, betray, break promises and
contracts, or commit adultery. (The dishonouring of parents and irreligi-
osity reflect more specific Greek social mores.) This is because his reason
governs his appetites, and that in turn is because he became habituated
from childhood to balance and control, thus becoming receptive to the
control of reason over appetite, rather than rebelling against it as if it
were an unfamiliar and unjustified bridle. While the focus here is on
psychic justice, there can be no behavioural justice – or willingness to
refrain from pleonectic greed for what belongs to others – without the
self-discipline to confine oneself to what is properly one's own. Self-
discipline is the underlying scaffolding of all the other virtues.[18] While
it is ideally completed by knowledge, which directs the self-controlled
person towards what is genuinely and not merely apparently good, it is
also the condition for making fruitful use of such knowledge. To adapt
some phrasing from a different subject, self-control without knowledge
may be blind, but knowledge without self-control is impotent. Like sustainability, self-discipline is not the highest good, but it is a condition for
achieving that good: indeed, it is a condition for its sustainable achievement over time.

Knowledge and the virtues

If justice and self-discipline are interdependent, both are for Plato inter-dependent, further, with wisdom or knowledge. Self-discipline must be intelligently directed, to what one knows to be one's proper limits and sphere, if it is to be valuable; otherwise it can too easily become a compla-cent apathy or a punitive austerity. Justice must likewise properly identify what belongs to oneself and one's own province, and what belongs to that of others: to do so requires cognitive insight. (Courage, too, though less central to my story, fits for Plato into the same interconnected template.) Being smart and self-aware, as we saw the modern handbook *Carbon Detox* prescribes, is vital to the moderate self-discipline necessary to keep self and society in harmonious, rather than destructive, relationship.

If knowledge is necessary, is it enough? Will the person who knows about climate change actually always, and thereby, do the right thing, or do we not sometimes act against what we know to be right? This is the classical problem which Aristotle baptized *akrasia*, often referred to as 'weakness of will', and describing the phenomenon of someone seeming to know or have decided that it is best to act in a certain way, yet acting otherwise. A standard way of telling the history of Greek philosophy – the way Aristotle himself told it – is to begin by saying that Socrates denied the possibility of *akrasia*, holding that people only act against what they know to be best 'by reason of ignorance', as if there were no other psychic motive forces other than knowledge or ignorance. This denial is taken to be stated most plainly in Plato's dialogue *Protagoras* (esp. 352a8–c7), where Socrates rejects a view he ascribes to the populist 'many', according to whom people often have knowledge but it fails to rule, being 'dragged about' by the emotions and appetites as if it were a slave.[19] The Socrates of the *Republic* then – it is often said, taking him to be a spokesman now for Plato – divided the soul precisely in order to be able to explain *akrasia*: with a tripartite soul, the knowledge of the rational part may be overcome by the superior forces of a rampant spirited or appetitive part bent on fulfilling irrational but powerful desires.[20] And Aristotle himself then gave the canonical explanation of *akrasia*.

Yet Aristotle's own solution ended up agreeing with Socrates in some sense, as he himself acknowledged: insofar as a person who knows acts wrongly against his knowledge, he cannot *really* have *fully* known at the time of wrongly acting. Instead he knew only in a derivative, imperfect sense, which Aristotle compares to the knowledge one has when drunk or asleep.[21] In the *Republic* too, a quotation from the *Protagoras* – a reference to the rational part of the soul being 'dragged along' by the two lower parts, using the same verb for 'dragged along' as the *Protagoras* – should be read not as rejecting the Socratic view, but rather as reinforcing it, by showing that this can only happen when the rational part of the soul lacks true and full knowledge.[22] Possession of true and full knowledge in active self-rule is then the point on which, contrary to the popular history of Greek philosophy reported above, 'Socrates' in Plato's *Protagoras*, Plato (that is, 'Socrates' again) in the *Republic*, and Aristotle all converge. And this in turn highlights the crucial relevance of knowledge to virtue. One can be largely virtuous by rote or habit, but to fully understand and grasp the right thing to do in each new circumstance demands knowledge to illuminate the correct contours of self-discipline, justice, and courage therein. We will return to the role of knowledge in Chapter 6.

The vices: the love of money

If we turn now from the virtues to the vices, depicted in the portraits of vicious cities and vicious individuals in *Republic* Books 8 and 9,[23] we immediately notice something which is often overlooked: this is the special place given to money in the economy, and moral and political theory, of the *Republic*, and the special status of the vice which love of money constitutes therein. It is true that some lovers of money are said by Socrates to be able to keep their addiction within bounds, using reason to calculate and control their appetites so that they go on accumulating without suffering the penalties of legal punishment or total social breakdown of relationships. Socrates acknowledges just this possibility of the person called the self-controlled oligarch in *Republic* Book 8 (considering the oligarch as the person driven by the accumulation of wealth, rather than as a figure in a distinctive kind of political regime as Plato also portrays him). Here is how Socrates describes him to Glaucon's brother Adeimantus as a prototype of the money-lover.

SOCRATES: '... the high reputation for honesty which he has in ... [certain] business transactions is due merely to a certain respectable constraint which he exercises over his evil impulses, for fear of their effect on his concerns as a whole. There's no moral conviction, no taming of desire by reason, but only the compulsion of fear.'

ADEIMANTUS: 'Very true.'

SOCRATES: 'And what is more, you are pretty sure to find evidence of [his giving in to his criminal desires] when a man of this kind is spending other people's money.'

ADEIMANTUS: 'Oh, very much so.'

SOCRATES: 'This sort of man, then, is never at peace in himself, but has a kind of dual personality, in which the better desires on the whole master the worse.'

ADEIMANTUS: 'True.'

SOCRATES: 'He therefore has a certain degree of respectability, but comes nowhere near the real goodness of an integrated and balanced character.'

ADEIMANTUS: 'I agree.' (554c–554e)

Could there be a better description of Bernard Madoff or Allen Stanford? These seeming pillars of respectability lacked the 'real goodness of an integrated and balanced character', the sort of character which would have respected the trust in which they were held to manage 'other people's money'. Instead, their 'high reputation for honesty' was due not to any 'moral conviction', not to the 'taming of desire by reason', but only to 'the compulsion of fear', which in their case was insufficient to keep them honest, but instead drove them to cover up their misdeeds until they were found out.

As the cases of Madoff and Stanford demonstrate, such characters are very often unstable and unreliable themselves. Even where they are not, where money-makers manage to control themselves enough to behave honestly, the inherent instability of their position is very often transferred to the next generation. Such characters are liable to suffer breakdown of relationships within the family (cue a high divorce rate and trophy wives) and pathologies among the next generation of such families, who learn no true self-control from their parents and so are liable to squander their money and their time as trust-fund brats. Socrates shows this too, describing the children of the oligarchs: '... their young men live in luxury and idleness, physical and mental, become idle, and lose their ability to resist pain or pleasure' (556c).

These are the young men who are liable to become what Socrates describes as 'democratic' characters. Again, our interest here is in their private lives rather than their significance as prototypes of a political regime. The 'democratic' youth, child of an oligarchic (capitalist, money-loving, as we may gloss this) father, is 'devoid of sound knowledge and practices and true principles' ... [intervention] and so their minds are 'filled instead by an invasion of pretentious fallacies and opinions ... [intervention] And back he goes to live with the Lotus-eaters' (560b–c).

This account has considerable sheer human plausibility. Socrates is relying not on arcane knowledge here, but on common-sense experience about child-rearing and business practice. Businessmen who are reliable only so far as it suits them are likely to be found out; their pampered children, who have no model of principle or work ethic in their parents, are likely to squander the family fortune. These are not absolutely necessary connections, but very likely ones, and when one adds to that the intrinsic happiness constituted by virtue and justice, the case for risking one's happiness, and most importantly the underlying health of one's agency, as well as one's reputation on unjust behaviour becomes far less compelling.

Consider now how Socrates' account might bear on debates about greed and consumption today. Greed is too often treated either as an aberrant feature of a 'tiny minority', or as an isolated moral lapse.[24] The assumption is that people could simply stop being greedy, perhaps if they exercised more willpower (a view of willpower too often divorced from the habit-forming structures of virtuous self-control). What the *Republic* shows is that greed is far more structurally entrenched in both character and culture for that to be easily done. In a society devoted to money-making, Socrates points out, there is a structural drive to maintain this dynamic: '... the rulers, owing their power to wealth as they do, are unwilling to curtail by law the extravagance of the young, and prevent them from squandering their money and ruining themselves; for it is by loans to such spendthrifts or by buying up their property that they hope to increase their own wealth and influence' (555c).

There is no easy path to controlling greed, and no way to do it without disrupting some of our cherished assumptions and habits about how the social world works and how we ourselves should be entitled to work.

Socrates goes so far as to say, in his next intervention, that: '... love of money and adequate self-discipline in its citizens are two things that can't coexist in any society; one or the other must be neglected' (555c–d). Notice that what Socrates says here is '*love* of money' (emphasis added). It is not money per se, but a damagingly unchecked passion for it, which is the problem (just as in the political analysis of the *Republic*, as I have argued elsewhere, it is not power per se, but the *love* of power which is the problem).[25] Today, however, love of money is rooted in and reinforced by the general way in which current financial and economic models operate. If we are serious about putting an end to the destructive effects of greed, then we have to be serious about reinstating a culture in which relationships matter more than acquisition, in which consumption is self-controlled, in which money is not a god. To do this, we need a culture of character which respects limits, instils self-control, and subjects appetites to rational scrutiny and discipline.[26]

This solution may still sound too easy, too smugly prescriptive. For a profound challenge posed by analysts of the modern economy is whether it is such as to be potentially controllable by such self-control at all, or whether it operates in a way which systematically undermines the very possibility of virtuous self-control. Such a challenge has been launched more or less simultaneously within several disciplines. One psychologist explains the 'hedonic treadmill' on which people find themselves trapped by arguing that modern materialism is inherently hostile to limits, in part because it is fuelled by a resistance to accepting the prospect of death.[27] He has argued further, together with an environmental strategist, that the environmental movement must for its part beware of appealing to materialist motivations, as these are inherently hostile to the very notion of intrinsic goods, intrinsic motivation, and identities based on anything other than the evanescent rewards of consumerism which environmental action (in my terms, virtuous action) demands.[28] Meanwhile, an economic historian has analysed 'the challenge of affluence' on the basis of British and American social experience since 1950: he sums up his case in the contention that 'affluence breeds impatience, and impatience undermines well-being.'[29] Affluence makes us impatient with the very commitments and commitment-devices which are needed to structure an intrinsically satisfying social identity. And so, thinking we can afford to jettison them, we end up undermining the very well-being which affluence was (on a shallow understanding) expected to produce.

In focusing on 'materialism' and 'affluence', these scholars are criticizing not any old pattern of consumption but specific patterns which are characterized not just by the acquisition of goods or money, but by what Plato called, as we saw, the 'love of money'. Money is an instrumental good which at best only allows the purchase of elements that support well-being, but it too easily becomes a goal in itself, so occluding the Platonic question of what is truly good. At the same time, the culture of modern materialism presents goods and services not merely as satisfying various needs or stable desires, but as the unique key to a well-being which is always just out of reach, since none of them once purchased proves to be able to supply it (not surprisingly, given that well-being depends in large part on virtuous activity, according not only to Plato and Aristotle but also to modern positive psychology, and this is something which cannot be bought). So it is a distinctive pattern and culture of consumption – call it materialism – which when enabled by affluence, serves to destroy the very well-being it pretends to purchase.

Plato did not, of course, know or predict the particular permutations of modern culture. He was however acutely aware of the danger of obsession with money both as an instrumental good mistaken for an intrinsic one, and also in terms of the seemingly limitless consumption which money seemed to promise.[30] The philosophers of Kallipolis may be indifferent to money in their love for learning, and will be deprived of it as rulers, but the rest of the city will have to engage with it, and so must do so on moderate terms. The virtues Plato propounded are not irrelevant relics from an age innocent of the challenges of unbridled consumption. On the contrary, they are prescriptions intended to prevent the very ravaging of psyche and society which such consumption, when loosed from the constraints of self-control, portends. Strikingly, the analysis of the economic historian quoted earlier closes with a call for the development of virtue to restrain and reverse the damaging trends he describes. Moderation is not out of date although – indeed because – it has become, in Nietzsche's sense, untimely.

To say this is not to damn consumption as such. Consumption is an inevitable part of the human condition, and caring about what we consume – how we dress, where we live, what we eat – is as well. What is dangerous is becoming trapped on the hedonist treadmill which seeks endlessly after evanescent pleasures or comforts, ignoring and so eroding the complex values of time, health, and sustainability. As lived out in the private realm, this hedonism today typically takes the form of materialism. And materialism condemns people to a rat-race of transitory satisfactions followed by a gnawing dissatisfaction which is filled only briefly by a new transitory pleasure before emptying out again.[31]

This transitory material rat-race, ignoring the need for balance which leads to true happiness in both psyche and body, was something which Plato well understood. We might say that materialism in this sense makes all the world into money. Goods and experiences become universally fungible, losing their individual character; their solidity dissolves in the very act of consumption, so that (again like money) they became inherently incapable of satisfying on their own, promising a satisfaction which is in fact endlessly deferred.

Such a generalized materialist attitude is expressed in Plato's dialogue *Gorgias* by the character Callicles, who thinks himself a tough, superior guy, someone who goes for the power to sate his appetites and is willing to outrage public opinion in order to do so.

> CALLICLES: 'the man who'll live correctly ought to allow his own appetites to get as big as possible and not restrain them. And when they are as large as possible, he ought to be competent to devote himself to them by virtue of his bravery and intelligence, and to fill them with whatever he may have an appetite for at the time.' (*Gorgias*, 491e–492a)[32]

But, Socrates points out, Callicles' appetites are never actually sated. His view of the happy life is of a life in which he must continually feed his recurrent hunger, scratch his itches, slake his sexual desires. Socrates tells the following story to dramatize the paradoxical misery of such a life.

> SOCRATES: 'Suppose there are two men, each of whom has many jars. The jars belonging to one of them are sound and full, one with wine, another with honey, a third with milk, and many others with lots of other things. And suppose that the sources of each of these things are scarce and difficult to come by, procurable only with much toil and trouble. Now the one man, having filled up his jars, doesn't pour anything more into them and gives them no further thought. He can relax over them. As for the other one, he too has resources that can be procured, though with difficulty, but his containers are leaky and rotten. He's forced to keep on filling them, day and night, or else he suffers extreme pain.' (*Gorgias*, 493d–4a)

The healthy, self-controlled man achieves a sufficiency and is content with that. The supposedly strong man whose appetites are constantly increasing finds that his supplies leak away: as fast as he refills his stocks, they drain away into the maw of his ever-increasing appetites. This is an excellent description of what modern psychologists call the 'hedonic treadmill'.[33] On that treadmill, we consume one pleasure only to be prompted to consume another. Psychologists today largely agree with Plato that this treadmill is, despite its apparent attractions, intrinsically unsatisfying and inappropriate as the basis for a healthy life. It may be difficult to step off the treadmill, especially when it is drawing power from so many pervasive social pressures and practices. Yet coming to know it is a path to nowhere is a crucial step in breaking its power, one which individuals can both take for themselves and model in order to encourage in others.

Against negligibility and indifference: summing up the Platonic case

Plato's appeal to the systemic consequences that one's own character has for the character of one's family, and so of the society, serves, in effect, to counter ideas of negligibility and indifference. We already saw an example of this in his account of the trust-fund babies of the oligarch. He makes the case more generally earlier in the *Republic*, where Socrates says:

> […] once we have given our system a good start … [his own interjection] the process of improvement will be cumulative. By maintaining a sound system of education and upbringing you produce citizens of good character; and citizens of sound character, with the advantage of a good education, produce in turn children better than themselves and better able to produce still better children in their turn … [omitting comparison to animals]. (424a–b)

The just social system is not only cumulative, but self-reinforcing, as Socrates points out later, when discussing the feedback effects of just actions on the psychology of the person who carries them out. Here he again draws the analogy to health.

SOCRATES: 'Healthy activities produce health, and unhealthy activities produce sickness.'

GLAUCON: 'True.'

SOCRATES: 'Well, then, don't just actions produce justice, and unjust actions injustice?'

GLAUCON: 'They must.'

SOCRATES: 'And health is produced by establishing a natural relation of control and subordination among the constituents of the body, disease by establishing an unnatural relation.'

GLAUCON: 'Certainly.'

SOCRATES: 'It seems, then, that excellence [virtue] is a kind of mental health or beauty or fitness, and defect [vice] a kind of illness or deformity or weakness.'

GLAUCON: 'That is so.'

SOCRATES: 'And each is in turn the result of one's practice, good or bad.'

GLAUCON: 'They must be.' (444c–e)

Thus Socrates completes the loop, showing that virtue is not just constitutive of psychological health and so of agency, but also self-reinforcing. In a word, the virtue of the *Republic* is sustainable virtue. Just actions not only issue from an internally just soul; they also reinforce the order of that soul, whereas unjust actions would tend to undermine or dismantle it ('don't just actions produce justice, and unjust actions injustice?'). Every action either reinforces a good habit or reinforces a bad one. To act unjustly, say by pursuing one's desire for money through sharp business practice, is to feed that appetite for money while simultaneously weakening (through disuse, through subversion) one's rational ability to control it. To act justly, by subduing one's appetites where good judgement says it is necessary, is to cultivate the ability of self-control and so to reinforce one's character and the happiness it constitutes.[34] Extended to the ecological context, we find that virtue is not only a path to sustainability; it is a sustainably self-motivating one.

In such a sustainable society, as understood by Plato, people are not best understood as at some times private consumers, at other times public-spirited citizens. The conceptual dichotomy between consumer and citizen fails to register the ways in which – in everything we do, public and private – we are either producing sustainably and so reproducing sustainability itself, or we are producing unsustainably and so reproducing unsustainability itself. We are not negligible individuals lost in the mass and entitled by our liberty to act indifferently to our effects. So while we sometimes buy as consumers (*idiotēs*, singular, for the Athenians), sometimes vote as citizens (*politēs*, singular), we cannot sever those identities from each other completely. The sustainability constraint enters into our consumer behaviour in order to make it possible for this to be reconciled with our public responsibilities as citizens. The values of a city being shaped by the dominant values of individuals within it, and those being shaped by them in turn: this is the fundamental relationship between the city and the soul which we can glean from the *Republic*, and which we moderns have tended at our peril to forget. In such a play of reciprocal interaction, no individual is negligible. Hence no one can afford to be indifferent to the social effects of her choices, nor complacent that those effects will somehow be indirectly socially beneficial whatever their direct impact.

We can now better appreciate the suggestion in Part I that we might best conceive ourselves as – at all times – co-producers, interacting so as to generate and reinforce virtuous, sustainable terms of action or their opposite in the market, the home, and the forum alike. Our characters and culture are not immune from the effects of our action in any of these domains. This Platonic understanding of ourselves as co-producers of our characters and culture can today underwrite an understanding of ourselves as *eco*-producers. We produce sustainability through the terms in which we interact, wherever we interact, or we produce its opposite. As eco-producers, we understand ourselves to be non-negligible, and to be responsible, in producing and reproducing the conditions for our own sustainable individual and social health.

Prologue to Chapter 6: Plato's Idea of the Good

'The highest? ... Is there anything higher than justice and the other qualities [i.e., the other cardinal virtues: wisdom, courage, and self-discipline] we discussed?' (504d). So Glaucon asks Socrates when the older man has told him that the rulers of the beautiful city will have to make efforts to 'reach the highest form of knowledge, which should be peculiarly his own' (504d). Glaucon's astonishment is understandable. The idea that cultivation of the virtues is the highest and most important thing to learn would readily have made sense to one of his ancient Greek contemporaries. If the virtues are, as we have been discussing, the keys to living a healthy life as an individual and to contributing to a healthy polity, it is hard to see what could be more important.

In the context of the *Republic*, too, the focus of the inquiry from the end of the first book to this point in the middle of the sixth has been, as we have seen, on whether it is justice or injustice which is more advantageous to the soul. This structuring of the dialogue suggests that the summit of its ambition will be an understanding of justice, and indeed, such an understanding seems already to have been achieved with the account of justice as one of the four virtues of city and soul in Books 2 to 4, as discussed above in Chapter 5.

For these reasons, Socrates' eventual answer to Glaucon's puzzled question as to whether there is anything more important than the virtues, produces even more astonishment in the young man. 'The highest form of knowledge is knowledge of the form of the good', says Socrates, since it is by relation to the Form of the Good that virtuous things 'derive their usefulness and value' (505a). Why is goodness the most important and highest thing to understand? It is because 'the good ... is the end of all endeavour, the object on which every heart is set' (505e).[1] This is

[handwritten marginalia at top: Therefore I have a knowledge of that which is good. People have THAT]

[handwritten marginalia at left margin: Good can be known if ... comparison]

so even when people lack knowledge of the good: they sense that there is something which is truly good or beneficial, and they are dissatisfied with anything less. Goodness or beneficialness is a sort of natural, genuine property, which people prize for its intrinsic consequences. To supply a modern analogy: if I am going to take medicine, I want it to be good medicine, not bad. I may not know be able to tell which medicine is good, but if I learn that I've been taking fake or faulty medicine, I will feel cheated and alarmed. Good medicine produces real benefit which bad medicine cannot.

Contrast, Socrates says, the way that people act with regard to what is thought good and with regard even to what is thought to be just or beautiful: 'when it's a matter of justice or value [also translatable as 'beauty'] many people prefer the appearance to the reality, whether it's a matter of possession and action or of reputation; but ... no one is satisfied to have something that only *appears* to be good, but wants something that *really* is, and has no use here for appearances' (505d). Socrates would doubtless think that people satisfied with the mere appearance of justice and beauty are also making a mistake: such people would be like those who covet the ring of Gyges' shield of invisibility, content to appear just while committing injustice with seeming impunity, but in fact disordering their own psyches by so doing. His point however is that many people don't instinctively care about whether or not they are making such a mistake when it comes to what is just or beautiful. They are satisfied to appear just or to present a beautiful façade, without being intrinsically motivated to ask or care about whether that façade corresponds to reality. (That is a question which they might come to ask only if prodded by Socrates or moved by reading the *Republic*.) When it comes to what is good, however, people do have an instinctive, intuitive desire to have what is genuinely good and to avoid being fobbed off by a mere façade. It doesn't take a philosopher to persuade me that I want good medicine, good food, or good friends: I am instinctively on the lookout for what is good in these domains and averse to what is bad.

Socrates isn't content to leave things at this level. After all, he had spoken at the outset of the 'Form of the Good', not, simply, what is good. What Plato means by the 'Forms' or 'Ideas' is, as noted earlier, a deep and complex question: many thinkers over the centuries have taken him to mean that the 'Forms' occupy a separate intelligible realm or dimension, although some have argued that he is only making an argument about predicating truth of a single existing world of phenomena.[2] For our purposes, we can say roughly that they are meant to signal what is real in contrast to what is merely apparent, and indeed to signify what is most real in contrast to what is less so, in the sense that the former is permanent and unchanging while the latter comes into being, varies with context, and passes away. So while good medicine is real *as* medicine, as contrasted with bad medicine which is not 'real' medicine, on a more abstract level even the goodness of good medicine is merely apparent, a contextually bound and so varying feature, which contrasts with the permanent and unchanging true reality of the 'Form of the Good'. The key insights are that what appears is not always what is real; that what appears good is not always what is good; and that we must therefore interrogate apparent goodness in doing our utmost to attain what is really good.

How, if at all, can Plato's treatment of the good in terms of the Form of the Good be appropriated today? Once again we must distinguish between the particular way in which he filled it out, and the general orienting questions which led him to offer such an account at all. Those general orienting questions give rise to the insights described above. It is the specific details which Plato went on to offer that are hard to save: that the Form of the Good be construed as 'beyond being' and that it be thought to be wholly permanent and unvarying, such that it could be grasped independently of any particular good thing. Some currents of later Platonism would come much closer to Aristotelianism in seeing goodness as immanent in particulars rather than as a transcendent form, and there is warrant elsewhere in Plato's dialogues for this, although there is also warrant for the more traditional transcendent reading.[3]

Part of the implication of the Form of the Good being presented as unvarying and beyond being is that it is only a few people – only the philosophers, in fact – who will be able to grasp it. That is, the problematic details emerge from the hierarchical nature of the *Republic*'s politics – resting as it does on an axiom that only a few people can be expected to be able to gain knowledge of any particular art or science. If goodness is a transcendent form knowable only by a few, then it is not enough that the good is 'the object on which every heart is set' (505e), since most of them cannot be expected to reach it. Instead only those few who have reached the heights of understanding the Form of the Good are able to serve as rulers, orienting their rule in light of the good and so able to make the other virtues, such as the justice and indeed also the beauty of the city, truly beneficial.

It was the political aspects of the beautiful city which the interlocutors had queried at the beginning of Book 5, leading Socrates to reveal three radical proposals which he had glossed over in the earlier presentation of the city–soul analogy. The first is that women who are capable of participating in ruling the city must be trained and employed to do so alongside the men with whom they share the same natural abilities: whether one is male or female is as irrelevant a criterion for political rule (and even for military service) as whether one is bald or not. The second, still more radical, is that the only way in which this ruling elite of men and women can be prevented from becoming corrupt is if they are deprived of any private property or familial interests. Their food and shelter should be supplied, austerely, by the political community whom they benefit as rulers. Likewise their children should be raised and even conceived for communal benefit, so that none of the adults have any knowledge of their biological kin, instead considering all of the children as their own and the community as a whole as a single family. The final most radical political proposal – the one which Glaucon finds most shocking – is that the rulers of the city should not merely be wise in an ordinary, everyday sort of way. Instead they must be philosophers: those defined by directing their love of knowledge not at any and every kind of knowledge, such as the trivia of popular culture (Socrates speaks disparagingly of the 'lovers of sights and sounds', the culture vultures, as one of my teachers called them, who love knowing everything about ephemeral events), but specifically at the knowledge of what is most real, as contrasted with mere appearance. And what is most real are the 'Forms', the 'Form of the Just', the 'Form of the Beautiful', and above all – 'beyond being' – the 'Form of the Good'.

The hierarchical politics of the *Republic* depends on the *Form* of the Good. Conversely, to save our own political model from imposing strict hierarchy, we can focus on the universal pursuit of goodness and its inescapable immanence in the everyday. We want good medicine and baby food, not bad; so too we want beneficial policies, not harmful ones. Yet we are liable to be confused and misled as to what is beneficial. Hence it is incumbent upon us ourselves to remain alert to the Platonic question of the difference between appearance and reality, without having to hand over all political power to an elite able to know the putative reality of the forms. Following in the footsteps of a modern programme of virtue ethics, one can value goods *as* and *because* they are good without treating all of them as mere means to or components of a single highest good. On this view, a good person will have a general disposition to value things that are good, 'that will blossom into love for some good things, and liking for others, and at least respect for most good things that catch her attention', an outlook 'likely to be accompanied by attitudes toward the good as such'.[4] Goodness can remain an orienting idea for us even without the univocal and eternal character with which the *Republic* endows it.

6

The Idea of the Good

To see how an appropriation of the Platonic idea of the good might serve us today, we need to delve further into the account which Socrates gives of the Form of the Good. I say 'account': in fact what he offers – saying that to arrive at his own view would be 'too big a topic' and he would fear looking ridiculous in trying to do so – is an account of the 'child and offspring of the good'. Or, since the word *tokos* means offspring both in the sense of a child who results from a parent, and in the sense of the interest which arises on capital, he is offering a down-payment of interest which is both derivative of and dependent on the true capital, the only true value, that of the Form of the Good.

One might expect that the offspring of the Form of the Good would be some ordinary, everyday case of goodness – such as the good medicine that I've been using as an example. Instead, the offspring Socrates has in mind is at a cosmic level. The Form of the Good is what makes the world intelligible; its offspring is the Sun, which is what makes the world visible. Let us see what he means by this.

When we act in pursuit of our aims, we take ourselves to be aiming at something which is (really) good, really worth having or doing. Put like this, as we saw in the prologue to this chapter, Plato seems to be canvassing an obvious truth, one with which utilitarians and even mainstream economists would not disagree. We pursue what we value, what we take to be (really) valuable, and we take it to be so even though we might not pause to ask ourselves explicitly whether it is really valuable or not. This is meant to be a simple, logical point about the relationship between ends and mean in action. Insofar as Sophia, say, is acting instrumentally, in order to get something, her action is only intelligible – that is, only makes sense – to others as to herself if she is understood to be aiming at something that she considers worth getting and having. The observers may think that she is wrong about its value; she herself may come to think that she has made a mistake, pursuing a game which was not in fact worth the candle. Nevertheless, if one asks someone her intention in acting instrumentally, ultimately one will get down to some category of fundamental value, and it is this which Plato is calling 'goodness'.[1]

Whether there is a single absolute good, or even a single person-relative good, is a controversial question which we cannot take Plato's argument here to have resolved.[2] Nevertheless, the structure of his account in relating goodness to reasons (leaving open whether there is a single or highest unitary account of goodness) remains instructive. Goodness is fundamentally about intelligibility: it is the evaluative term in which we make sense of our actions, the actions of others, and the world.

'Making sense' is precisely one of the two roles for goodness which Socrates goes on to identify by using the parable of the Sun: '[the Sun] bears the same relation to sight and visible objects in the visible realm that the good bears to intelligence and intelligible objects in the intelligible realm' (508c). 'Intelligible' here is to be understood simply on a par with the everyday meaning of 'visible'. Nothing can be clearly seen, without being seen in a particular light, which for Plato (in a pre-electronic age) is primordially the light of the Sun. Just so, nothing can be clearly understood (for that is the simple meaning of 'intelligible'), without being understood in a particular light, that is, in the light of goodness.

This thought connects directly with the discussion of the political imagination in Part I. Nothing can be rationally decided without being decided in some light or other, that is, in the light of a view about value – even if minimally the value in question is the value of one currency against another, or if the value is seemingly obvious. Even to hold that it is rational to prefer more of something than less is to make a presumption about value (in this case, the sheer value of quantity: imagine a Buddhist monk who systematically prefers the less, for example because it is a lesser burden). Goodness is a *sine qua non* for the evaluation of reason: no reason is ultimately intelligible except in its light.

Now in the case of the light of the Sun, Plato may seem to have fudged his point. While he wrote more than two thousand years before electric light, he and his society knew many other sources of light: what we would now explain as the electrically caused light of lightning, for example, and more significant for Plato, the artificial light of fire, which featured in his parable of the cave. So while it is true that nothing can be visibly seen without being seen in some light or other, it doesn't follow that nothing can be seen except in the light of the Sun. Much may be seen in the light of a candle, or a compact fluorescent bulb.

In fact, Plato has an answer for this. As Socrates goes on to explain: the Sun 'not only makes the things we see visible, but causes the processes of generation, growth and nourishment, without itself being such a process' (509b). This is a good answer. Sunlight is indeed nutritive for life and growth in a way that firelight and candlelight are not. Indeed, Plato is right in attributing a fundamental causal force to the Sun in the process of life; as two industrial designers put it, 'All of nature's industry relies on energy from the Sun, which can be viewed as a form of current, constantly renewing income.'[3] But appealing to a parallel between the Sun and the good may seem to make it even harder to make the parable as a whole make sense. For Socrates applies the same point to the good: just as the Sun is the cause of growth of plants and animals, so too the good 'is the cause of knowledge and truth', and is the source 'not only of the intelligibility of the objects of knowledge, but also of their being and reality' (508e, 509b). What can this mean, that just as visible things only grow in the light of the Sun, so too intelligible matters only come into being in the light of the good?

The remark about growth puts a further condition on the nature of the end that may constitute an ultimate value. It suggests that such a value cannot be self-undermining. If pursuing some end undermines one's ability to go on pursuing it (and/or the ability of others to do so), then this is not an end which can grow, and so its very intelligibility as an ongoing end is compromised. For example, if I pursue the end of raising money by selling myself into slavery, I undermine my very ability to go on pursuing this end, and so I can no longer understand this as a truly intelligible end. It is intelligible only in a short time window, and in a self-undermining fashion. And here we come to the punchline. The condition that value must be both intelligible and a source of growth is a condition that value must be sustainable. The highest good for Plato is what is of ultimate value, not sustainability per se. But that highest value must be sustainably valuable: it must be capable of generating indefinite growth and of continuing to make sense in the course of such generation. Sustainability can actually be perceived to be built as a condition into Plato's understanding of goodness.

I am not claiming that Plato had in mind ecological sustainability in making this point: the notion of sustainability just identified is rather a logical condition accompanying Plato's analysis of goodness as an object of pursuit. Nevertheless, the notion that other values can be understood only insofar as they are sustainable – that sustainability is one of the conditions on sheer intelligibility of value *as* valuable – is highly suggestive. Plato can here be constructively interpreted as identifying sustainability as the condition for healthy, ongoing growth. Unsustainable growth not only puts an end to the accumulation of value, but can also, in the crisis of its collapse, destroy much of the value that it had originally produced. Financial crises are recurrent testimony to this point.

Sustainability, then, is best understood as a condition on goodness. It does not constitute or replace an ultimate good; on the contrary, as was observed in Part I, the very definition of sustainability depends on presupposing some notion of the good or value that is worth sustaining. Yet, as was also remarked in Part I, the modern ethos has tended not only to deny or ignore the question of what is ultimately good, but also to deny or ignore the condition of sustainability.

To defend a complete substantive account of the common good is beyond the scope of this book. I limit myself here to the claim that society cannot afford the luxury of indifference to the conditions for its own survival and growth. Insofar as sustainability is a condition on the good, so is it also a condition which any account of society's overall purpose (including a lack of overall purpose) must respect. Just as one cannot affirm an individual value which would be self-undermining and so deny growth, so one cannot affirm a social value of the same kind.

This can be seen by adapting another argument made by John Stuart Mill. In Chapter 2 we considered Mill's harm principle, according to which individuals should generally be free to do anything that does not harm others. But he limited it by a further contention which virtually all liberals accept today: that people should not be allowed to sell themselves into slavery, because to do so is to use liberty to destroy itself, and liberty cannot be preserved if exercised so as to commit suicide. It is less often asked, however, whether there is a parallel political case. Are there acts which societies should not be allowed to commit, because to do so would be to use liberty to destroy themselves?

To the extent that this question has been asked at all, it has been asked in terms of what we might call the 'political conditions' of social survival. In Germany (and previously in West Germany), for example, assaults on the historical truth about the crimes of Nazi Germany are banned; political theorists there and abroad debate whether such bans are legitimate. My question by contrast is about what we might call the 'ecological conditions' of social survival, referring to the physical, material conditions of a society's continued existence. Are there acts and policies which societies should not be allowed to pursue, because to do so would be to use liberty to destroy the ecological conditions of their existence and so of their liberty?

I argue that any society worth defending must answer this question in the affirmative, while leaving open to public debate exactly what those acts and policies are. That is, the good of its own existence is not merely a matter of the good of its internal social relations, but also requires the good of the conditions for its continued physical and material existence above a certain threshold of well-being. This latter good is one which sets limits on the range of acceptable policies. While it is to be adopted through public debate and interpreted through public debate, its role in principle is no more debatable than Mill's ban on selling oneself into slavery (which is likewise enforceable only through the public process of legislation).

Ecological sustainability, in other words, is an indispensable part of the common good. To instal it as such does not violate strictures about liberal neutrality or pluralism, because it constitutes conditions without which any social order (including a liberal one) cannot survive. To act so as to promote or facilitate catastrophic, runaway climate change is to commit suicide as a society and as a species – as Pete Postlethwaite speaks of 'suicide' in the film *The Age of Stupid*.[4]

Does this argument mean that individual and collective goods will always and necessarily coincide? It would be naïve to argue this. In fact, it would have been naïve to argue this also in ancient Athens, where citizen-jurors, for example, were constantly asked by citizen-prosecutors to consider whether some defendant's actions were inimical to the city's laws or welfare. Plato's effort in the *Republic* to establish a perfect harmony between the interests of the individual and the polity is an arduous one, and in this respect it is more realistic to consider the ongoing social conflicts within democratic Athens as our guide. Both in ancient Athens and in modern societies, the individual good and the common good may come apart: this is one of the reasons for the proceduralism, distribution, and delineation of social and political roles, and rule of law approach which we find in a basic form already in Athens as well as today.

So while we can't logically deny either the theoretical notion of a common good, or the corollary that such a good must be sustainable, it does not follow that we will all agree about it, nor that each person will in fact consider her individual good to be harmonious with the common one. Such harmony is not naturally given: producing it is the very task of the virtues, which will remain as incomplete and contested as it is necessary. Nevertheless, even in situations of conflict about the good, or conflicts between an individual's good and that of the society, the condition of sustainability remains effective. I can't rationally be indifferent to at least that aspect of the common good which serves to sustain my own, even though I may disagree with others about what that requires and how it fits into any bigger picture. Sustainability as a condition of the good is more like a structural element of any rational worldview than a given substantive account.

An excellent illustration of the role of the good in such a structural context today is offered by the architect and designer Bill McDonough. His book *Cradle to Cradle*, written with Michael Braungart, explains in the title of its second chapter 'Why Being "Less Bad" Is No Good'. How to be less bad – how to design a slightly less toxic bath toy, for example – is the dominant goal of current industrial eco-efficiency. But even if what is bad can only ultimately be understood in light of the good, to act *towards* the bad is to turn one's back on what we all ultimately care about, the only thing that can benefit us: what is actually good. As McDonough and Braungart write, in terms inspiring a central thesis of this book: 'to be less bad is to accept things as they are, to believe that poorly designed, dishonorable, destructive systems are the *best* humans can do. This is the ultimate failure of the "be less bad" approach: a failure of the imagination.'[5]

A sustainable culture is born only when we stop trying to make things a little less bad, stop relying on the shield of legal protection for our currently defined organizational roles, stop indulging in the whims of choosing without thinking about our overall goal or the needs of society. To aim at the good – to step up and reorient oneself in its light, moving steadily towards it and not settling for any excuses or illusions along the way – is the only way to achieve an individually healthy and collectively sustainable society. Instead, consider the challenge which these designers set, as an echo and even a radicalization of Platonic terms: 'What about an entirely different model? What would it mean to be 100% good?'[6]

In light of the relevance of this question, we might even reconsider the abandonment of the notion of the Platonic 'Forms' which I suggested earlier. For the 'Forms' were meant by Plato to indicate a reality beyond what appears to be everyday reality. Plato, indeed, took this intelligible reality to lie beyond the visible world of nature, but he also treated the most fundamental features of the visible cosmos as the highest embodiments of the good that are accessible to us through the senses. For if goodness is ultimately what makes the world intelligible, it is also tangible in what is beautiful.[7] The harmonious beauty and order of the cosmos, visible in the regular, mathematically defined orbits of the heavenly bodies, gives us a path via perception towards a grasp of what is intelligible. Thus despite what is usually thought of as Plato's scorn for nature and this world compared to the forms, in fact nature itself has some Platonic claim to be a path to the Forms, an intimation of what is good.

That claim is telling today. In a world where most urban-dwellers live largely cut off from nature, taking airports and asphalt to be reality, nature itself in its complex yet intelligible principles of interaction may be a worthy successor to the Platonic Forms. If the precariously integrated, but in fact highly vulnerable, system of human habitation on the planet is part of what constitutes our cave, together with a reliance on linear effects which understates the causal complexity of the world around us, realizing the dependency of our fragile human perch on the bigger, older, and far more complex system of nature is part of what it would mean today to leave the cave. To know nature is to be a scientist; to understand our reliance on nature is, perhaps, to be today what a modern Plato might have meant by a philosopher – however paradoxical this might have seemed from the vantage point of the ancient Greek author himself.

The role and rule of knowledge

So far we have focused on the nature of the good for Plato. Yet it is equally important to inquire into what he had in mind in saying that it was *knowledge* of the good that the philosophers would acquire and be able to incorporate into the city – and what role knowledge can play today in a democratic society. Our sociology of knowledge is far more complex than Plato's: diverse sources of authority and expertise, which are variously constructed and socially evaluated, mean that we cannot invoke Plato's simple model of a direct hot-line to knowledge of the Forms and of the Good (even though he held that this hot-line would have to be hard-earned by study and practice). It might be thought, therefore, that Plato's discussion of knowledge is wholly irrelevant to modern democratic society, at least. Our politics are predicated precisely on denying his claim that some have a special political status enabling them to enlighten us once and for all.

Yet we cannot simply abandon the idea of knowledge and its role in governing individual and polity altogether. Virtue itself, as we have been arguing, has an inescapable cognitive dimension: if we don't know what is worth aiming at, our virtues in achieving our aims will be hollow. And while virtue is primarily the task of the individual, we have also seen that unless the individual and the culture fit together with sufficient congruence, the virtues of each will be unstable to the point of being undermined. Thus if Plato's ethics are to serve as any sort of model, we must investigate the kind of knowledge needed today and how it might relate to the revival of the virtues.

The knowledge involved in the case for sustainability – and the transition to it – is of several kinds. First there is the scientific knowledge of global systems: for convenience, let's focus solely on knowledge of climate change. This knowledge is composed in part of observations, in part of theoretical judgements of probability, in part of laws of physics, chemistry, and biology. Science develops, but it also reaches widespread consensus as a basis for further development. That process is actually unusually clear in the case of climate change, because of the IPCC, which was established precisely in order to coordinate and approve (one might say baptize) an authoritative set of scientific studies as a basis for political deliberation. The model of scientific consensus (which is never 100 percent, but is in the case of the IPCC overwhelming), combined with political involvement and approval, gives our knowledge of climate change a unique status. This is not merely knowledge from outside the political tent, which politics may take account of or not as it wishes; it is knowledge already organized and vetted for political use, while at the same time meeting an accepted standard of scientific credibility (the IPCC reports are further tested by the ordinary processes of science).

Thus, knowledge today is understood as a product of complex forms of social interaction, depending heavily on testimony and not simply on individual observation or reasoning. While knowledge itself is not evenly distributed, access to it is very widely available. Or at least this is how we would put it today, in that we typically use the word 'knowledge' quite loosely.

Plato saw knowledge as something which only a very few people were likely to possess: it was inherently difficult to achieve, and while its achievement might involve engaging with others (as in the one-to-one discussions with Socrates, or the notion of dialectical discussion more broadly), its object was eternal, invariable, and independent of human constitution. He would have denied the title of 'knowledge' to the IPCC reports, a denial not credible to our understanding of science today. But more plausibly, he would have denied the title of 'knowledge' to my understanding (as a non-scientist) of the IPCC report. Plato would have called this true belief, rather than knowledge, insofar as the person with true belief lacks full understanding of what she believes. Here, his distinction has some merit: as a non-scientist, it is hard for me fully to understand the physics of the loss of Arctic summer ice, even if I can cite its rate accurately. Thus I am arguably more justified in saying that I have true beliefs about the science of climate change acquired from the IPCC than in claiming to have 'knowledge' of it, given that I lack the full understanding that knowledge should involve.

The reason that the Platonic distinction is helpful here, despite the fact that it goes against our everyday broad usage of the word 'knowledge', is the accompanying emphasis placed by Plato on the fact that true beliefs are typically *unstable*. I may lose them, and perhaps more importantly, I may lose my focus on their importance. They are not rooted in my mind in firm connection with other things that I know and care about; so they are easily destabilized, and tend to slip behind other concerns. And this is even more the case when emotions such as fear and anxiety begin to reshape my mental landscape. It's easier to avoid and repress true beliefs which we do not understand – and do not want to understand, for fear of their implications – than it would be true knowledge. So even though knowledge has been so widely democratized and also downgraded in what it requires, this does not enable us to escape altogether from Plato's problematic about knowledge.

Thus, rather than distinguish simply between those who know and those who do not know, we today confront the Platonic issue of knowledge about sustainability in the form of a distinction which is at least fourfold:

- those with full knowledge and understanding, who can't help but integrate this knowledge into their framework for belief and action (scientists, at least some, though they too may be liable to temptations to downplay or repress what they know);
- those with true beliefs, who are willing to keep these beliefs front and centre even though in tension with much else of what they (in practice) believe and care about and desire (convinced/immersed policymakers);
- those with true beliefs (at least some), who are disposed to ignore or neglect these beliefs and their implications at least much of the time, perhaps out of fear or other emotions (most of us, most of the time);
- those lacking either knowledge or true beliefs, or whose beliefs are piecemeal and incoherent, and for whom the issue is not a matter of concern (deniers; those with their heads in the sand).

Reasons and beliefs remain vulnerable to inconsistencies with emotions and desires so long as full cognitive understanding has not been achieved. 'Knowledge' in our everyday loose sense, in which it roughly equates simply to information, is never going to be a reliable basis for promoting change in action because it is, as Plato knew well, unstable and therefore ineffective in integrating behaviour with outlook. Yet insofar as full cognitive understanding of the science of climate change is difficult for most non-scientists to achieve, we can appreciate how difficult the task of getting coherent individual, let alone political, action in response to it will be.

It follows that one underestimated task for those wanting to tackle climate change is actually to work on their own understanding first. Only by achieving as integrated and stable a grasp of the whole predicament as possible, which will then work to transform one's grasp of reasons, one's sense of identity, and one's emotions and desires alike, is one actually likely to achieve a platform for real individual change or for consistently demanding and working for real political change. We may never achieve true knowledge according to the most demanding Platonic standard, but the further we can travel in that direction away from the instabilities of true belief, the better the prospect for both personal and social virtue. Virtue must be understood as, in large part, a cognitive achievement. At this point of the argument this should be no surprise. We can now better appreciate the thinking at work underneath the *Carbon Detox* challenge to act sustainably out of savviness, not duty: acting well really is a matter of acting smart, but to do so is not merely a matter of acquiring information (as on the deficit model of social change), but rather of integrating cognitive and emotional outlooks into as close an approximation of stable and pervasive understanding as possible.

Let us return now from knowledge in general to knowledge of the good. However the good may be manifest at the cosmic level, how is it manifest in the dimensions of everyday individual and social life? We consider this in the fundamental dimensions of the physical and the temporal – the body and time – before uniting them in an idea which is a fundamental issue for a sustainable society: how to reconceive, or to re-imagine, the idea of growth.

Re-imagining the body

Health is not merely an analogue for the sort of complex valuation of sustainability that we need. A sustainable society will also revalue physical health, and the condition of the body, in ways which the dominance of financial metrics alone has distorted or obscured. For the emphasis on the abstractly assessable and countable, in place of more complex, sophisticated systems of valuation, has led to a denigration of the bodily as such.

To some extent, the downplaying of the bodily has had good motives and valuable results. For privileging the body can easily lead to an aristocratic norm of beauty which is contemptuous of those who fail to meet it. That was a fault in the society of ancient Greece: the ancient Greeks were so enamoured of beauty that they struggled with the idea that Socrates' ugly face and body could nevertheless be animated by the most valuable intelligence. Beauty remains a powerful implicit norm for people today: psychologists have shown how more attractive people are systematically favoured, judged to be smarter and more proficient, more likely to be offered jobs, and so on. But that norm, we have rightly come to recognize, has immense costs for those who fail to meet it: for the congenitally disabled, the accident victims, those of races whose features typically differ from a prevailing aesthetic. And so laws and cultural norms have slowly changed to root out discrimination on the basis of physical features. The treatment of the body as an index to the value of the soul has been rightly abandoned.

All this is admirable. But it has had an unfortunate unintended consequence. Gender, race, physical capability, obesity: all of these are officially (though not always in practice, as the aforementioned psychology studies show) expunged from judgements of worth. But expunged too is the notion that the body has any relation to the soul at all. Instead we have a conception of the person in terms of featureless, bodiless rationality. And this is a mistake.

Of course, needless to say, bodies do not reflect souls (by which I mean minds and characters) in any uncomplicated way. A beautiful body is compatible with ignorance, vanity, or spite. A less beautiful body may belong to a person of great intelligence and charm. An obese body is not necessarily a sign of lack of willpower: it may result from deliberate choice, from the aftermath of pregnancy, from genetic predisposition, from medical side-effects.

Nevertheless, the body is not irrelevant to the welfare of the person. Mind and body are intimately interrelated. Calming the body through meditation can stimulate the mind; an anxious mind will deprive the body of sleep. Mirror neurons and pheromones make us highly susceptible even to being unconsciously influenced by the actions and attitudes of others around us. It is easiest, in the prevailing culture, to make these points in medical language. People are more likely to accept that obesity is a problem when its links to a range of other diseases can be demonstrated. But to accept only that much is to close one's eyes to the need to restore a richer connection between the body and the good per se.

The role of the body in relation to the good is again something which Plato celebrated. He was well aware of the points made earlier about the danger of exaggerated respect for beautiful bodies. The *Republic* character

Glaucon specifies that an educated man will not be attracted to someone with a defect in character, but 'if [the person has] a physical defect, he will not let it be a bar to his affection' (402d–e), and Socrates later makes the converse point, that 'physical excellence does not of itself produce a good mind and character' (403d). However, he asserts that 'excellence of mind and character *will* make the best of the physique' one is given (403d, italics added to Lee translation). And so physical training – gymnastics, as the Greeks generically called it – is essential for good education. Focusing on those who will become the soldiers of his imagined society, Socrates advances a rather spartan (and indeed Spartan-influenced) conception of the physical education required to train them for war. But this is only a special case of a more general conception of physical education (including diet and exercise) and health. Just as 'simplicity in music produces discipline of character', so 'simplicity in physical education [produces] health of body' (404e). Both mental and physical education primarily aim at training the mind (410c), and indeed the character, harmoniously adjusting both the mind and the body to the right degree of interplay between athletic and philosophical (physical and intellectual) qualities, so as to achieve 'a proper harmony between energy and initiative on the one hand and reason on the other, by tuning each to the right pitch' (412a).

The delicate balance between initiative and reflective judgement, the need to restrain those entrepreneurial types who are eager to act so as to tame their ambitions to the good, while at the same time to energize Yeats's 'best' who 'lack all intensity', is something the importance of which recent financial and political travails have reminded us. Education and public policy need to remember the importance of the body and the way that slothful, untrained, and self-indulgent bodies can undermine the physical as well as cultural and social health of the society. Indeed, scientists now estimate that obesity itself is costly to the environment. One study has concluded that (as the *Guardian*'s headline put it on 20 April 2009) 'population fatness has an environmental impact'. This is primarily because fatter populations need more food energy and use cars more often. Their research concludes that the current global population of approximately one billion overweight people may, on certain assumptions, 'be considered to be responsible for a third, or possibly half of total global GHG [greenhouse gas] emissions'.[8]

Despite the significance of the body of which Plato can remind us, this is a source of value which is consistently overlooked in most policy-making, including putatively sustainable policies. Even for children, the role of play, art, music, and dance in the curriculum has been steadily eroded, and for adults the physically fit agenda still seems something of an afterthought, not properly integrated into building design, workplace hours, commuting structures, or the other 'serious' topics of political economy. Only when we remember that the body must be part of any complete conception of value, will we be able to restore the bodily dimensions of our lives to sustainable personal and social health. A truly sustainable society will be impossible to achieve while the importance of bodily fitness and health is marginalized in public policy (even if it is a personal obsession for certain classes of the population).

Re-imagining time

A further way in which the body has suffered is from the popular addiction to convenience as the dominant measure of time. Fast food is the obvious example: food no longer as an end, as a value embedded in relationships (the family meal, the business lunch), but as a means (the TV dinner, the sandwich snatched at the desk or on the run). As this illustrates, the dimensions of value do not lie merely in the monetary, nor even in the material. Time itself is a dimension of value. Do we value time sustainably? What would it mean to do so? How could we bring alive the Platonic and Aristotelian notion of the *kairos*, the opportune or correct moment for action, which Aristotle defines as the good in the category of time?[9]

The dominant modern paradigm of time has been convenience and efficiency. Efficiency is the more developed idea, with a strict definition in economics: according to the dominant (Pareto) standard of efficiency, it characterizes a distribution of goods such that no one can be made better off without making someone else worse off. But as a recent generation of economists have pointed out, this definition is empty with respect to any other value. A distribution of cake giving two children half each is efficient; but so is a distribution of cake giving all of it to one child and none to the other. Efficiency in this formal sense serves to eliminate any unexploited sources of social welfare. It guarantees that we don't limit each child to a quarter of the cake and leave half to go stale. But this ignores any reasons that we might have to limit them to a quarter of the cake for their health – even at the cost of letting some of it go stale. Equally, it ignores the reasons we might have to press more on one child (perhaps our guest) than on another, the type of reason which has led in many societies to the notion of potlatch, or gifting regulated by display rather than narrow reciprocity. And it ignores the reasons we might have to positively value the giving up of some of the cake to no one's use at all: such as the religious principle of sacrifice. In short, efficiency begs the question of our ultimate values. A society organized around efficiency is a society which has forgotten to ask about its ends in its obsession with means.

The same is true of the less formalized, but still immensely powerful, notion of convenience. Convenience is the less exacting cousin of efficiency: it is a comparative notion, not governed by an all-or-nothing standard like Pareto efficiency. Yet it is no less powerful in its effects for that. In the months and years before 11 September 2001, convenience was the dominating drive of the American airline industry. The airlines had resisted some attempts to upgrade security on the grounds that this would slow down passengers whose supreme demand was ever-more-conveniently abbreviated check-in times, shortened security queues, and simplified travel routines.[10] Of course, the passengers themselves were making those demands against the backdrop of their own assumptions about normality: that the existing regulations were adequate for safety, that there were no terrorist plots about. And equally, airport security will always be a balancing act between security and convenience. It is impossible to provide absolute security (and questionable whether some of the measures introduced since 9/11 have actually enhanced security), and certain forms of security (requiring all tickets to be purchased six months in advance to allow for individual profiling, for example) would be more inconvenient than most people would tolerate.

Nevertheless, the current and often clumsy attempt to balance security and convenience is a significant shift from the dominant discourse before 9/11, when in the public imagination, and that of the airlines, convenience was god and security something to be pursued only at ever-reducing cost to convenience. In an inversion of what one would expect, security had in that now seemingly innocent age come close to becoming a means (tested constantly for cost and burden) to convenience as the end. Yet convenience is no proper end. To fetishize convenience is to substitute a concern with the means for a genuine conception of an end. It is only useful to save money and time if one is saving them for some purpose. A society which fails to ask about that purpose, which suppresses the very question in favour of a constant effort at streamlining the means, is not healthy. It is not sustainable to pursue means without debating the value of the ends – quite apart from the (un)sustainability of the means themselves.

So, in the recent public imagination, time has been transmuted into convenience, the invaluable and irreplaceable mortal time of a finite life dissolved into an ever-hurrying effort to get to the next place faster, losing its link to the question of where it is (towards what good) we are trying to go. It is in reaction to this that religious fanatics proclaim that the absolute and eternal bliss of the next life trumps the mundane time of this one – a mundane time which most Westerners have not been honouring or valuing themselves. But fanaticism is not the only answer. An alternative is for Western societies to restore honour and value to mundane time. The slow food movement is part of an attempt to do just that. So[11] is the recurrent appeal of Zen, or kabbala, or any meditative practices. For the only good which we cannot actually buy or sell or bank is our time. When we 'buy time' through convenience, what we are actually doing is using time now in a certain way, with the expectation (but far from certainty) of being able to use future time differently as a result. But the language of 'buying time' and 'saving time' misleads us into thinking this is a purely future-oriented transaction, tucking away safe slices of future time, rather than a transaction which is itself taking place in the present and using up present time. Consider the tale of a Buddhist monk who was visiting a Western city. His host suggested that they take the metro rather than walk, in order to save time. The monk agreed. But when they emerged from the underground, the monk sat down on a wall and looked around him. His host was perplexed: what was the monk doing? The monk smiled, saying, have we not just saved time? How else should we use it? In fact, as the monk's playful gesture points out, time cannot be banked: it can only be lived. When we eat fast food or rush through the streets in order to 'buy' time, what we are really doing is spending time on fast food and rushing. All time is spent, or better, lived, not bought or saved: the only question is how we live it.

By recalling that time is at its best when suffused by goodness, when it offers the demarcation of festival from everyday, of anticipation and fulfilment, rather than simply the rat-race of convenience, we can use our free time – the free time with which liberal society has invaluably endowed us – to make ourselves truly free. Indeed, research on happiness and time demonstrates that celebrating festive occasions with family and friends, and doing so over time so that one builds up a stock of happy memories, is one of the best ways to consolidate a positive perspective on one's past that translates into confident goal-setting and achieving in the future.[12] Time off for holidays is not something which translates neatly into a cost-benefit metric of value. It is nevertheless a measure of well-being which should be at the heart of a sustainable society.

Time is only valuable in how we use it, however, and time off for holidays may simply be frittered away in trips to the shops, rather than used to build up a stock of happy family memories. Why don't we use our time for meaningful leisure rather than convenient consumption? To some extent, this is the human condition: we are striving animals, not fully attaining or achieving ones, and we are unlikely ever to live in a condition of perfect self-realization. Imperfection, failure, slacking off will never go away, and no social ideal should depend on assuming that they will do so. But there is also a paradox to the way that liberal societies have developed which has fostered the growth of convenience over true leisure.

This is the subordination of the self to its options. In identifying the liberal self as a choosing self, the high aspiration to autonomous choice has too often and easily degenerated into the trap of multiple consumption decisions. The value of the individual herself erodes into the value of her multiple choices, which in turn becomes too easily fleshed out as the value of her multiple consumables alone. Giving people choices can enslave them to the need to choose between just these options (this washing powder or that one?), blinding them in turn to the question of what broader life choices they might make.[13]

There is a second way in which time plays a role in sustainable outlooks or, as at present, in unsustainable ones: this is in terms of the time horizon which it demarcates. Sustainability requires concern for a long time horizon. Yet too many of the roles and requirements of modern society dictate time horizons which are ridiculously short when compared to the magnitude of the challenges which face us. The Long Now Foundation is in the process of building a 10,000-year clock to attempt to recalibrate our temporal imaginations.[14]

Consider the time horizons of democratic politicians, which reflect the attempt to strike a balance between corruption and knowledge which we considered earlier. Politicians are ideally given long enough to make their mark, to bring to bear the knowledge and ideas which they have to offer, but not so long as to begin to believe themselves politically immortal in a way which would conduce to corruption. Relatively short terms of office (between two and five years for legislators, and normally four to five years for independent executive roles) mark the way this balance has been struck. Term limits are another attempt to strike the balance, which are interestingly ambivalent in their effects: intended to exert more control over politicians, they can have the effect of freeing final-term politicians from electoral concerns. Early in the first term (so that the damage can be assimilated or forgotten) or during the last term (when electoral constraints do not bind one personally) are likely to be the best times for initiating drastic change. But while term limits give some shape and definition to the temporal horizon of politicians, other less formal limits concentrate their minds in ways which may be less productive. The time horizon for ministers to make their mark in a parliamentary system, for example, is dramatically short:[15] many ministers only serve one or two years, and they are keen to imprint their own legacy rather than to carry on consistency with the policies of their predecessors (even of the same party). The same is generally true of cabinet secretaries and lower appointees in a presidential system.

The upshot of these various horizons is that many politicians sincerely believe themselves to be severely disabled from acting in the long-term interest of society. They take politics to be notoriously and necessarily short-termist in its patterns of incentives, and contrast themselves with business, who are taken to be able to take a longer view in line with their long-term investments (at least in some cases). But of course, within the business community, the view is just the reverse. The pressures of quarterly reporting and, even more, the importance placed by analysts on quarterly results (an importance which has grown in recent decades), make business leaders feel themselves to be severely constrained from long-term thinking. Even pension funds, with a mission to invest for the long term in which their monies will eventually be used, often do not differ as much from other investors in being swayed by short-term signals as one might expect. The lure of short-term gain, or simply the fear of losing out while others accrue it, is in the current mindset hard to resist.

Meanwhile the time horizon of the public is also foreshortened, some-times by what is perceived to be individual interest, sometimes out of pure time-preference for jam today rather than jam tomorrow. It is, I think, misleading to believe that we can only address climate change if we can bring ourselves to care about the interests of future generations: the effects of climate change are being felt in our own lifetimes, in our own generation, so we have sufficient reason to care about it now, irrespec-tive of the long-distant future. It is temporally akin to pensions policy, involving a concern for our own future well-being. Yet that comparison raises problems of its own, for democratic publics are notoriously bad at funding their own pensions compared with competing goods which they could have today. The problem of caring about the future remains even when it is a question of our own future selves rather than anonymous future generations. But cost is not the only measure of radicality. The Stern Review's estimate of the amount of investment needed now year-on-year was extremely modest. It is the sunk imaginative costs which we can't bear to give up on – irrational though we know it is to be influenced by sunk costs at all. It is too frightening to admit that the current model, into which we've all bought to some degree or other, and in which many of us have succeeded quite well, is radically flawed.

Here is a Platonic reconceptualization of the problem of time hori-zons. In the dimension of time, goodness is lastingness. Plato considered this the eternal. Yet in the *Symposium* (208c–209e), in a speech which Socrates voices in the name of the priestess Diotima, he acknowledges that for many people, the children, creative works, and memories of virtu-ous deeds which they will leave behind them is as close as they will come to immortality. 'Everything mortal is preserved, not, like the divine, by always being the same in every way, but because what is departing and aging leaves behind something new ... anyone will do anything for the sake of immortal virtue and the glorious fame that follows' (*Symposium* 208a–e).[16]

Legacy is the operationalized version of human immortality. And one's legacy is an abiding human concern, invoked by multitudes of leadership, management, and personal growth tracts, despite the fact that it escapes the short-term maximization perspective which purportedly dominates our practical lives. Quarterly reporting cycles, even lifetime investment goals, are not the sum of human time horizons. The usual, and important, dimension of this topic in the climate change ethics literature is cast in terms of the value to be accorded to future generations. Without denying the importance of that question, I focus here on a different one: the question of what one will oneself leave behind, which is a motivational question for many people of the highest order.

This goes one step beyond concern with the welfare of one's future self of the kind that makes pension planning rational. A concern with legacy may sometimes be objective and isolated: I may care about what I leave behind just as I care about what I contribute to today, irrespective of whether or not anyone else knows or cares about it. But it is more often and characteristically an intrinsically social concern, in the shape of a concern with how one is going to be remembered by others. Here self-interest and concern with the interest of others come together: for I am unlikely to be remembered lovingly unless I have in my lifetime benefited others. True, there is scope for me to try to manipulate or shape what they will count as benefit, just as there is scope for them to be mistaken about that (they may revere me as a great warlord even if I led the community unnecessarily into destruction). Nevertheless, in thinking about my legacy, my sense of self-interest necessarily expands to a concern with the way in which my doings affect others.

Ordinary accounts of self-interest do not comprehend the power of this concern, especially when it is linked to a concern for the endurance of an institution or a commitment with which we have identified ourselves. Why should executives care about building a company which will last? Thin accounts of self-interest cannot explain this: it would seem much more rational in the short term to be concerned with maximizing their own profits rather than taking the legacy and lastingness of the company into account. The same can be said of politicians who care about the legacy of their party, and of anyone who contributes to building institutions – or planting trees – that will persist after they are gone. The legacy question arises from a different place within us, the desire for meaning, not only interest, that seeks not only jam tomorrow as well as jam today but building something which will endure. Plato spoke about this as the desire to create and to procreate which is animated by our love for what is beautiful and good. We are not just consuming animals, but creative ones, creators and producers of objects and structures built to last.

The legacy dimension is one which we recognize better in practice than in theory. We can't explain why companies (or the executives within them) should care about their own longevity, but we know they do: this is why appeals to the legacy which a CEO will leave can be very powerful ways of getting such a person to consider change. One way to crystallize the legacy dimension is to ask the uncomfortable question of how one wishes one's obituary to read, what it is that will be carved on one's tombstone. In thinking about this it is crucial to remember that while we can think about how we would like our obituary to read, the second fact of life – beyond death itself – is that we do not get to write our own obituary. Someone else will write it, based on the evidence of what we have actually achieved or failed to achieve, not on the hopes or self-delusions which we entertained along the way. And at present the likely obituary to be written by the next generation for those active today is not a happy one, for it may well read:

Killed the Earth. RIP.

The question of legacy brings the Platonic concern for wholeness into the domain of time. It is a challenge to re-imagine the temporal horizon of our action, from the short-term rewards and responsibilities to the pressing concern of what we will leave behind.

This can be put powerfully in yet another way. Consider the conclusion reached by Viktor Frankl, who survived Nazi concentration camp internment by studying the psychological experience of himself and his fellow inmates. Frankl concluded that the paramount question is not what we ask of life, but what life asks of us. Life is asking our generation a historic question. Will we be the ones on whose watch the human impact on the earth set off down a dangerous trajectory of no return? Do we really want our tombstone to read, 'Failed to respond'?[17]

Re-imagining growth

Body and time unite in the process of growth. Growth is not a bad thing, on the contrary: it is a condition of life, inasmuch as living organisms either grow or die. Yet growth as a process of material production and consumption, in which economic health is measured most publicly in GDP (gross domestic product) per capita, is a poor surrogate for health, and even poorer for sustainability. As many economists and politicians have begun to point out (though theirs is not yet the dominant wisdom), GDP is liable to count an increase in environmental bads as if it were good (valuing as 'output' the product of polluting industries, for example), while failing to count many goods as such (not valuing as 'output' greater time spent by parents with their children, for example).

For Plato, the condition of growth is intelligibility, modelled as the light of the Sun. Plants can only grow if exposed to the illumination of pure sunlight, the condition for their photosynthesis and so for their growth. Just so, Plato argues (or at least suggests: the argument here is obscure), people can only grow in wisdom and understanding if exposed to the illumination of the good, the condition for their being able to make sense of the world insofar as possible. In other words, we might say that for Plato, growth must make sense, it must be meaningful, otherwise it is not growth in any good sense but an anarchic cancerous sprawl. Rather than posit 'growth' and 'health' as rival scenarios for global development, as an Oxford study has done, the Platonic message is that healthy growth is the only growth to which it is sane to aspire.[18]

How, in the light of meaning which is provided by sustainability, might growth today make sense? One provocative answer has been offered by the ecological economist Herman Daly. He suggests (among many other important reflections) two fundamental revisions to the way we think about what economic growth means.[19] The first is that we stop treating production as a good; instead treat it as a cost, to be minimized. This is because producing any good uses up resources and energy, hence costs us these, as well as depriving us of their substitution possibilities. Why produce whenever production of a new widget is not absolutely necessary? This turns the ideology of GDP on its head. If GDP is a measure of a peculiarly perverse form of growth, Daly's proposal is a far better measure of wealth, in which transaction costs are minimized and the wealth of resources and energy stock is preserved wherever possible. The second is that we treat advertising as a social bad: tax it as a pollutant, rather than (as in many jurisdictions) allowing it to be written off as a business expense.

These sorts of ideas can help us to re-imagine and reinterpret the constituents of growth. Growth may nevertheless pose a crunch point for the general Platonic thesis of the interdependence of individual and society. For if it is true that individuals must go on growing in some sense, or die, it may not be true that society should or can go on growing *ad infinitum*. Indeed, the inevitable death of individuals, while society as a whole need not die – until the sun itself collapses – is itself a deep point of divergence between individual and society.

The question of what society would look like without aggregate growth has puzzled and intrigued philosophers and political economists for years. John Stuart Mill mused on it in the nineteenth century in his *Principles of Political Economy* (Book IV, Chapter 6). Mill suggested that the end of productive growth was at some indefinite time in the future inevitable, and was far from unreconciled to it, even suggesting that its earlier achievement by decision rather than by necessity should be welcomed. Society could continue to grow in learning, in musical activity, in conversation and leisure; a stationary state would mean only that it ceased to register net growth in its physical outputs. Because of the modern configuration of employment and economic demand, the way to make this work on a macroeconomic scale is still a matter of hot debate. Clearly, it could not happen on the basis of current expectations of consumption, for neither the growth in output to supply such consumption, nor the levels of income to support its demand, would be sustainable. For this reason, sustainability advocates have tended to stop short of a fully 'stationary state', pinning their hopes instead to renewable energy and to 'decoupling' of production from physical energy and resource use. The hope of some is that production and consumption could continue on such a dematerialized basis; others, more radically, follow Mill in beginning to ask what a real end to growth would mean.

How would reflecting on Plato orient us in this debate? If asked what growth looks like, Callicles – the insatiable and arrogant Platonic character we met above – would answer that growth is getting fatter and fatter as one consumes more and more. But that image of growth as untrammelled obesity is one which liberal societies are finally waking up to as an illusion. Growth that consists in adding fat (growing wider, not taller, as it were) is not normally valuable growth, but dangerous and destructive. So too the analogue of obesity in the public sphere: untrammelled consumption. That is not valuable growth, it is dangerous and destructive. That is not to say that consumption per se is bad; but only consumption which is limited and balanced can maintain the health both of the body and of the ecosystem. Any other notion of growth is nothing but a hedonic con. Luxury is not having more than enough; it is having enough (which may involve occasional indulgence but not perpetual breaking of limits) and living well. True luxury is health and peace of mind. That is the message of the *Republic*, and it is the message of modern psychology and of most of the world's religions too. It is time – indeed, well past time – to heed it in our politics and in our personal lives as well.

PART III

INITIATIVE

Prologue to Chapter 7: Revisiting Plato's Cave

Recall the Platonic image of the Cave introduced at the outset of this book, which we are finally prepared to consider in more depth. This is not merely a generalized image of the human predicament. Rather, as one scholar has demonstrated, Socrates introduces the Cave as an illustration of the democratic city and of the 'education' (514a) which the city affords, not just in its schools, but in its public culture.[1] The details of this illustration are worth considering.

SOCRATES: 'Imagine[2] an underground chamber like a cave, with a long entrance open to the daylight and as wide as the cave. In this chamber are men who have been prisoners there since they were children, their legs and necks being so fastened that they can only look straight ahead of them and cannot turn their heads. Some way off, behind and higher up, a fire is burning, and between the fire and the prisoners and above them runs a road, in front of which a curtain-wall has been built, like the screen at puppet shows between the operators and their audience, above which they show their puppets.'

GLAUCON: 'I see.'[3]

SOCRATES: 'Imagine[4] further that there are men carrying all sorts of gear along behind the curtain-wall, projecting above it and including figures of men and animals made of wood and stone and all sorts of other materials, and that some of these men, as you would expect, are talking and some not.'

GLAUCON: 'An odd picture and an odd sort of prisoner.'

SOCRATES: 'They are drawn from life ... For, tell me, do you think our prisoners could see anything of themselves or their fellows except the shadows thrown by the fire on the wall of the cave opposite them?'

GLAUCON: 'How could they see anything else if they were prevented from moving their heads all their lives?'

SOCRATES: 'And would they see anything more of the objects carried along the road?'

GLAUCON: 'Of course not.'

SOCRATES: 'Then if they were able to talk to each other, would they not assume that the shadows they saw were the real things?'

GLAUCON: 'Inevitably.'

SOCRATES: 'And if the wall of their prison opposite them reflected sound, don't you think that they would suppose, whenever one of the passers-by on the road spoke, that the voice belonged to the shadow passing before them?'

GLAUCON: 'They would be bound to think so.'

SOCRATES: 'And so in every way they would believe that the shadows of the objects we mentioned were the whole truth.'

GLAUCON: 'Yes, inevitably.' (514a–c)

The reader may feel that Glaucon gets it right in calling this an 'odd picture'. And yet it has had a compelling hold on the subsequent political imagination of all those overlapping traditions in which Platonic thought has been received, whether Jewish, Christian, or Islamic, republican, liberal, or authoritarian. The key is to realize that the 'prisoners' are imprisoned by the horizon of their city or political regime: of the artifacts, images, language, and values which the city educates them to believe exhaust reality. The 'carriers' of the statues are the artists, artisans, and rhetoricians, who parade images before the citizenry and so give shape and form to their culture. By positing that the citizens are trapped and unable to move, the Cave models their inability to escape the limited, artificial horizon of the existing (in Plato's day, democratic) city, lit by the distorting light of a man-made fire rather than by the limpid and natural light of the Sun.

Socrates goes on to argue that these artificially fixed values define the prisoners' motivations and ambitions, speaking of the 'honour and glory to be won among the prisoners, and prizes for keensightedness for those best able to remember the order of sequence among the passing shadows and so be best able to divine their future appearances' (516c–d). Pursuing vain ambitions which are irrelevant or toxic to the overall social good, meeting sales targets for selling environmentally destructive products

– these are examples of the sort of thing that would go on in such a cave today. To connect this argument to the discussion in Parts I and II: embedded in the images and artifacts and rhetoric of the puppeteers (some of whom are said to speak) are socially determined values, such as the current understanding of harms, costs, and benefits which shape our own political and social contests and the 'honours, praises, [and] prizes' which are earned within them.

In the image of the Cave, Plato suggests that it is the 'opinion-makers', as we might say, who are responsible for fixing the imaginative horizon of a democratic society. Ordinary citizens are portrayed as powerless, trapped within a given set of values and images, resistant to change: Socrates says that they would ridicule, and even kill, anyone who challenged the validity of their worldview (516e–517a). Another image which Socrates uses elsewhere in the *Republic*, however, complicates this story. There, the *dêmos* or citizen body are portrayed as a large beast, with the politicians and artists and artisans as its attendants. Like lion-tamers in a circus, these men must 'learn when to approach and handle [the animal], when and why it was especially savage or gentle, what the different noises it made meant, and what tone of voice to use to soothe or annoy it' (493b). That image suggests that the people do have some role in shaping their own society, but it is a confused, inarticulate, and inchoate role. The beast-tamers have to try to intuit the nature of the beast in order to control it, so they will not come up with just any set of values and images, but choose those to which the beast most readily responds, 'calling what pleased it good, what annoyed it bad' (493c). Still, this is a very dark and limited picture of democratic autonomy. Although in this image the people are not portrayed as prisoners, they are no more than an inarticulate mob manipulated with skill by those most adept at discerning and responding to their inchoate desires.

Plato, here, is condemning democracy, together with any other kind of regime which is not ruled by those who have genuine knowledge. Any such regime will be controlled by the ideological choices of its leaders and opinion-formers – among them, the men the Greeks called 'sophists' – even if these in some way play upon the instinctive needs and wants of the people. According to this reading of the *Republic*, the only way to instil rational values which cohere in the light of truth, is to establish an undemocratic regime in which self-appointed guardians rule from above.

Can democracy defend itself against these charges? Can we give a plausible account of democratic culture-change, in which this is not merely manipulation, but rather responds to an emerging understanding of real constraints and the choices thereby required? If not, if democratic societies are content to wallow in the status quo irrespective of its contradictions and dangers, then it is not Plato, but we ourselves, who will have condemned the value of democracy.

7

Initiative and Individuals:
A (Partly) Platonic Political Project

In this chapter, we explore ways in which individuals can take the initiative in helping to reshape the political imagination in a more sustainable direction – using the Platonic model as continued inspiration and suggestion. Initiative is not a standard topic in political theory, despite the suggestive remarks made by the philosopher Hannah Arendt about the importance of natality (birth, connected with newness) in politics.[1] Yet a focus on initiative is important in two respects. First, it highlights the role of the individual in making any political system function, and in shaping which way it will lean – within given constraints – when confronting challenges.[2] Anyone who has served on committees knows that committees are otiose unless someone is active in informing their agenda and following up on their decisions. Second, it highlights the importance of aiming at the full achievement of some good, rather than simply complying with procedural standards of legitimacy. Taken together, these two dimensions yield an account of initiative which is not a defence of any and every kind of initiative, but is rather a defence of initiative relating to the good understood as shaped by sustainability and oriented to the whole achievement of that good. By 'initiative' in what follows, I mean unless otherwise specified to refer to the aim to achieve an actual and substantive good, not to any initiative at all. The initiative taken by those unnamed figures (or the force of necessity) in Plato's text who, or which, compel a prisoner to leave the cave; the initiative which that prisoner shows in going back into the cave to try to enlighten his or her fellows:

both of these are initiatives which are valuable only because and insofar as they help to orient people to an intelligible perspective on, and goal of, the whole good.

Initiative requires a combination of knowledge to recognize urgency, the self-discpline to prioritize, the justice to care about contributing to the common good, and the sheer courage to step forward. Each of these is currently in short supply. Distorted judgements of self-interest deprive us of urgency in addressing sustainability; the limitations of our collective imagination and the laxity of our commitments to self-discipline and justice make it hard for us to prioritize drastic and systemic change; and the courage to step forward is hobbled not only by cowardice and fear, but also by a misplaced understanding of political propriety. Many people fail to step up because they don't believe that it is their role to do so; instead, they believe that it is their right – or even their duty – to hold back. Political entities, for their part, are defined by capacity rather than agency: structures give us the possibility of action, but only agents within them can make action happen. We will consider aspects of these failures, and ways in which initiative on behalf of the good could be regained, beginning with a consideration of the neglect of initiative in the basic models of modern political theory.

Neglect of initiative for the whole good: the myopia of liberals, democrats, and republicans

The inertia–initiative axis of political organization delineates a domain in which collective action problems arise. The problem of sustainability can be analysed both as a coordination problem (in which we share the same fundamental interests but need a mechanism to coordinate with each other in pursuing them) and as a prisoners' dilemma (in which we have interests which diverge from each other's at least in part). Both of these are most easily solved by the imposition of coercive action: the state as saviour. But that solution in turn fails to address a further question: what if the state itself fails to act? The state is a mechanism, an opportunity, rather than an agent in the true sense of the word; though we personify the state as an actor, political scientists know that it really consists of a huge number of individual actors jostling and contesting to earn the right to act in the name of the state. If none of these micro-agents takes the initiative to pursue sustainability – or if those who do are drowned out or ignored – then the coercion solution to collective action will necessarily fail. The need for initiative is dramatized, not replaced, by an analysis of the need for state action to address sustainability.

Yet the broad range of current political theories in the academy takes insufficient notice of this question. Such models are systematically hobbled by neglect of the inertia–initiative axis, focusing primarily on some alternative dimension of political analysis: the corruption–control axis which preoccupies liberals; the elitism–participation axis which preoccupies democrats; or the domination–freedom axis which preoccupies republicans (each of these groups should be understood as representing a normative position in academic discourse, not a particular political party). Liberals attack elites for abusing power; democrats attack elites for denying or minimizing public participation; 'republicans' identifying themselves in a Roman tradition of freedom from domination attack tyrants and other bodies who arbitrarily dominate political life. Each represents a powerful and important line of analysis of modern politics, yet none of them prioritizes the actual, full, and urgent attainment of any particular political or ethical aim, beyond that of freedom itself. Power can be controlled, people empowered, and arbitrary domination curbed – all valuable achievements – without initiative being taken to pursue any overall good. Achieving liberal control, democratic empowerment, and republican liberty would not necessarily prevent the polity from being crippled by inertia.[3] If the main concern of liberals, democrats, and republicans is with fat cats of various kinds, the inertia–initiative axis has a different concern: the danger of becoming an ostrich. The ostrich, with her head in the sand, is not the only political danger, nor does it minimize or replace the myriad threats that come from fat cats and even tyrants who indulge in the corruption, disinformation, and manipulation which can do so much damage. It is however one which is too easily overlooked.

Thus the concern for initiative oriented to a holistic understanding of the good as a response to inertia lies at an oblique angle to liberal democracy and to its republican variants. It seeks not to replace democratic politics and liberal principles but to orient them in a further dimension than those to which they are normally angled. And this oblique relation between initiative and dominant existing approaches to political theory helps us further to address the challenge to any use of Plato in thinking about modern politics. That challenge, as we have seen, runs as follows: insofar as modern politics is democratic, how can the notoriously anti-democratic Plato be any use to thinking about it? But if the problem that concerns us is not the nature of democracy per se, but rather how to orient any political regime towards initiative for what is good, then Plato's critique of democracy is irrelevant to the main issue at stake. It will be hard to integrate initiative into *any* regime. Democracy may pose particular difficulties, but it like any other type of regime must face up to this challenge.

Modern resources for understanding initiative: how norms change

The neglect of initiative by modern political theories on the grand scale does not mean that modern social science has nothing to contribute to our understanding of it. On the contrary: sociological and legal studies of changes in norms offer illuminating perspectives on how it is that individual initiative can lead to widespread social change. While, as remarked earlier, such studies of change tend to focus on discrete norms rather than the broader and vaguer panorama of the political imagination as a whole, they are still informative as to the micro-dynamics of social change, and in particular, of change in informal rules and standards which lie partly or wholly outside the current power of state agents to penalize. Such norms are enforced by informal sanctions administered by individuals or groups on other individuals or groups, in order to 'please their audiences'.[4] Yet, for diverse reasons, some individuals can decide to challenge existing norms, either out of personal conviction or position, or responding to changing circumstances or knowledge, and these initial challenges can sometimes engender a 'bandwagon' for change. As one scholar summarizes the dynamics involved, using the technical language and the micro-rational perspective characteristic of 'new norms' scholars in economics and law (some of whom would challenge aspects of this account):

The basic scenario of a successful bandwagon is this: An exogenous change creates new cost-benefit conditions that favor a switch to a new norm. Various change agents, employing advocacy or exemplary acts or enforcements, offer up competing norms to govern the new conditions. The first change agents to supply new norms are self-motivated leaders, who will attain net tangible benefits from a shift, and norm entrepreneurs, who have the best technical info about the aggregate advantages of possible changes. Over time, members of the audience assess these competing offerings and confer esteem on worthy change agents. Because the first change agents to move are challenging traditional ways, for a time ordinary members of the audience may accord them less esteem than previously. The change agents' early losses tend to be mitigated, however, by their relatively low supply costs (arising from their low discount rates and special knowledge and skill) and by their awareness of the existence of appreciative experts who soon will be according them higher esteem. Opinion leaders – those with the best social intelligence – then play a key role. They notice that the technical experts have been gravitating toward the new norm, a sign that it is one that other audience members eventually will learn to appreciate. Hopping on the bandwagon, the opinion leaders begin to supply the new norm and to esteem the change agents who have been pushing it. An ordinary member of the group observes all these moves and for a number of reasons eventually infers that it would be prudent to join the cascade. First, because technical experts are approving the change, it is likely to be good for the group. Second, social experts, those who best understand where the crowd will end up, also are on board, and it is socially risky not to follow them. The mass of ordinary members ultimately conforms to what their respected leaders have been doing. The informational and reputational cascades both crash to completion.[5]

I quote at such length because this analysis illuminates many aspects of initiative: the way in which it may, or may not, be taken up; the fact that it may be taken up for diverse reasons by diverse agents, not all of whom share the original motivating vision or interest; the way in which it can 'cascade', a development which can't be guaranteed in advance, but which follows recognizable patterns once it does get off the ground. The initiative of one, or a few, people, can be traced as the origin of the change of norms about duelling, footbinding, smoking, and many other such phenomena, as remarked in Chapter 1. Norms which have been kept in place by high costs for those who depart from them, and by the inertial imaginative entrenchment of the status quo, can be slowly or rapidly transformed by these initiatives if and when they catch on.

The diversity of motivations is an important point to underline. For Plato, social change must begin with a few people seized of a philosophical vision, yet it can only spread and stabilize if the majority of people come to understand and accept the basic order of social arrangements designed and oriented by philosophers towards the good. The original motivation of the philosophers, driven by their love of learning and knowledge, will never be fully shared by the others.[6] Yet all can come to accept the same basic principles and values of the new regime.

Note that in the description cited at length above, the spread of a new norm is presented as entirely voluntary and independent of political structures (though in other cases studied in the literature on norms, the state plays a role with both voluntary and coercive measures). This is a potential point of divergence from the Platonic model, where the philosopher-rulers are to engage in wholesale culture change. Yet the changes they bring about must meet with popular acceptance, albeit that the exact nature of such acceptance, and how it is to be brought about, remains contested among scholars of Platonic thought. Even if there are reasons for resisting the accusation that manipulation and deception are fundamental to bringing about the *Republic*'s regime – as was argued in Part II – still the way in which acceptance is to be brought about among non-philosophers remains somewhat opaque. Much emphasis is placed upon education, to the extent that at one point Socrates says that the 'quickest and easiest' way to bring the new city about will be to exile everyone over the age of ten to the countryside, enabling the city to be populated solely by children educated so as to be receptive to its ideas and structures (540e–541a).[7] Yet this is said to be (only) the quickest and easiest way, not necessarily the sole way, and while other mechanisms remain opaque, Socrates stresses throughout that acceptance in the form of harmonious concordance is essential if neither state (432a) nor individual (442c) is to become tyrannical. What it means for change to be voluntary, and the complex, partly unconscious, way in which people react to and act upon one another in transmitting and inculcating norms and values, is a subtle point which both contemporary norms scholars and Plato before them have struggled to articulate.

Both Plato and current scholars in psychology, as well as in the economic and legal study of norms, further stress that motivations may change as and because people become involved in a new set of social practices. How one conceives of oneself and one's own motivation is not static or fixed: it is continually reshaped as a person reacts to new circumstances and incorporates those reactions into an understanding of oneself. So while, on the one hand, values shape reasons which in turn shape behaviour, on the other hand behaviour can also shape values.

Plato described this, as we saw in Part II, as people accustoming themselves to the shape and feel of certain values expressed in behaviour – such as the children imitating fools or knaves who risk accustoming and habituating themselves to such actions and reactions. As Socrates says to Adeimantus, children – he is speaking in particular of the children being groomed to become philosopher-rulers, but the point applies more generally – must not 'be clever at acting a mean or otherwise disgraceful part on the stage for fear of catching the infection in real life. For have you not noticed how dramatic and similar representations, if indulgence in them is prolonged into adult life, establish habits of physical poise, intonation and thought which become second nature?' (395c–d).

An influential group of modern psychologists describes the mechanism differently, focusing on the cognitive rationalization of behaviour rather than merely on habit, and arguing that people infer their values from the behaviour in which they engage. On this view, our identity is continually reshaped by inference from the evidence of our actions; it is not so much sheer habit, but the unconscious or partly conscious drive for consistency, which shapes future conduct. One experiment designed to test this theory found that people primed by having been asked, and who agreed, to make a small commitment illustrating a new value (putting a tiny card in their window in favour of safer driving) were subsequently far more likely than the control group to allow a large unsightly sign to the same effect to be erected in their front yards. Once people have formed a commitment to a certain kind of behaviour, they reshape their conception of their own identity, and from there identity reshapes their reasons, making new reasons become salient to them.[8]

Despite the differences between them in matters of detail, Plato and these modern psychological theorists agree that as people begin to act differently – for a variety of different motives, whether individual conviction, social pressure, or state regulation – so they will come to see reasons and the world differently. As one modern scholar puts it:

They will convince themselves that it is the correct way to be and will begin
to pay attention to facts they hadn't noticed before ... They will make themselves available to hear arguments they hadn't heard before ... and will find
such arguments more persuasive than before ... What is important about
this process of generating additional reasons to justify the commitment is
that the reasons are *new*.[9]

Call this bootstrapping. It describes a path by which a small set of changes
can spiral into a much more comprehensive transformation, both in the
individual case and in the social one.

Yet, as remarked earlier in this book, contemporary studies of such
processes leave certain questions unanswered. What is it, exactly, that
motivates certain people to become 'change agents'? The scholar quoted
at length above on the bandwagon effect remarks further that such
people tend to be characterized by a certain perspective on time. They
value the future (in technical terms, they have 'relatively low discount
rates and long time horizons') and so it makes sense for them to engage
in social change that may take time to reap benefits, if at all.[10] While
important, this observation still leaves opaque the motivations which
lead people to adopt a particular cause. If individuals are crucial to initiating the process of social change, it is equally crucial to understand
what it is that motivates such individuals to do so. A revised process
of imagination, so this book has argued, is one fundamental source of
such initiative.

Changing roles in light of the whole

We have seen reason to believe that a few individuals can sometimes kickstart a complete transformation of a single norm (new norms scholars)
or even a complete social transformation (Platonic model). Yet often,
such attempted transformations may not take off. They may stop short,
affecting a small group but not finding sufficient resonance or support to
take root in society as a whole. Hence we must ask: what are the ethics of
responsible initiative in a society as yet untransformed, still in the throes
of contestation between norms and values old and new?

Platonic guidance would suggest that the responsibility is to reorient one's understanding of existing social roles in light of one's emerging
understanding of the whole, of what the overall good requires (and in
the case which we have been tracing throughout this book, specifically
the element of the good which consists in sustainability). This in turn
suggests two principal tasks in the domain in which one acts: to press
towards an understanding of the whole, and to press towards action in
relation to it. Let me elaborate on each in turn.

Responsible initiative in one's own domain would engage in radical,
integrated, and systematic prioritization of the good in question (in this
case, sustainability). At the moment, sustainability is one among many
other issues competing for individual, corporate, charity or non-profit, and
government attention, and it is still judged intellectually and politically
permissible (perhaps ill-advised, but permissible) for each to prioritize
other goals. For example, the politicians and civil servants who designed
the 2009 budget measure in the United Kingdom offering a £2000 grant
for people to trade in their old cars for new ones, and a similar 'cash for
clunkers' programme in the United States, aimed primarily to help the
car industry and stimulate the economy, and this aim compromised the
fullest possible achieving of a green end. True, the goal was to replace less
fuel-efficient cars with newer and more fuel-efficient ones, but the policy
was indifferent as to whether incentives for people to buy new cars would
end up in swamping those relative efficiency gains – what if without the
incentive, more people would have given up their cars altogether? That
calculation was simply deemed irrelevant because the focus of that particular policy was on the car industry and not on climate change. Call this
tunnel vision: the idea that sustainability is an issue which government
can choose its moment to address, and can afford to downplay when
convenient for other issues.

A similar distortion afflicts approaches adopted by leaders in both
business and government who dwell on relative improvements in carbon
emissions, for example, rather than absolute ones. Reducing the carbon
intensity of particular technologies is a worthy goal. Indeed it is essential
to an overall solution. But it is not enough in itself. For the overall emissions of that technology may nevertheless continue to grow, whether due
to increasing population, increasing specific demand, or simply general
economic growth. Increased efficiency can even itself generate a 'rebound
effect', as when consumers respond to more energy-efficient refrigerators

by buying an extra one – which although unlikely to wipe out all net gains, must be taken into account. This is a problem especially in relation to win-win business strategies which seek to increase profits at the same time as, and indeed by means of, improving performance on measures of sustainability. The first phase of such strategies almost always aims for continued growth in sales, and this very often means that the relative efficiency gains of the win-win will be swamped by a rise in absolute emissions due to such growth. Scarcely any business has actually incorporated sustainability in the sense of an absolute limit on emissions into its business strategy (for one example to the contrary, see the discussion of Interface below).

Almost all current approaches to climate change – itself only a single facet of sustainability, as noted in Part I – fall into one of these two categories: it is not consistently prioritized, and where it is, relative reductions in carbon intensity are accepted as adequate. Such a piecemeal, on-and-off approach fails to measure up to the scale and nature of the changes required. I will draw on some recent scientific and policy analysis to illustrate this point: I do so for the sake of illustration alone, as this book is not in the business of prescribing specific changes, but rather of illuminating what the nature and implications of any such changes would have to be.

The best way to appreciate the scale of the change needed is to begin as does Cambridge physicist David MacKay, by making rough calculations ('guerrilla physics') of energy demand and then working out what sources of low-emission energy supply could potentially stack up to meet it.[11] That then sets the challenge of working out systemic ways of allocating those available energy resources. One well-worked-out proposal argues that it makes most sense to decarbonize the transport sector completely by moving to all-electric vehicles, linking into existing electricity grids and operating on mobile-phone-like contracts for central battery charging and swapping; use hydrocarbons in power plants with carbon capture and storage technology; and reserve sustainable biofuels for aviation where their energy density is most needed.[12] This sort of integrated and comprehensive plan makes sense on many levels: it concentrates the point sources of emissions in relatively few places (power plants) rather than spreading them out across millions of cars, and so allows them to be far more easily controlled; it makes most efficient use of hydrocarbons, rather than the more energy-wasting (though at the moment financially lucrative) transformation of them into liquids such as petrol from oil or coal-to-liquids processes; and it is swiftly achievable through government procurement and existing regulatory frameworks, which could quickly require refitting petrol stations as battery-charging and transfer stations plugged into the national grid and simply banning the manufacture of non-electric vehicles. The report even suggests that electric vehicles charged off-peak could become net energy-value producers by releasing that energy at peak times back into the grid. This is not net new production, but it is a way of gaining maximal cost efficiency as well as energy efficiency, and materially encapsulates the people as co-producers mentioned in Part I.

Whether or not the details of plans like these are the very best way to go – a debate which this book does not propose to enter – the point is that only plans of this sort of scale and systematicity will be able to make the necessary difference. Encouraging individuals to swap old cars for more efficient ones is an important starting point, but it must be a starting point to a comprehensive strategy, not an end in itself. What is required is an integrated plan that can be shown to make a significant and overall contribution to the kind of drastic emissions-reductions trajectory required to get the world to a significantly less dangerous emissions pathway (though 2 degrees may now be out of reach).

Hence the vital interplay between individual, initiative, and the good. While individuals are the only ones who can, in the final analysis, take or prompt any initiative, the initiatives they take need to be conceived in light of the largest possible framing and understanding of the good. This is the relevance of Plato's vision of the whole to confronting the psychosocial dimension of sustainability. Rather than accepting a limitation of responsibility to one's own patch, giving up responsibility for the way in which that role is defined and it relates to the whole problem and possible solution, the challenge is to act locally while thinking as globally as possible in terms of the systemic shifts and their implications that sustainability requires.

That brings us to the second task set by the vision of the whole: that of rethinking the responsibilities associated with whatever particular roles one occupies. At present, the assumption that existing role boundaries relieve us of responsibility is all too pervasive, and all too convenient. Whatever role or roles one occupies within the system – politician, parent, entrepreneur, employee, public official – each role is very often interpreted as setting strict horizons on what one needs to take into account. Believing our role to be bounded by its current definition, and our duty to consist in pursuing that role as defined, we are led to abjure, sometimes on principle, concern for the health of the broader system. Indeed, we are easily led to believe that we are doing our best by *not* asking those broader questions, that our duty consists in playing our part as currently defined – even pushing to the limits of what the law allows us to do – rather than in asking questions about how well those definitions serve any broader purpose.

Duties of reporting, for example, confine themselves to what we have done within our role rather than to whether we have considered whether the effect of our position is to undermine larger goods, and what we have done to alter that effect if so. Even regulators and policy-makers confine themselves to considering issues in isolation. Pesticide regulation is one example, in which individual licensing decisions are taken for the effects of products considered one by one in isolation, without requiring consideration of the interactive effects of widespread multiple applications of myriad chemicals which might individually be safe enough.[13]

It is understandable how such tunnel vision has evolved. In a complex society, it is easiest and can seem most efficient (from some points of view, even including certain definitions of accountability) to devolve and disentangle different decisions, licensing diverse agents to proceed according to limited briefs. But this division of labour works only if the division has been made responsibly and thoroughly, and if it includes a role for continual assessment of how well it is meeting the ends of the whole. Without such a role or responsibility, the result is that no one is considering the whole. Worse, no one is required to consider the whole. Even worse, what people *are* required to consider can positively militate against their considering the whole, requiring them to blinker themselves even to the obvious long-term or overall impact of their actions.

Clearly, such tunnel vision is not the only blockage on the road to a more sustainable society: there is plenty of resistance generated by short-term self-interest and by ideological disagreement as well. All these causes of resistance demonstrate the fact that leadership is intrinsically paradoxical. One has to get people to do what they would not otherwise have done, to respond to arguments or appeals which did not previously motivate them. In democratic leadership the paradox is of an even more acute kind: a politician is supposed to serve the people at the same time

as leading them, to respect their will or interests or preferences or con-
clusions in the very act of moving them to new positions and actions.
How far ahead of the public a democratic politician can get – and should
get – is both theoretically and practically problematic.

Plato, notoriously, intimated that this relationship is inherently catastrophic: democratic politicians will be servile to the people, flattering and
pandering to them in order to win their support, whereas only politicians
who do not themselves desire or seek power can be trusted to serve them
in the true sense of governing them for their benefit. We can be more
charitable while still preserving the insight which he identified. Some
politicians will not want to lead, being content to pander. Others are afraid
to lead, not sure of whether the people will follow. Still others are willing
to follow if some of the people lead from below. Fear and deference are
key factors in producing the passing-the-buck deadlock.

Can the Platonic model outline a path from tunnel vision to a vision
of the whole? Recall Plato's vision of the Sun. In Part II we focused on
the notion of the Sun as an image for the Good, stressing the need for a
structural account of goodness including sustainability as one of its condition. Here, we may draw out another aspect of the Platonic vision. This
is the importance in taking up a perspective on the whole, as opposed
to any piecemeal part of one's understanding. The Good, like the Sun,
integrates in casting its light over the whole of a field of vision, whether
perceptible vision in the case of the Sun or the vision of what we can
understand (intelligible vision) in the case of goodness. No perspective
which fails to rise to that height will be able to understand the place of
what it is considering in light of the whole. So it is not only goodness but
also wholeness, the unifying understanding which can produce a unified
personality and a unified city, which is the lesson of the *Republic*.[14]

Wholeness is the antidote to tunnel vision. In a world whose interdependence is proving so instantaneous and breathtaking, we can no longer
afford to license indifference to the effects of one's own patch on others.
We need a new ethics of the division of labour, no longer writing off the
overall effect of one's actions as outside one's concerns, and building an
awareness of the whole and the goal into everyday choices. We can no
longer afford to think of organizations such as corporations (and indeed
NGOs) as adequately serving society simply by the blinkered pursuit of
their allotted social role, blind to the broader functioning of the society
which those roles are meant to serve. There is a fundamental ethical duty

to consider the role that one's organization is playing in the broader social context. Playing the game is not enough. One has to play in a way which strengthens the rules, rather than threatening to undermine them.

This is an ethical duty on individuals which is simultaneously a duty on their organizations. It means thinking through the mission and definition of one's own roles, and of one's organizations and their roles, and working to expand, revise, and implement those roles in relation to as full as possible an understanding of the good. Let me illustrate with the case of those who have positions in corporate organizations which, to make the case as challenging as possible, are organized to make a profit for their shareholders. What would it mean to live out this role in light of the good of sustainability, and how might the role be revised in light of that good?

One implication is that such companies should be held accountable for acting in terms which broadly help to sustain the viability of the financial, social and ecological system as a whole, in those areas to which their activity is most relevant. This could begin as a matter of required reporting: demonstrating in the annual report that managers and board members have reasoned about the aspects of the broader social system in which the company engages, have identified the areas where their actions have most impact, and are able to detail the range of information and views they took into account in deciding on their actions. Such reporting would include the direct and indirect ecological footprint of products and services; lobbying and advertising; and financial practices, including full disclosure of all tax arrangements and taxes paid. Of course, this is an open-ended requirement which would need further specification. The NGO sector could play a key role in developing best-practice model reports for each sector, so that reports would increasingly become comparable and standards would quickly emerge.

The requirement to disclose reasoning would have two effects. It would make managers and board members engage in that reasoning in the first place, thus opening their eyes to the wide range of social impact of what they do; and it would provide evidence for external stakeholders to engage the company. The difference from current CSR reporting is that often this is limited to what companies do, as opposed to how they think; it is most often measured in comparative and relative terms, rather than in terms of the absolute scale of the problem; and it is focused on particular areas of operation, so that it might trumpet community involvement but neglect to report on lobbying efforts. The new model would require companies to demonstrate that the overall effects of their business model and operation not only contribute social value (including, but not limited to, producing wealth, goods, and services), but also do not detract from that social value in their systemic effects so as to yield a net negative result.

An objection to this view of ethics is that it requires controversial judgements. Who is to say what is public benefit, and so how can companies know what it is, or be held accountable for considering it? This is the origin of the view that companies should be answerable to the law and law alone, widely held on both the left and the right. But as we've seen, the law is imperfect, slow, and incomplete, and it was ever thus. The way forward is to formulate this ethical duty along the lines of European, not American, generally accepted accounting standards: cast in terms of principles, not specific rules. So long as a company provides a reasonable interpretation of its social role, regulators and courts should accept it (though wider stakeholders may press for more stringent interpretations). The requirement can be interpreted loosely and broadly, as in the formulation of the test of business judgement itself, where courts are typically very deferential to management decisions even where these are relatively poor. Nevertheless, some germane reasoning would have to be documented.

A second implication is the corporate choice of sustainability achievements and targets. It is not good enough to report mere percentages or numbers of improvement: trumpeting a 10 percent cut, or the equivalent of 30,000 cars off the road. That is equivalent to validating the effort one feels like making without measuring it against the total magnitude of the task that needs to be achieved. Reporting must set targets in relation to a broad and systemic analysis and report them in relation to the achievement of a substantive goal, not in mere feel-good percentage terms divorced from any standard of 'enoughness'. As Winston Churchill is reported to have said, 'It is no use saying, "We are doing our best." You have got to succeed in doing what is necessary.'[15]

Rethinking the duties of reporting, and the broader duties of engagement, is all the more urgent because companies haven't been completely indifferent to policy and regulation. Instead they've engaged with it for their own benefit, not social benefit. They can lobby to tilt the rules in their direction, do aggressive tax planning, do all they can to capture policy or starve governments of resources, support trade associations which lobby for Neanderthal policies behind the scenes while companies tout their progressive credentials in front of them – and none of that has been covered in CSR codes. The sustainability of the system is not a corporate concern. It's left to the regulators, and if the regulators are outnumbered, out-resourced, or just unable to keep up with the latest manoeuvres, well, that's the name of the game.

One solution to this would be to ban corporate lobbying altogether. Robert Reich made a powerful case, ignored in Washington, that any Wall Street firm rescued by federal funds should be banned from using their resources to lobby on how they should be run.[16] He was anticipated by two centuries or so by Adam Smith, whose insight into the productive value of the division of labour was matched by his less celebrated insight into the dangers of merchants combining to change the political rules for their own benefit.[17]

Where the local legal understanding of free speech allows it, this is an attractive solution. It is not inevitable that companies be viewed, as they are in the United States, as corporate persons entitled to many of the same Bill of Rights protections as natural persons. The differences in kind between natural persons and corporate persons could be construed to justify significant differences in their legal entitlements. Unlike natural persons, after all, corporate persons are potentially immortal, with corresponding deep and potentially non-time-limited pockets. They are not subject to physical injury which can curtail their lives, and where incorporated through limited liability, not liable to reduction of welfare in the same proportion as natural persons even through legal or financial penalties. In other words, as an eighteenth-century lord chancellor of Britain put it, corporations have 'no soul to be damned, no body to be kicked'.[18] Were all companies to be banned from direct lobbying and limited in their forms of political speech, it would relieve disproportionate fear of the business lobby on the part of government and level the playing field between corporate and natural persons.

Nevertheless, where corporate lobbying either can't be banned on constitutional grounds or isn't banned for other reasons, the challenge falls on companies themselves to use it constructively, and on politicians to design regulatory and lobbying rules that can support them in doing so. The vicious circle in which government allows itself to be trapped by a self-proclaimed business lobby with antediluvian policies on the environment can be broken if government designs lobbying rules more intelligently and an enlightened corporate sector uses them to step up to the plate, lobbying for changes to rules in which the more sustainable companies will be better placed and incentivized to succeed. After all, not all business interests are the same. For every loser in the old economy there will be a winner in the green economy. The rise of a business lobby opposed to a third runway at London's Heathrow Airport – in contrast to the official Confederation of British Industry position – gave government some space to consider the arguments rather than simply kowtowing to a single business voice. Likewise, the Prince of Wales's Corporate Leaders Group on Climate Change has been calling for more and faster regulation to introduce a carbon price and bring down emissions across the whole economy, both in the United Kingdom and in the European Union.[19] Both cases show how important it is to have public business voices backing a policy change which goes against the conventional grain. Both showcase business using its convening power for an ethical purpose, taking responsibility for shaping the architecture of the system to good ends, not subverting it for private ends. And this is where economic and ecological sustainability come together. Both require us – individuals and organizations alike – to reorient our everyday licensed actions to take account of a greater good.

An individual and corporate odyssey: Ray C. Anderson and the story of Interface

Such corporate rethinking, like all rethinking, begins with individuals: individuals who, whether in corporations or other bodies, rethink the demands of their roles and of the goals which those roles direct them to serve. The best example is that of Ray C. Anderson, who was founder and CEO of Interface, an American carpet company serving businesses and based in the state of Georgia. Like the message of *Carbon Detox* discussed in Part II, Anderson's story is an unwitting Platonic parable: one which combines reorientation to the whole good with knowledge in a transformative reconceptualization of his role as CEO and of his company's role in the office services economy, the American economy, and ultimately the global economy.

Anderson's retelling of his journey begins where we began, with the harmful inertia constituted by current neglect of sustainability in defining the scope of harm and the concomitant scope of permissible corporate action. Stunned by reading Paul Hawken's *The Ecology of Commerce* in the course of what had begun as a perfunctory attempt to reply to a client's queries about the firm's stance on sustainability, Anderson realized that he was 'a *legal* thief [emphasis original]. The perverse tax laws, by failing to correct the errant market to internalize those externalities such as the costs of global warming and pollution, are my accomplices in crime.' That led him to challenge the firm to a radical goal: 'to convert Interface into a restorative enterprise, first to reach sustainability, then to become restorative … doing good to Earth, not just no harm – by helping or influencing others to reach towards sustainability'. The Platonic goal of doing good defines the enterprise's new 'mission'. And just as in Plato, and as in *Carbon Detox*, this is presented not just as right, but as '*smart*': several times Anderson compares the insight and goal of sustainability – his new strategic 'ultimate purpose' – to the insight and goal of the value of carpet tiles which had inspired his original corporate strategy.[20]

The new strategy does not abandon the old strategy's goal of attaining value. Rather, it redefines the parameters of value, by adopting a target of zero waste and radically redefining what waste means: 'We define waste as *any* cost that goes into our product that does not produce value for our customers. Value, of course, embraces product quality, and more – aesthetics, utility, durability, resource efficiency. Since in pursuit of maximum value any waste is bad, we're measuring progress against a zero-based waste goal.' The redefinition of waste goes even further: the company later 'declared *all* energy that is derived from fossil fuels to be waste, waste to be eliminated systematically, first through efficiency improvement and, eventually, to be replaced by renewable energy'. Finally, Anderson's reflections on the dynamic process involved in attaining a sustainable economy are a perfect illustration of the process of changing norms analysed above. Regulation is needed to get the pricing of carbon emissions (for example) right. 'But', Anderson asks, what in turn will drive the creation of tax shifts and other politically derived financial instruments? It seems to me that those will ultimately be driven by a public with a high sense of ethics, morality, a deep-seated love of Earth, and a longing for harmony with nature. When the marketplace, the people, show their appreciation for these qualities and vote with their pocketbooks for the early adopters, the people will be leading; the 'good guys' will be winning in the marketplace and the polling booth; the rest of the political and business leaders will have to follow.[21]

As an exemplar for other businesses, potential customers and rivals alike, Anderson's way of thinking about the changes made at Interface models the scope for individual and organizational rethinking of one's goals in light of the good and the whole which a Platonic model of politics demands.

The challenge of the whole for individual ethics

The average reader who is not a CEO may find the Anderson story impressive but too remote to be inspiring or instructive. It's possible for a CEO to determine a new strategic purpose for his company. But what is a middle manager or salesperson or factory worker, caught within the confines of her existing role, to do? Such a person may feel that she can take, at best, only very incomplete measures towards the demands of the whole that Plato models for her to perceive. And that frustration may lead to an inhibition about taking any initiative in this direction at all. Ironically, there is a tendency to judge both oneself and others more harshly for taking half-measures towards a radical challenge that has been acknowledged, whereas those who simply deny the challenge insulate themselves from such criticism.[22] Insisting on an holistic assessment of sustainability may simply seem to make matters worse. If someone reaches such an assessment, yet the actions open to her are simply inadequate to the scale of the problem, will she be paralysed on pain of hypocrisy from either taking the possible half-measures or acknowledging the true scope of action needed?

It is in answer to this question that many of the threads of this book can be drawn together. The fear, paralysis, and inertia in such cases typically reflect a sense that one's contribution is hopelessly inadequate, even negligible, in relation to the scale of the problem. Yet the possibility of serving as an exemplar for others, of reorienting one's roles and organizations to some extent, and of contributing to change the ideological and political climate so as to make further political action possible, is a possibility without inherent limits on success. History demonstrates again and again that the effects of individual action and the paths of social change are far from wholly predictable. In such circumstances, compounded by the fact that our knowledge of the pathways of climate change and other scientific dimensions of sustainability does not allow us to predict their exact future course, it is both irresponsible and untrue to let oneself off the hook by concluding in advance that one's actions are irrelevant or inadequate. The only certainty is that doing nothing to change the course of business as usual is a mistake. To penalize those who try to effect change for failing to be radical enough, while letting others who do not try at all off the hook, is to sacrifice social complexity on the altar of an arid logical consistency. It is surely better to be partially, and unpredictably, effective than to be wholly inert. As the eighteenth-century statesman Edmund Burke is reported to have said, 'No man can make a greater mistake than he who did nothing because he could do only a little.'

Conclusion

Let us take stock. In what respects do the arguments of this book follow the contours of the Platonic political project of the *Republic*, and in what respects do they depart from its paths? We can sum up three principal planks in the Platonic project. First is that, contrary to stereotypes of him as an egghead intellectual, Plato was, as the nineteenth-century philosopher Friedrich Nietzsche would call him, a 'political agitator'.[23] He wrote to provide models of social transformation and even to practice such transformation in the effects of his writings themselves. Second, however, he was not *merely* a political agitator, nor concerned merely with jostling for his party's advantage. Rather he was *simultaneously* a political agitator and a philosopher in the literal sense – a 'lover of wisdom' – and he saw politics consisting ideally in an internalization of the rule of knowledge, a knowledge rooted in a holistic conception of the good. Third, his vision was that of a self-identified elite leading top-down and paternalistic social change. That elitism made him sceptical of democracy, as a benighted or at best chaotic political and ideological system which could not, he feared, effect the kinds of transformative changes required (though nor could any of the other actually existing regimes of his time).[24]

We have seen grounds in the course of this book to adopt the first two elements of the Platonic model: the challenge of sustainability is one which requires both political art and philosophical insight to address, and no one could succeed in meeting that challenge without a knowledge of the scientific, but also the ethical, demands which it makes. It is the third plank which I have questioned, and where I have attempted to reshape the Platonic model to be useful to those beginning from a liberal and democratic perspective. That doesn't mean assuming that everyone can be expected to share the same motivation, or to have the ability, leisure, and education to study and analyse the demands of sustainability in detail. (Formal education may prove less essential, and sometimes more inhibiting, than curiosity- and value-driven autodidacticism, nevertheless.) A bottom-up project will still be started by a few, whose motivations will be different, as suggested earlier in this chapter, from those who for mixed and diverse reasons decide to follow their lead. If this remains structurally elitist, it is an elite open to anyone able to grasp the urgency and scale of the problem, and to begin experimenting with being part of the solution. My bet is that it is possible to effect social change in the requisite political and philosophical dimensions by starting from the bottom up (not only from the top down, as Plato would have it), and that such change can be made while still respecting the fundamentals of personal liberty. That bet may yet fail. It will certainly fail if we do not try it, concluding in advance that it is impossible for it to succeed or for us to make a difference in its doing so.

Coda: on the ridiculous

This book has canvassed a range of elements in the current political imagination which sustain inertia and inhibit initiative. There is one, however, which we have not yet emphasized – yet which the story of the

Cave already demonstrated. This is the fear of being thought ridiculous, for example by taking initiatives that might seem outlandish or unnecessary or ostentatious to those still mired in denial. Plato was acutely sensitive to the fact that not just high-flown values and principles are at stake in dramatic social change: so too is the sheer sense of the absurd. He dramatized this in relation to a particular and peculiar Athenian social norm: that while adult men should routinely exercise naked in public, as should young girls in prescribed ritual contexts, adult women should not be seen naked in public. Socrates proposes in Book 5 of the *Republic* that in the new city he is describing, adult women should exercise naked alongside the men (one reason is that some women as well as some men are potentially suitable to serve as philosopher-rulers of the city, and so both eligible groups have to receive military training). He immediately admits that this will look ridiculous to those who are listening to him:

> SOCRATES: 'And won't the most ridiculous thing of all be to see the women taking exercise naked with the men in the gymnasium? It won't only be the young women; there will be elderly women too, just as there are old men who go on with their exercises when they are wrinkled and ugly to look at.'
>
> 'Lord!' he [GLAUCON] said, 'that's going to be a funny sight by present standards.' (452a–b)

Glaucon's response gives the clue to how Socrates proposes that they should jointly respond to the imagined critics of the new society, critics who will condemn it as ridiculous. For as the boy says, it is only 'by present standards' that this is a funny sight. Standards of the ridiculous change over time, sometimes dramatically within the same society. And so Socrates encourages him by reminding him that very different standards prevailed in Athens even in the recent past.

> SOCRATES: '... it was not so long ago that the Greeks thought – as most of the barbarians [non-Greeks] still think – that it was shocking and ridiculous for men to be seen naked. When the Cretans, and later the Spartans, first began to take exercise naked, wasn't there plenty of material for the wit of the comedians of the day?'
>
> GLAUCON: 'There was indeed.'

SOCRATES: 'But when experience showed them that it was better to strip than to wrap themselves up, what reason had proved best lost its absurdity to the eye. Which shows how idle it is to think anything ridiculous except what is wrong. Indeed, anyone who tries to raise a laugh at the sight of anything but what is foolish and wrong will never, when he is serious again, make goodness the object of his admiration.' (452c–e)

The key sentence leaps off the page: 'what reason had proved best lost its absurdity to the eye.' Here is Socrates summing up the process of bootstrapping changes in the political imagination which we have described. Argument, or other inducement to act differently, can change the way we see the world, what we count as reasons, and what we see – or do not see – as ridiculous. If the arguments are compelling, we should not be afraid to change, because change is almost certain to come anyway, and we can be part of the vanguard of a new sense of the ridiculous. The choice is not so much between change and no change, as between surfing the waves of change versus being swamped by them. An early twentieth-century scholar of Plato and shrewd university administrator identified a rhetorical fallacy to which we are all susceptible, 'the Principle of Unripe Time': 'that people should not do at the present moment what they think right at that moment, because the moment at which they think it right has not yet arrived'.[25] If we resist the Platonic call for individual virtue and initiative, indulging ourselves in the plaintive, shamefaced prayer of another sometime Platonist, St Augustine – 'Grant me ... continence, but not yet' – we risk missing the *kairos*, or what Plato and his contemporaries knew as the crucial opportune moment for action in light of the good.[26]

Notes

PROLOGUE TO CHAPTER 1: PLATO'S CAVE

1   Translations of the *Republic* are, if not otherwise noted, quoted with per-
    mission from Plato, *The Republic*, 2nd edn, transl. Desmond Lee, introduc-
    tion by Melissa Lane (London and New York: Penguin, 2007), a choice
    made to facilitate readers' engagement with an easily accessible translation.
    Other translations of Plato are, if not otherwise noted, quoted under the 'fair
    use' doctrine from Plato, *Complete Works*, ed. John M. Cooper with D. S.
    Hutchinson (Indianapolis: Hackett, 1997), with individual translators being
    acknowledged when a work is first cited.

2   Millennium Ecosystem Assessment, *Ecosystems and Human Well-Being:
    Synthesis* (Washington, DC: Island Press, 2005). A good introduction to the
    relationship of biology and ecology to climate change is Jonathan Cowie,
    Climate Change: Biological and Human Aspects (Cambridge: Cambridge
    University Press, 2007).

3   I use this term in the sense coined by Eli Sagan, 'Citizenship as a Form of
    Psycho-Social Identity', in John A. Koumoulides, ed., *The Good Idea: democ-
    racy in ancient Greece* (New Rochelle, NY: A. D. Caratzas Press, 1995), 47–60,
    at 47, elaborated by Danielle S. Allen, *The World of Prometheus: The Politics of
    Punishing in Democratic Athens* (Princeton and Oxford: Princeton University
    Press, 2000), 333 n. 3: 'The word "psychosocial" [connotes] the ways in which
    an individual's participation in social practices and ideas interacts with the
    individual psyche (or meets the needs of the individual psyche) and serves to
    foster *social cohesion*. The word indicates how social cohesion at once sup-
    ports individual cognitive and psychological mechanisms and needs their
    support' [quoting Allen's paraphrase of Sagan with her emphasis; note that
    she misprints the page number to which she is referring in Sagan as 147].
    (A similar appropriation, which reminded me of Allen's reference, is made
    by Christina H. Tarnopolsky, *Prudes, Perverts, and Tyrants: Plato's* Gorgias

and the Politics of Shame (Princeton and Oxford: Princeton University Press, 2010), 8 n. 31.)

4   I owe this phrase to Alan Knight, speaking at the Prince of Wales's Business and the Environment Programme, Madingley Seminar, 2009; quoted with permission.

1 INTRODUCTION:
INERTIA AS FAILURE OF THE POLITICAL IMAGINATION

1   On the 'great moderation': Ben S. Bernanke, 'The Great Moderation' (speech, meeting of the Eastern Economic Association, Washington, DC, 20 February 2004); James H. Stock and Mark W. Watson, 'Has the Business Cycle Changed and Why?', *NBER Macroeconomics Annual* 17 (2002). On the end of 'boom and bust': '... we today in our country have economic stability not boom and bust ...' Gordon Brown, 'Budget for Enterprise' (speech at the TGWU Manufacturing Matters conference, 28 March 2002).

2   A PDF of the letter is available via http://www.britac.ac.uk/news/newsrelease-economy.cfm; I was a co-signatory to a letter written in reply on 26 August 2009, pointing out that the financial crisis must be addressed in light of the broader brewing ecological crisis, for which see: http://www.abundancypart-ners.co.uk/2009/08/open-letter-to-the-queen/.

3   Peter Head of ARUP, speaking at the Prince of Wales's Business and the Environment Programme, Madingley Seminar, 2008; quoted with permission.

4   Dean Kamen, the inventor of the Segway: 'Technology is easy to develop ... Developing a new attitude, moving the culture from one mental model to another, that's the difficult part. You give people a solution to a problem and the great irony to me is that even though they're unhappy, they have high inertia. People don't like change. The reason it takes technology 15 or 20 years to come in is because 15 years is the time it takes a kid who saw it when he was young to become a functioning adult' ('Mr Segway's Difficult Path', *Economist*, 10 June 2010). An excellent overview of the broad field of ethics and the environment is Dale Jamieson, *Ethics and the Environment: An Introduction* (Cambridge: Cambridge University Press, 2008). Among many books on ethics and climate change is James Garvey, *The Ethics of Climate Change: Right and Wrong in a Warming World* (London and New York: Continuum, 2008). On political theory and the environment, a leading author is Andrew Dobson: see his *Green Political Thought*, 4th edn (London and New York: Routledge, 2007), and Andrew Dobson and Robyn Eckersley

(eds), *Political Theory and the Ecological Challenge* (Cambridge: Cambridge University Press, 2006).

5 These comments were made under 'Chatham House rules' and so cannot be attributed without permission. However, public attestations of the same sentiment can also be found: for example, WWF-UK has initiated a 'Strategies for Change' project looking, among other things, at 'the myths we live by' – see http://www.wwf.org.uk/research_centre/research_centre_results. cfm?uNewsID=2224 – and John Grant has called for the deliberate creation of 'counter-myths' in *The Green Marketing Manifesto* (London: John Wiley and Sons, 2007).

6 One exception is the identification by Mike Hulme, former director of the Tyndall Centre in Britain, of four 'myths' by which people do and may interpret climate change: as Eden, apocalypse, Babel, and jubilee. These myths are limited to the phenomenon itself rather than relating to broader dimensions of political value and identity. See his stimulating book *Why We Disagree about Climate Change: Understanding Controversy, Inaction and Opportunity* (Cambridge: Cambridge University Press, 2009), 340–65.

7 G. A. Cohen, *Rescuing Justice and Equality* (Cambridge, MA: Harvard University Press, 2008), 123. In Part III, we will explore the further dynamics to which Cohen later alludes, that actions shape ethos, which in turn shapes norms, which in turn shapes action: 'our everyday actions greatly affect the ethos, because they change the norms to which we fall subject', 381.

8 Nicholas Stern, *The Economics of Climate Change: The Stern Review* (Cambridge: Cambridge University Press, 2007), 452. Compare, in the context of ecology, Dale Jamieson's identification of the 'system of values' which 'specifies permissions, norms, duties, and obligations; … assigns blame, praise, and responsibility; and … provides an account of what is valuable and what is not' as 'like an iceberg – most of what is important may be submerged and invisible even to the person whose values they are.' Jamieson considers such a system of values to be generally 'a cultural construction rather than an individual one', one in which '[t]he vast areas of agreement [among people] often seem invisible because they are presupposed or assumed without argument' (Dale Jamieson, 'Ethics, Public Policy, and Global Warming', in Jamieson, *Morality's Progress: Essays on Humans, Other Animals, and the Rest of Nature* (Oxford: Clarendon Press, 2002), 282–95, quoting from 290–1). This essay is reprinted in a slightly modified form from its original appearance in *Science, Technology, and Human Values* 17:2 (1992), 139–53.

9 Stern, *The Economics of Climate Change*, 27.

10 During the early phase of the European Union Emissions Trading Scheme, the cap was set too high and carbon credits were over-allocated. As a result,

though there was a reduction in carbon emissions, the amount of abatement was modest. See A. Denny Kellerman, et al., *Pricing Carbon: The European Emissions Trading Scheme* (Cambridge: Cambridge University Press, 2010), 158–92.

11 I have learned much about the centrality of social communication to the human animal from Philip Pettit and Victoria McGeer. See for example their jointly authored article, 'The Self-Regulating Mind', *Language and Communication* 22 (2002), 281–99.

12 See especially articles on 6 and 7 January 2009: Martin Delgado, 'An energy saving bulb has gone – evacuate the room now!', 6 January 2009; Beth Hale, 'Yes I found some … but it wasn't light work', 6 January 2009; Michael Hanlon [on website also given as Micheal Hanlon], 'Analysis: So are these really such a bright idea?', 7 January 2009; David Derbyshire, 'The low-energy bulbs that won't fit your light sockets', 7 January 2009; and David Derbyshire, 'Revolt! Robbed of their right to buy traditional light bulbs, millions are clearing shelves of last supplies'. For the United States, see Julie Scelfo, 'Any other bright ideas?', *New York Times*, 10 January 2008, and Edward Wyatt, 'Give up familiar light bulb? Not without fight, some say', *New York Times*, 11 March 2011.

13 'Heavy baggage', *Economist*, 31 January 2009, 62, quoting J. K. Dadoo, the senior bureaucrat in Delhi's environment department. In 2002 Ireland was the first country to impose a tax on plastic bags; the tax is currently 44 euro-cents per bag. Also in 2002, Bangladesh imposed a ban on plastic bags. In the United States, there are no state-wide bans on plastic bags; a bill to ban plastic bags in California was defeated on grounds of higher cost in 2010. See The Associated Press, 'California: Backers of Plastic Bags Prevail', *New York Times*, 2 September 2010.

14 The importance of 'status quo bias', as documented by psychologists, for law and politics has been emphasized by Cass R. Sunstein, for example in his 'Preferences, Paternalism, and Liberty', in *Preferences and Well-Being: Royal Institute of Philosophy Supplement* 81 (Cambridge: Cambridge University Press, 2006), 233–64.

15 Dr Mayer Hillman, author of a 2010 Policy Studies Institute report entitled *Making the Most of Daylight Hours: the Implications for Scotland*, observed that the objections to a proposal to extend British Summer Time through the winter 'are part of the nature of the very conservative society we live in. When new ideas come up they are scrutinised for perfection. If that perfection is not found, they are rejected for the status quo, which if scrutinised in the same way would fare much worse' (as reported in Patrick Barkham, 'Wouldn't changing our clocks make our lives better?', *guardian.co.uk*, 20 December 2010).

16 See Daniel Kahneman, Jack I. Knetsch, and Richard H. Thaler, 'The Endowment Effect, Loss Aversion, and Status Quo Bias: Anomalies,' *The Journal of Economic Perspectives* 5 (1991), 193–206; Amos Tversky and Eldar Shafir, 'Choice under Conflict: The Dynamics of Deferred Decision', *Psychological Science* 3 (1992), 358–61; William Samuelson and Richard Zeckhauser, 'Status Quo Bias in Decision Making', *Journal of Risk and Uncertainty* 1 (1998), 7–59.

17 See, for instance, Christopher D. Stone, *Should Trees Have Standing?: Law, Morality and the Environment*, 3rd edn (Oxford: Oxford University Press, 2010).

18 Others have explored what the Greeks did think, or might have thought, about nature and the environment. See John M. Rist, 'Why Greek Philosophers might have been concerned about the environment', and Daryl McGowan Tress, 'The Philosophical Genesis of Ecology and Environmentalism', both in Laura Westra and Thomas M. Robinson, eds, *The Greeks and the Environment* (Lanham, MD, New York, Boulder, and Oxford: Rowman and Littlefield, 1997), 19–32 and 33–42.

19 The phrase 'fiduciary responsibility' comes from the Nobel Prize-winning economist and philosopher Amartya Sen, 'Why Exactly is Commitment Important for Rationality?', in Fabienne Peter and Hans Bernhard Schmid (eds), *Rationality and Commitment* (Oxford: Oxford University Press, 2007), 17–27, at 25: 'We can have many reasons for our conservational efforts – not all of which are parasitic on our own living standards and some of which turn precisely on our sense of values and of fiduciary responsibility.'

20 Strictly speaking, the contents created by an act of imagination should be called an 'imaginary', as is done by Charles Taylor, *Modern Social Imaginaries* (Durham, NC, and London: Duke University Press, 2004), who uses 'social imaginary' to describe 'what enables, through making sense of, the practices of a society'. There is a more extensive discussion of the 'cultural imaginary' across literary, psychoanalytic, and cultural studies, stressing the unconscious roots of such contents. One of the books in this area however uses 'l'imaginaire social' or 'social imaginary' in a similar sense to 'cultural imaginary': see Cornelius Castoriadis, *The Imaginary Institution of Society*, transl. Kathleen Blaney (Cambridge: Polity Press, 1987).

21 Edmund Burke, *Reflections on the Revolution in France* (London: Penguin Books, 2004), 171.

22 For example, the author Gertrude Himmelfarb collected her essays under the title *The Moral Imagination* (New York: Ivan R. Dee, 2006); reflections on peacebuilding were published under the same title by John Paul Lederach two years earlier (Oxford: Oxford University Press, 2004); earlier still, the philosopher Martha C. Nussbaum organized a study of Henry James and

her broader reflections on philosophy and literature in terms of this idea, in essays collected in her *Love's Knowledge: Essays on Philosophy and Literature* (New York and Oxford: Oxford University Press, 1990), especially but not only "'Finely Aware and Richly Responsible": Literature and the Moral Imagination', 148–67; and before that the phrase was closely associated with the 'liberal imagination' celebrated by literary critic Lionel Trilling – to give a far from complete list.

23 Barack Obama, 'Remarks of the President at the Acceptance of the Nobel Peace Prize' (speech, Oslo, Norway, 10 December 2009), available at www. whitehouse.gov/the-press-office/remarks-president-acceptance-nobel-peace-prize; 'Remarks by the President at a Memorial Service for the Victims of the Shooting in Tuscon, Arizona' (speech, Tuscon, Arizona, 12 January 2011), available at www.whitehouse.gov/the-press-office/2011/01/12/remarks-president-barack-obama-memorial-service-victims-shooting-tucson.

24 Sheldon S. Wolin, *Politics and Vision: Continuity and Innovation in Western Political Thought* (Boston and Toronto: Little, Brown and Company, 1960).

25 Danielle S. Allen, *Talking to Strangers: anxieties of citizenship after Brown v. Board of Education* (Chicago and London: University of Chicago Press, 2004), 53. See the further elaboration of these ideas in Allen, *Why Plato Wrote* (Malden, MA and Oxford, UK: Wiley-Blackwell, 2010).

26 The former volume mentioned is Ira Katznelson and Gareth Stedman Jones (eds), *Religion and the Political Imagination* (Cambridge: Cambridge University Press, 2010), a volume arising from a project at the Centre for History and Economics at the University of Cambridge with which I have long been associated. The latter volume mentioned is that of Raymond Geuss, *Politics and the Imagination* (Princeton: Princeton University Press, 2010), which argues for 'the importance of the imagination in all forms of politics' (x) and observes that 'the reality of the modern state arose in part from a construction in imagination' (69), citing there the equally relevant thesis of Benedict Anderson in *Imagined Communities* (London: Verso, 1983). Geuss several times uses the phrase 'political imagination' (15, 33) but primarily to refer to a distinctive individual conception rather than a shared and wide-spread social one.

27 Contrast the higher level of institutional contrast which interests Charles Taylor, between something like feudalism on the one hand, and the modern state and market economy on the other. Taylor, *Imaginaries*, 12, also draws a contrast between a Platonic state, in which the differentiation of social roles itself has normative worth, and the modern state in which it is a contingent and non-normative matter. However, as made clear below, I reject this aspect (the fixed and normative hierarchical nature) of the Platonic state.

28 Dale Jamieson 'Ethics, Public Policy, and Global Warming', 291, where he also perceptively observes that a system of values is 'like an iceberg' in that 'most of what is important may be submerged and invisible even to the person whose values they are'.

29 The cultural theory of risk has been developed particularly by Mary Douglas and Aaron Wildavsky, classically in their book *Risk and Culture: An essay on the selection of technical and environmental dangers* (Berkeley: University of California Press, 1982); the quotations summarizing it here are by Mike Hulme, *Why We Disagree about Climate Change: Understanding Controversy, Inaction and Opportunity* (Cambridge: Cambridge University Press, 2009), 185, 186.

30 Hulme, *Why We Disagree*.

31 Michael Hechter and Karl-Dieter Opp, 'Introduction', in their *Social Norms* (New York: Russell Sage Foundation, 2001), xi–xx, at xiii.

32 Christine Horne, 'Sociological Perspectives on the Emergence of Norms', in Hechter and Opp (eds), *Social Norms*, 3–34; all quotations in this sentence from 4.

33 On footbinding and infibulation, see Gerry Mackie, 'Ending Footbinding and Infibulation: A Convention Account', *American Sociological Review* 61:6 (1996): 999–1017. I am grateful to Gerry Mackie for sharing his expertise and resources about norms with me. For an accessible discussion of changing norms, including these, see Kwame Anthony Appiah, *The Honor Code: How Moral Revolutions Happen* (New York: W. W. Norton & Company, 2010).

34 The term is central to the theory of Eric A. Posner, *Law and Social Norms* (Cambridge, MA: Harvard University Press, 2000), 29–32 and *passim*. Other 'new norms' scholars include Cass Sunstein and Richard McAdams. A useful review and intervention by a founder of the focus on norms in the legal academy is Robert C. Ellickson, 'The Evolution of Social Norms: A Perspective from the Legal Academy', in Hechter and Opp (eds), *Social Norms*, 35–75.

35 World Commission on Environment and Development (WCED), *Our Common Future* (Oxford: Oxford University Press, 1987), 43.

36 As argued in Jared Diamond, *Collapse: How Societies Choose to Fail or Survive* (London: Allen Lane, 2005).

37 This is discussed in Lawrence Hamilton, *The Political Philosophy of Needs* (Cambridge: Cambridge University Press, 2003).

38 See http://www.forumforthefuture.org/what-is-sd, last accessed 29 June 2009.

39 As Dale Jamieson remarks, in 'Ethics, Public Policy, and Global Warming', 285, 'the problem we face is not purely a scientific problem that can be solved by the accumulation of scientific information. Science has alerted us to a problem, but the problem also concerns our values. It is about how we ought

to live, and how humans should relate to each other and to the rest of nature. These are problems of ethics and politics as well as problems of science.'

40 Note Amartya Sen's cautionary words : '... sustaining living standards is not the same thing as sustaining people's freedom to have – or safeguard – what they value and to which they have reason to attach importance' ('Why Exactly', 23).

41 See the important reading of Plato from this point of view, to which the revision of the manuscript for this book is indebted, by Allen, *Why Plato Wrote*.

42 I discuss the methodological role of the *paradeigma* in another work of Plato's in M. S. [Melissa] Lane, *Method and Politics in Plato's* Statesman (Cambridge: Cambridge University Press, 1998). I translated the word there as 'example', but have since been persuaded that 'model' is a better translation: see Mary Louise Gill, 'Models in Plato's *Sophist* and *Statesman*', *Plato: The Internet Journal of the International Plato Society* 6 (2006), online at http://gramata. univ-paris1.fr/Plato/spip.php?article27.

43 J. G. A. Pocock, 'Quentin Skinner: the history of politics and the politics of history (2004)', in *Political Thought and History*, 123–42, at 140; I cite this point in my forthcoming article, 'Constraint, freedom, and exemplar: history and theory without teleology', in Jonathan Floyd and Marc Stears (eds), *Political Philosophy versus History? Contextualism and Real Politics in Contemporary Political Thought* (Cambridge: Cambridge University Press, forthcoming).

44 A rich reading of Aristotle as a theorist of the mutual constituting of self and polity is offered by Jill Frank, *A Democracy of Distinction: Aristotle and the Work of Politics* (Chicago and London: University of Chicago Press, 2005). This reading has stimulated and enlightened my study of Plato in turn.

45 See the useful comparisons between consequentialist, deontological, and virtue ethics in Marcia W. Baron, Philip Pettit, and Michael Slote, *Three Methods of Ethics: A Debate* (Malden, MA: Blackwell, 1997). I don't however defend virtue ethics in the strong form described there, according to which virtue is the means by which value is defined, not merely the means by which it can be attained.

46 The philosophical case against the existence of the virtues in a certain understanding thereof has been made most strongly by Gilbert Harman, for example in 'Moral Philosophy Meets Social Psychology: Virtue Ethics and the Fundamental Attribution Error', *Proceedings of the Aristotelian Society* 99 (1999), 315–31. A thoughtful response, arguing for a different understanding of the virtues and drawing on Plato to do so, is offered by Rachana Kamtekar, 'Situationism and Virtue Ethics on the Content of Our Character', *Ethics* 114 (2004), 458–91.

47 There are many important works on virtue ethics; one foundational work is Philippa Foot, *Virtues and Vices* (Oxford: Blackwell, 1978). For an application of this approach to ecological questions, see Louke van Wensveen, *Dirty Virtues: The Emergence of Ecological Virtue Ethics* (Amherst, NY: Humanity Books, 1999). Not yet published at the time this book was completed was James Connelly, *Sustainability and the Virtues of Environmental Citizenship* (New York and London: Routledge, forthcoming).

48 I discuss the common rejection of treating political theories as blueprints in political theory, and defend their role in electoral politics, in Lane, 'Constraint, freedom, and exemplar'.

49 Consider the Cambridge Platonists in the seventeenth century and the Oxford new liberals in the nineteenth. Suggestive of the more general role of Greek ethical schools in the early modern period in Europe is this remark about their role in the eighteenth century: 'ancient philosophy [specifically, in context, ancient ethics] was the only available alternative to Christianity for thinking about the relationship between morality and politics', made by Michael Sonenscher, *Sans-Culottes: An Eighteenth-Century Emblem in the French Revolution* (Princeton: Princeton University Press, 2008), 63.

50 For discussion of this point in Plato – for example at *Republic* 422e–423a, where Socrates says there that all cities other than the ideal city are in reality two or more cities, inherently divided and so lacking the unity which characterizes a city – see Melissa Lane, 'The rule of knowledge as self-knowledge in Plato's *Protagoras*', in Fiona Leigh (ed.), *Self-Knowledge in Ancient Philosophy: Proceedings of the Eighth Keeling Memorial Colloquium* (Leiden: E. J. Brill, forthcoming).

51 That 'Plato invents the regime of community interiority in which the law is the harmony of the ethos, the accord between the *character* of individuals and the *moral values* of the collective', and so invents the sciences that we call psychology and sociology, is advanced as a fundamental criticism of the role played by his thought in political philosophy by Jacques Rancière, *Disagreement: Politics and Philosophy*, transl. Julie Rose (Minneapolis: University of Minnesota Press, 1999), 68. Rancière takes democracy to be the essence of politics understood in turn as 'the sphere of activity of a common that can only ever be contentious', contrasted with the attempted abolition of conflict and contingency by Platonic 'archipolitics' (14, 65 respectively). By contrast, I take it that while a full archipolitics would indeed be incompatible with democracy, the absence of any common ethos uniting character and collective values is equally inimical to a viable political order, including a democratic one. For an alternative critique of Rancière, stressing that it is the characters of the dialogue who institute these static fantasies, while the dialogue itself works to dramatize this process and disrupt it, see Christina

Tarnopolsky, 'Plato's Politics of Distributing and Disrupting the Sensible', *Theory and Event* 13:4 (2010).

AN UNCONSCIOUSLY PLATONIC PROLOGUE TO CHAPTER 2:
CARBON DETOX

1   George Marshall, *Carbon Detox: Your Step-by-Step Guide to Getting Real about Climate Change* (London: Gaia Books, 2007), 134, 135.
2   Marshall, *Carbon Detox*, 135.
3   Another meditation on climate change and the virtues, centring on the Christian virtue of hope rather than the classical Greek virtues, is Alastair McIntosh, *Hell and High Water: Climate Change, Hope and the Human Condition* (Edinburgh: Birlinn, 2008).

2 FROM GREED TO GLORY:
ANCIENT TO MODERN ETHICS – AND BACK AGAIN?

1   Michiko Kakutani, 'Greed Layered on Greed, Frosted with Recklessness', *New York Times*, 16 June 2009, reviewing Gillian Tett, *Fool's Gold: How the Bold Dream of a Small Tribe at J. P. Morgan Was Corrupted by Wall Street Greed and Unleashed a Catastrophe* (New York: Free Press, 2009), and Daniel Gross, *Dumb Money: How Our Greatest Financial Minds Bankrupted the Nation* (New York: Free Press, 2009).
2   The Greek word *sōphrosunē* is not easily translatable into English: it connotes the virtue of balanced self-control and self-possession, in particular in relation to bodily appetites, and is often translated by 'self-discipline', 'temperance', or 'moderation'. The Penguin translation primarily quoted in this book uses 'self-discipline' and 'discipline', which captures some aspects well yet is less clearly a 'virtue' in English than other possible translations. Hence I shall sometimes refer to moderation or temperance when discussing the concept.
3   Speech by the Chancellor of the Exchequer, the Rt. Hon. Alistair Darling MP, at the Mansion House on 17 June 2009, available at http://www.hm-treasury. gov.uk/press_57_09.htm.
4   Quoted in Binyamin Appelbaum and David M. Herszenhorn, 'Financial Oversight Bill Signals Shift on Deregulation', *New York Times*, 15 July 2010.
5   Ferdinand Mount, *Full Circle: How the Classical World Came Back To Us* (London: Simon and Schuster, 2010), 2 and 3 respectively. Mount traces these

similarities in a wide range of domains, including the body, sex, religion, and the dialogic expectations of citizenship and other forms of social interaction, some of which I will also discuss. He does not however identify the idea of city–soul interrelation as a key similarity, instead focusing directly on Greek virtues and duties of citizenship as something we do not fully share.

6 Bernard Williams, *Shame and Necessity*, with foreword by A. A. Long (Berkeley, CA: University of California Press, 2008), 159 and 7 respectively.

7 Williams, *Shame and Necessity*, 166.

8 On concern for Athenian *pleonexia* as a central feature of the *Republic*, see Jill Frank, 'Wages of War: On Judgment in Plato's *Republic*', *Political Theory* 35 (2007) 443–67.

9 Ryan K. Balot, *Greed and Injustice in Classical Athens* (Princeton: Princeton University Press, 2001) is an excellent discussion of greed and *pleonexia*; he notes (4) that neither Homer, Hesiod, nor Solon used the term *pleonexia*, which is extant only in Attic prose literature.

10 Albert O. Hirschman, *The Passions and the Interests: Political Arguments for Capitalism before its Triumph* (Princeton: Princeton University Press, 1977).

11 See the essays collected in Kathryn A. Morgan (ed.), *Popular Tyranny: Sovereignty and Its Discontents in Ancient Greece* (Austin, TX: University of Texas Press, 2003).

12 See for example Plutarch, *Life of Lycurgus*, section 30.

13 For an introduction to Sparta, see Paul Cartledge, *The Spartans: An Epic History* (London: Pan Books, 2003).

14 Nadia Urbinati, 'Thucydides the Thermidorian: democracy on trial in the making of modern liberalism', in Katharine Harloe and Neville Morley (eds), *Thucydides: Reception, Reinterpretation, Influence* (Cambridge: Cambridge University Press, forthcoming).

15 Benjamin Constant, 'The Liberty of the Ancients Compared with that of the Moderns', speech given at the Athénée Royal in Paris in 1819 and published in a collection of his writings in 1820. A good translation is available in Constant, *Political Writings*, transl. and ed. Biancamaria Fontana (Cambridge: Cambridge University Press, 1988), 309–28.

16 The habitual scholarly neglect of the fact that Constant's analysis was explicitly said to apply least of all to Athens is emphasized in Mogens Herman Hansen, 'The Ancient Athenian and the Modern Liberal View of Liberty as a Democratic Ideal', in *Demokratia: A Conversation on Democracies, Ancient and Modern*, eds Josiah Ober and Charles W. Hedrick (Princeton: Princeton University Press, 1996), 91–104, at 96.

17 Jean-Jacques Rousseau, *Emile or On Education*, transl. and ed. Allan Bloom (New York: Basic Books, 1979), 40.

18 Hansen, 'The Ancient Athenian and the Modern Liberal View', 99.

19 The exchange over the theatre in Geneva was with Jean le Rond d'Alembert, who had written an article on Geneva in Diderot's *Encyclopédie* in 1758 advocating establishment of a theatre there. Details may be found in Jean-Jacques Rousseau, *Letter to D'Alembert and writings for the theater*, ed. and transl. Allan Bloom, Charles Butterworth, and Christopher Kelly (Hanover, NH and London: University Press of New England, 2004).

20 Bernard Mandeville, 'The Fable of the Bees: Or, Private Vices, Publick Benefits', was first published in 1714 (based on an earlier poem by Mandeville, 'The Grumbling Hive', of 1705), and is now most easily available in *The Fable of the Bees*, ed. F. B. Kaye, 2 vols (Indianapolis: Liberty Fund, 1988). Adam Smith, *An Inquiry into the Nature and Causes of the Wealth of Nations,* was first published in 1776 and is now available ed. R. H. Campbell and A. S. Skinner, 2 vols (Indianapolis: Liberty Fund, 1981); it should be read in conjunction with Smith's earlier *The Theory of Moral Sentiments* (orig. 1759), ed. D. D. Raphael and A. L. Macfie, 2 vols (Indianapolis: Liberty Fund, 1982), both of which are online at The Online Library of Liberty at http://oll.libertyfund.org. Jeremy Bentham's voluminous work may be approached via his *An Introduction to the Principles of Morals and Legislation* of 1823, published by the Clarendon Press of Oxford in 1907 in a version which is now available online at The Online Library of Liberty http://oll.libertyfund.org.

21 On this shared vision, see Emma Rothschild, *Economic Sentiments: Adam Smith, Condorcet, and the Enlightenment* (Cambridge, MA, and London: Harvard University Press, 2001).

22 See also Christina Tarnopolsky's remark on the '*ethos* of greed (*pleonexia*) behind the kind of lending and borrowing that had been going on for many years prior to the global credit crisis', in her '*Mimêsis,* Persuasion, and Manipulation in Plato's *Republic*', in *Manipulating Democracy*, eds John Parrish and Wayne S. LeCheminant (Routledge: 2010), 155, n. 52.

23 Deirdre N. McCloskey, *The Bourgeois Virtues: Ethics for an Age of Commerce* (Chicago: University of Chicago Press, 2006), 24.

24 See for example Furedi's appearance in 'Against Nature', Martin Durkin's 1997 series for Channel 4 on British television.

25 This passage was recalled to me by Antony Hatzistavrou.

26 The idea of co-production of social services has become popular in British policy circles: see the discussion in David Halpern, *The Hidden Wealth of Nations* (Cambridge: Polity Press, 2010). I am interested in taking this idea both to a more abstract level of co-production of social ideas and practices, as well as to the more material level exemplified by feed-in tariffs that allow citizen co-generation of electrical power.

27 A good survey of geoengineering is Eli Kintisch, *Hack the Planet* (Hoboken, NJ: John Wiley and Sons, 2010).

28 Jonathon Porritt, *Capitalism as if the World Matters* (London: Earthscan, 2005).

3 UNDERPINNING INERTIA: THE IDEA OF NEGLIGIBILITY

1 Richard Tuck, *Free Riding* (Cambridge, MA and London: Harvard University Press, 2008) reviews this development in economics and its broader influence in social science.

2 In fact, Huxley held that this was true of only certain fisheries, contrasting the sea fisheries with others such as river ones. The full context of the quotation, from the Inaugural Address he delivered to the Fisheries Exhibition, London, 1883, is: 'I believe, then, that the cod fishery, the herring fishery, the pilchard fishery, the mackerel fishery, and probably all the great sea fisheries, are inexhaustible; that is to say, that nothing we do seriously affects the number of the fish. And any attempt to regulate these fisheries seems consequently, from the nature of the case, to be useless. [new paragraph] There are other sea fisheries, however, of which this cannot be said.' Quoted from http://alepho.clarku.edu/huxley/SM5/fish.html, and originally called to my attention by Paul Warde in a paper given at a seminar of the Centre for History and Economics, King's College, Cambridge.

3 Constant, 'The Liberty of the Ancients', 314.

4 Constant, 'The Liberty of the Ancients', 316.

5 Joseph Alois Schumpeter, *Capitalism, Socialism, and Democracy*, 6th edn (London: Unwin Paperbacks, 1987).

6 Intergovernmental Panel on Climate Change, *Aviation and the Global Atmosphere* (Cambridge: Cambridge University Press, 1999).

7 As quoted in 'Airlines stage fightback on environmental criticism', *guardian. co.uk*, 3 June 2008.

8 As quoted in editorial, 'End of the Runway', *Guardian*, 10 June 2008. The government was eventually persuaded to commit to the inclusion of shipping and aviation in the UK Climate Change Bill.

9 This estimate comes from data provided by the US Energy Information Administration for 2009, available at http://www.eia.gov/cfapps/ipdbproject/ IEDIndcx3.cfm?tid=90&pid=44&aid=8.

10 US emissions from the consumption of energy in million metric tons were 5424.530 in 2009; the UK's emissions were 519.944, India's 1602.122 and China's 7710.504 million metric tons. However, US and UK emissions per

capita were higher than those of China and India. Available at tonto.eia.doe. gov/cfapps/ipdbproject/IEDIndex3.cfm?tid=90&pid=44&aid=8.

11 The case of imperceptibility is one of those rebutted in the influential discussion of Derek Parfit, *Reasons and Persons* (Oxford: Clarendon Press, 1984), 67–86; Parfit also argues that even a small chance of being pivotal in the outcome should be assessed in terms of the overall benefit that would be thereby achieved and so supports the rationality of pursuing such a chance. I would like to thank Alex Guerrero for discussing Parfit with me and also for his role in helping me articulate the argument of this section.

12 For the case of global poverty and the moral duty to contribute to ending it which is not defeated by the the 'chronic horror' which may continue irrespective of my contribution, see Peter Unger, *Living High and Letting Die: Our Illusion of Innocence* (New York and Oxford: Oxford University Press, 1996).

13 A brief account of the innovative mayoralty of Antanas Mockus can be found in Maria Cristina Caballero, 'Academic turns city into a social experiment', *Harvard Magazine*, 11 March 2004, online at: http://www.news.Harvard.edu/gazette/2004/03.11/01-mockus.html.

14 See Atul Gawande, 'The Hot Spotters', *New Yorker*, 24 January 2011, 40–51.

15 Translated by C. J. Rowe, in Plato, *Complete Works*, ed. Cooper with Hutchinson.

16 Alexander A. Guerrero, 'The Paradox of Voting and the Ethics of Political Representation', *Philosophy and Public Affairs* 38:3 (2010): 272–306, at 296.

17 Here I contest the argument of Walter Sinnott-Armstrong, 'It's not *my* fault: global warming and individual moral obligations', in *Perspectives on Climate Change: Science, Economics, Politics, Ethics*, eds Walter Sinnott-Armstrong and Richard B. Howarth, Advances in the Economics of Environmental Resources vol. 5 (Amsterdam: Elsevier, 2005), 285–307, who argues that the individual has no reason to reduce her emissions voluntarily where her contribution to solving the problem of climate change by so doing is negligible.

18 Compare the discussion in Paul Lucardie, 'Why Would Egocentrists Become Ecocentrists? On individualism and holism in green political theory', in Andrew Dobson and Paul Lucardie (eds), *The Politics of Nature: explorations in green political theory* (London and New York: Routledge, 1993), 21–35, at 30–1, who surveys the spectrum from holism to individualism within the green movement, distinguishing ontological, psychological and strictly ecological forms of holism. He remarks on the way that adopting a holist or deep ecological perspective would change one's identity and so one's reasons, seeing this as probably limited to an elite, with other forms of motivation needed for the masses: 'why would rational individuals (without

children) sacrifice the use of a car, a daily bath, meat, ski-ing in the Alps, colour television, aerosol and so many other polluting luxuries which they [31] enjoy? In most cases it is not in their own immediate interest to renounce these pleasures – except in return for praise of significant others, or to avoid unpleasant sanctions such as fines or additional (ecological) taxes. Hence their individual freedom would have to be restricted – whether by social control, ethical norms or environmental policies. Deep ecologists, however, need not restrict their individual freedom, as their individual identity has been broadened to incorporate the whole earth … deep ecology might be restricted to certain groups in society, more sensitive or saintly than others perhaps, who share the mystical experience of identification with Nature. Other people still need environmental ethics, if not ecological taxes and fines, to change their anthropocentric wasteful behaviour.'

19   Stephen S. Pacala and Robert Socolow, 'Stabilization Wedges', *Science* 305 (2004), 968–72, identify fifteen already feasible measures or 'wedges' to stabilize emissions, each of which would save one billion tons of carbon emissions per year, and seven of which would be enough to stabilize global emissions at a certain level. Since the division into wedges is arbitrary, we can easily imagine requiring fourteen wedges rather than seven (say if we put almost all of Pacala and Socolow's existing options into effect, but more slowly or less fully than they envisaged), in which case each wedge would solve just over 7 percent of the total problem. That is not far off from the levels of 2 or 4 or 6 percent which we have seen industry and government pooh-pooh as minor and relatively insignificant contributions from UK aviation or from Liverpool.

20   Whether carbon emissions contribute to a problem defined by a sufficiency threshold is a matter for science; although rising emissions contribute to rising temperature in some sort of positive relationship, this relationship is unlikely to be simply linear, and there may well be sufficiency thresholds for certain feedback effects to kick in, though we do not know with certainty where they are. However, political efforts to mitigate climate change impose their own sufficiency thresholds, which are more or less closely related to science (the notion of stabilizing at 450ppm so as to hold global temperature rise down to 2°C is already probably out of reach).

21   Focus group recounted in Stewart Barr, *Environment and Society: Sustainability, Policy and the Citizen* (Aldershot, Hampshire, UK and Burlington, VT: Ashgate Publishing, 2008), 244.

22   As recounted in Barr, *Environment and Society*, 121.

23   I draw here on Guerrero, 'The Paradox of Voting', who argues that it is rational to seek to increase the 'normative mandate' enjoyed by one's candidate (linking this to an account of the ethical entitlement of political representatives

to act more like trustees, and less like delegates, the higher their manifest normative mandate). A similar idea is advanced in Gerald Mackie, 'Why It's Rational to Vote', forthcoming in a festschrift for Jon Elster, which argues that the idea of advancing one's cause by increasing the 'mandate value' of one's preferred candidate is the key to why people vote, as they do, even when they know their candidate will lose. In the case of climate change, I interpret an equivalent to the idea of 'manifest mandate value' as the visibility of the cause, contributing to unexpected possible tipping points in terms of the social perception of its normality and so also to possible unpredictable political change as politicians gain confidence in advancing the cause. This view makes voters rational even in standard instrumental terms, concerned with their interests, in contrast to the attempt to rescue voting as an 'expressive' act disconnected from actual interests, applied to climate change for example by Geoffrey Brennan, 'Climate Change: A Rational Choice Politics View', *Australian Journal of Agricultural and Resource Economics* 53:3 (2009) 309–26. Brennan takes voters' interests to be against climate change regulation, even though their values may endorse it, whereas I argue that one's values and imagination can reshape one's interests.

24   The classic argument is by Anthony Downs, *An Economic Theory of Democracy* (New York: Harper and Row, 1957), 274. A variant suggests that while people have no rational reason to vote because they have a negligible chance of being decisive in the election, they may instead rationally indulge their irrational pet theories and preferences when doing so: see Bryan Caplan, *The Myth of the Rational Voter* (Princeton: Princeton University Press, 2007).

25   See Casey B. Mulligan and Charles G. Hunter, 'The Empirical Frequency of a Pivotal Vote', *Public Choice* 116:1 (2003) 31–54, to which I was directed by a paper by my Princeton undergraduate student Benjamin Cogan.

26   Here I am considering the argument of Tuck, *Free Riding*, whose own solution depends on the idea of a sufficiency threshold to which it is rational for individuals to seek to contribute. However, as argued in the main text, this entails radically different reasons for voting where one has no reason to expect that one's candidate can win, which seems implausible. Tuck's formulation depends on the existence of a sufficiency threshold: one which is sharp in the case of voting, vague in the case of the classical problem of whether it makes any difference to add a grain of sand to a pile in determining whether or not it is a heap.

27   I thank Jonathan Wolff for this objection, though again, he is not responsible for the way that I have answered it. Compare Frey, *Not Just for the Money*, on elections and popular referendums being cases where 'the cost of pursuing environmental morale [ie acting on one's intrinsic motivation] is low': 'Each voter only has a minuscule impact on the total vote outcome and therefore

casting a vote in favour of environmental projects is nearly costless' (both quotations, 59). Frey here, in line with Caplan and Brennan cited in notes above, and other scholars in a similar vein, suggests the inverse of Tuck, that, to the extent that voters consider their likely impact on the election negligible, this will encourage them to vote for intrinsic or value-based reasons independent of their rational interests.

28 See for example Ernst Fehr and Simon Gächter, 'Fairness and Retaliation: The Economics of Reciprocity', *Journal of Economic Perspectives* 14:3 (2000) 159–81.

29 There is a significant debate about this in the philosophical literature. Some, such as Liam Murphy, have argued that if others fail to play their part, I am not morally liable to do more than I would have owed had they done so. But others, such as Tim Mulgan, argue that this is not true when the obligation owed is to third parties: if others fail to contribute to alleviating global poverty, my moral obligation as a willing donor does change. See Tim Mulgan, *The Rejection of Consequentialism* (Oxford: Clarendon Press, 2001), esp. 117–20.

30 Cohen, *Rescuing Justice and Equality*, 10, 61; Cohen identifies his version of the idea of a personal prerogative with what Samuel Scheffler calls an 'agent-centred prerogative' in *The Rejection of Consequentialism: A Philosophical Investigation of the Considerations Underlying Rival Moral Conceptions*, rev. edn (Oxford: Clarendon Press, 1994).

31 John Stuart Mill, 'On Liberty', in Mill, *On Liberty and Other Essays*, ed. John Gray (Oxford: Oxford University Press, 1998), 14.

32 See 'The Liberty of the Ancients Compared with that of the Moderns', in Benjamin Constant, *Political Writings*, 307–28.

33 Constant, 'The Liberty of the Ancients', 317.

34 See Catriona MacKinnon, 'Climate Change and Corrective Justice', in *Jahrbuch für Recht und Ethik/Annual Review of Law and Ethics* 17 (2009), 259–77, in a special part-issue of the journal on the topic of compensation edited by the present author.

35 The first stage of the EPA's carbon regulations went into effect on 2 January 2011. The regulations affect large greenhouse-gas-emitting industries planning to build new facilities or make major renovations to existing ones. In December 2010, the EPA issued its plan for the next stages of regulation, with proposals for power plants and refineries expected in July and December 2011, respectively, and finalized standards expected in May and December 2012, respectively. Environmental Protection Agency, 'EPA to Set Modest Pace for Greenhouse Gas Emissions,' news release, 23 December 2010; 'EPA Completes Framework for Greenhouse Gas Permitting Programs,' news release, 23 December 2010.

36 Dan M. Kahan, 'Gentle Nudges vs. Hard Shoves: Solving the Sticky Norms Problem', *University of Chicago Law Review* 67:3 (2000): 607–45.

37 This distinction and its application to changes in environmentally related behaviour is articulated in a brief article by Robert B. Cialdini, 'Crafting Normative Messages to Protect the Environment', *Current Directions in Psychological Science* 4 (2003), 105–9; for one experiment reported there, see R. B. Cialdini, R. R. Reno and C. A. Kallgren, 'A focus theory of normative conduct: Recycling the concept of norms to reduce littering in public places', *Journal of Personality and Social Psychology* 58 (1990), 1015–26.

38 In September 2009, a 2nd US Circuit Court of Appeals panel ruled in favour of a coalition in their lawsuit against coal-burning utility companies (*Connecticut v. AEP*), the first climate change tort case to be brought and won, creating a new judicial remedy against the creation of a 'public nuisance' in the form of climate change. (A panel of the 5th Circuit followed suit the following month in deciding *Comer v. Murphy Oil Co.*, which was later vacated for technical reasons, though a district court meanwhile rejected similar reasoning in another case, *Kivalina v. Exxon Mobil Corp.*, which is now in appeal.) At the time of writing, however, the Supreme Court was considering the appeal of AEP, an appeal which was actually supported by the acting Solicitor General of the Obama administration on the ground that the original case rested on the fact that the EPA was not regulating greenhouse gas emissions, which it has since begun to do. For these cases, see the Greenwire reports available through the *New York Times* website. For the British context and the development of scientific arguments to support such cases, see David Adam and Afua Hirsch, 'Oil giants could soon face lawsuits over climate, says Oxford University scientist', *Guardian*, 9 December 2008, now online as 'Science paves way for climate lawsuits', http://www.guardian.co.uk/environment/2008/dec/09/oil-business-climate-change-flooding?INTCMP=SRCH.

39 Here I focus on defining costs and benefits. There is also much work to be done on how to calculate and weigh them in a more complex and enlightened way, of the kind sketched in Richard L. Revesz and Michael A. Livermore, *Retaking Rationality: How Cost-Benefit Analysis Can Better Protect the Environment and Our Health* (Oxford: Oxford University Press, 2008).

40 Solitaire Townsend, founder of the Futerra consultancy, on a BBC radio interview in 2007, as quoted in Tom Crompton, *Weathercocks and Signposts: the environment movement at a crossroads*, WWF-UK's Strategies for Change Project, April 2008, 15. Available at wwf.org.uk/strategiesforchange.

41 Tom R. Tyler, *Why People Obey the Law*, 2nd edn (Princeton: Princeton University Press, 2006).

42 Frank H. Easterbrook and Daniel R. Fischel, 'Antitrust Suits by Targets of Tender Offers', *Michigan Law Review* 80 (1982), 1155–78, at 1177 n. 57.

43 For an expanded version of this argument on which the present paragraphs draw, see Melissa Lane, 'The Moral Dimension of Corporate Accountability', in Andrew Kuper (ed.), *Global Responsibilities: Who Must Deliver on Human Rights?* (New York: Routledge, 2005), 229–50, at 240–3.

44 Compare Cohen, *Rescuing Justice and Equality*, 140: 'personal choices to which the writ of the law is indifferent are fateful for social justice.' Cohen's argument is, again, that an ethos shaping individual choice according to the principles of justice must be part of the conceptual structure of justice itself. My primary claim is parallel only to an extent: it is causal rather than conceptual, arguing that an ethos shaping individual choice according to the principles of sustainability is necessary in order for sustainability to be realized. However, I will also argue in Part II that such an ethos, and the political imagination which nourishes it, is necessary for the psychosocial sustaining, as it were, of ecological sustainability. Combined, the claim is that the ethos as reshaped by the imagination is necessary both for achieving and for sustaining a more ecologically sustainable society.

45 John Stuart Mill, *On Liberty*, cited from *On Liberty and Other Essays*, ed. John Gray (Oxford: Oxford University Press, 1991), 1–128, at 120 for both quotations; I am grateful to Tim Mulgan for reminding me of this discussion.

46 Amartya Sen, 'Freedom and Coercion', *University of Chicago Law Review* 63 (1996), 1035–61.

47 On the importance of identifying the relatively rich high-emitters across all nations, rather than simply classifying nations themselves as high or low emitters, see S. Chakravarty et al., 'Sharing Global CO2 Emission Reductions Among One Billion High Emitters', *Proceedings of National Academy of Science* 106: 29, 11884–8, a paper brought to my attention by one of its co-authors, Rob Socolow.

48 Mill himself stressed that public pressure by the state as well as by other social actors was legitimate even where the state use of coercion was rejected, as is brought out by Corey Brettschneider, 'When the State Speaks, What Should It Say? The Dilemmas of Freedom of Expression and Democratic Persuasion', *Perspectives on Politics* 8 (2010), 1005–19, at 1012.

49 Compare again Jamieson, 'Ethics, Public Policy, and Global Warming' (294), who argues that 'we should focus more on character and less on calculating probable outcomes' precisely because doing the latter means that 'We can each reason: since my contribution is small, outcomes are likely to be detetermined by the behavior of others ... When we "economize" our behaviour in the way that is required for calculating, we systematically neglect the subtle and indirect effects of our actions, and for this reason we see individual

action as inefficacious. For social change to occur it is important that there be people of integrity and character who act on the basis of principles and ideals.'

PROLOGUE TO CHAPTER 4:
POST-PLATONIC PERSPECTIVES ON THE REPUBLIC

1   This was a phrase used by George Kateb in commenting on a presentation of an earlier draft of some of this material in Princeton in November 2010. I think he mischaracterized the details of the *Republic*'s ideal city in referring to 'universal poverty'; it is the guardian-rulers who are to live deprived of private property, while the artisans and farmers they rule will be able to accumulate wealth and property within limits. But the phrase captures the spirit of one widespread view of the *Republic*.

2   Melissa Lane, *Plato's Progeny: How Plato and Socrates still captivate the modern mind* (London: Duckworth, 2001), quoting from and paraphrasing 97–8.

3   On the uses of Plato within the Stefan George circle, see Melissa S. Lane, 'The Platonic politics of the George-Kreis: a reconsideration', in Melissa S. Lane and Martin A. Ruehl (eds), *A Poet's Reich: Politics and Culture in the George Circle* (Rochester, NY: Camden House, forthcoming); for a broader overview of the political uses of Plato in the nineteenth and twentieth centuries, see Lane, *Plato's Progeny*, 97–134.

4   MEET PLATO'S REPUBLIC

1   This is not to say that there is nothing in Plato which could be relevant to a reconsideration of our relationship with nature. Gabriela Roxana Carone, *Plato's Cosmology and Its Ethical Dimensions* (Cambridge: Cambridge University Press, 2005), argues that in other dialogues – in particular the *Timaeus* – the presentation of the cosmos itself as an accessible, perceptible model of the Forms available to everyone can inspire us with a new appreciation of nature (194–5). Similar points are made about the *Timaeus* by Madonna R. Adams, 'Environmental Ethics in Plato's *Timaeus*'; about the *Critias*, by Owen Goldin, 'The Ecology of the *Critias* and Platonic Metaphysics'; and about Plato generally by Timothy A. Mahoney, 'Platonic Ecology, Deep Ecology', all in Laura Westra and Thomas M. Robinson (eds), *The Greeks and the Environment* (Lanham, MD, New York, Boulder, and

Oxford: Rowman and Littlefield, 1997), 55–72, 73–80, and 45–54 respectively. However, this is not the focus of the present book.

2   This was already true of Part III of John Rawls, *A Theory of Justice* (Cambridge, MA: Harvard University Press, 1971). Rawls changed his view of what stability required and how it could legitimately be achieved in *Political Liberalism* (New York: Columbia University Press, 1993).

3   In giving these dates, I follow the account of Plato's life given in Debra Nails, *The People of Plato: a prosopography of Plato and other Socratics* (Indianapolis: Hackett, 2002).

4   A subtly different account of the authority of philosophy in the *Republic*, stressing its affinity with (rather than repudiation of) a new conception of the authority of poetry, was offered by Jill Frank, 'Vying for Authority in Plato's *Republic*', a paper presented at the 2008 Annual Meeting of the American Political Science Association. I have learned a great deal from her despite our disagreements.

5   I have added the words 'in speech' to translate a Greek formulation (*logô*, with an iota subscript) which is for some reason omitted from Lee's translation of 369a.

6   Allen, *Why Plato Wrote*, offers an extensive discussion of the Line analogy. For a helpful account of the relation between Sun and Line, see Nicholas Denyer, 'Sun and Line: The Role of the Good', in G. R. F. Ferrari (ed.), *The Cambridge Companion to Plato's* Republic (Cambridge: Cambridge University Press, 2007), 284–309.

7   Friedrich Nietzsche, 'What I Owe to the Ancients', in Nietzsche, *Twilight of the Idols/The Antichrist*, transl. R. J. Hollingdale (Harmondsworth: Penguin, 1999), 117.

8   Christina Tarnopolsky, '*Mimêsis*, Persuasion and Manipulation in Plato's *Republic*', 135–56, at 141, quoting an excerpt from Danielle S. Allen, 'Envisaging the Body of the Condemned: The Power of Platonic Symbols', *Classical Philology* 95:2 (2000): 133–50, at 263.

9   Allen, *Why Plato Wrote*, 4.

10 Allen, *Why Plato Wrote*, 6 and *passim*. See also Murray Wright Bundy, *The Theory of Imagination in Classical and Mediaeval Thought*, University of Illinois Studies in Language and Literature, vol. 2 (Urbana, Ill.: University of Illinois Press, 1927), 19–59.

11 Karl Popper, *The Open Society and Its Enemies*, vol. I: *The Spell of Plato* (London: Routledge, 2003 [1945]).

12 See Lane, 'Introduction' to Plato, *The Republic*.

13 I have also discussed this issue in Melissa Lane, 'Plato, Popper, Strauss, and Utopianism: Open Secrets?', *History of Philosophy Quarterly* 16:2 (1999) 119–42.

14 Allen, *Why Plato Wrote*, 20–2, 63–8, 108.
15 Plato, *Republic*, ed. G. R. F. Ferrari, transl. Tom Griffith (Cambridge: Cambridge University Press, 2000), 107 n. 62, to 414c.
16 See the interpretation of the 'noble lie' in Malcolm Schofield, *Plato: Political Philosophy* (Oxford: Oxford University Press, 2006).
17 Allen, *Why Plato Wrote*, 22.
18 I discuss the founding of the *Republic's* ideal city as legislating in Melissa Lane, 'Founding as legislating: the figure of the lawgiver in Plato's *Republic*', in *Plato's* Politeia. *Proceedings of the IX Symposium Platonicum*, eds L. Brisson and N. Notomi (Berlin: Akademie Verlag, forthcoming).
19 Compare Christina Tarnopolsky's remark that 'taken within its immediate context of the discussions of myths and fictions in *Republic* 2 and 3, it [the noble lie] encapsulates Plato's teaching that the best citizens or guardians of a regime are those who continually question its authoritative myths and fictions', in her '*Mimêsis*', 150; she also offers a relevant discussion in Christina H. Tarnopolsky, 'Plato's Mimetic *Republic*: A Preliminary Treatment of Plato's Preliminary Treatment of the *Gennaion Pseudos*', a paper presented at the 2009 Annual Meeting of the American Political Science Association, available through the SSRN (Social Science Research Network) (http://ssrn.com/abstract=1448923).
20 Popper, *The Open Society and Its Enemies*, vol. I: *The Spell of Plato*.
21 One such exception is Stephen Macedo, *Liberal Virtues: Citizenship, Virtue, and Community in Liberal Constitutionalism* (Oxford: Clarendon Press, 1990).

PROLOGUE TO CHAPTER 5: PLATO ON WHY VIRTUE MATTERS

1 M. F. Burnyeat, 'Culture and Society in Plato's *Republic*', in *The Tanner Lectures on Human Values*, vol. 20, ed. Grethe B. Peterson (Salt Lake City: University of Utah Press, 1999), 217–324; the subsequent discussion in the main text is indebted to this work.

5 THE CITY AND THE SOUL

1 But not of course unique. See the suggestive contrast of 'growth' with 'health' scenarios in Angela Wilkinson, *Beyond the Financial Crisis: The Oxford Scenarios*, undated report of the Institute for Science, Innovation and Society, Oxford University, available under a Creative Commons licence at: http://

www.sbs.ox.ac.uk/centres/insis/projects/Pages/financial-scenarios.aspx. See also Tim Jackson, *Prosperity without Growth? The transition to a sustainable economy*, published by the Sustainable Development Commission of the United Kingdom (2009).

2   A good overview may be found in Julia Annas, *The Morality of Happiness* (New York: Oxford University Press, 1993).

3   An influential account from economics has been Richard Layard, *Happiness: Lessons from a New Science* (Harmondsworth: Penguin, 2005); from psychology, Martin E. P. Seligman, *Authenic Happiness: Using the New Positive Psychology to Realize Your Potential For Lasting Fulfillment* (New York: Free Press, 2004). An overview is in Felicia A. Huppert, Nick Baylis, and Barry Keverne (eds), *The Science of Well-Being* (Oxford and New York: Oxford University Press, 2005). For applications to sustainability, see the Happy Planet Index (http://www.happyplanetindex.org/) and the decision of the King of Bhutan to make 'gross national happiness' (rather than the more usual 'gross national product') his nation's principal national measurement and goal (http://www.grossnationalhappiness.com/).

4   See Jon Elster and John E. Roemer (eds), *Interpersonal Comparisons of Well-Being* (Cambridge and New York: Cambridge University Press, 1991).

5   For one account of the philosophical underpinnings of this transformation, see Richard Tuck, *Free Riding*.

6   This is not to say that it is uncontroversial. One important virtue ethics theorist, for example, rejects the Platonic assertion of the unity of the virtues: see Robert Merrihew Adams, *A Theory of Virtue: Excellence in Being for the Good*, 2nd edn (New York: Oxford University Press, 2009). While it's plausible that not all virtues can or need be possessed in order to possess any, I take the Platonic thesis to focus on the four cardinal virtues and in particular on the integration of three of them with wisdom. In this light, it is more persuasive to think that without wisdom one doesn't fully possess courage or justice or self-discipline.

7   The idea that too much pleasure ceases to be pleasure at all is well established in modern psychology. As Jon Elster wrote in *Ulysses Unbound: Studies in Rationality, Precommitment, and Constraints* (Cambridge: Cambridge University Press, 2000), 263: 'Up to a point, more is more; beyond that point, more is less.' This is quoted here from a discussion of the general point in Avner Offer, *The Challenge of Affluence: Self-Control and Well-Being in the United States and Britain since 1950* (Oxford: Oxford University Press, 2006), 56. See also the extensive discussion in Tibor Scitovsky, *The Joyless Economy: An Inquiry into Human Satisfaction and Consumer Dissatisfaction* (New York: Oxford University Press, 1976), for example at 25: 'the most pleasant level of total stimulation is intermediate between too much and too little.'

8   Helen Rappaport, *Joseph Stalin: A Biographical Companion* (New York: ABC-CLIO, 1999), 361.

9   This is also broadly the argument developed by Offer, *The Challenge of Affluence*, who puts it in terms of affluence itself undermining the habits and techniques of self-control necessary for happiness. Scitovsky, *Joyless Economy*, puts it rather in terms of certain kinds of sub-optimal pleasures – which he calls 'comforts' – undermining the willingness to risk and change necessary to enjoy real pleasure, joy, and happiness.

10 On how to treat the central books in relation to the *Republic*'s overall argument, see David Sedley, 'Socratic intellectualism in the central books of the *Republic*', in a forthcoming volume of essays in honour of Christopher Rowe, ed. Christopher Gill, Dimitri El Murr, and George Boys-Stones.

11 Among important work in virtue ethics, in addition to that cited earlier, see the early revival by Peter Geach, *The Virtues* (Cambridge: Cambridge University Press, 1977), and the extensive work by Rosalind Hursthouse, including *On Virtue Ethics* (Oxford: Oxford University Press, 1999). The focus of virtue ethics appealing to the Greeks has been overwhelmingly on Aristotle, as for example in Timothy D. J. Chappell (ed.), *Values and Virtues: Aristotelianism in Contemporary Ethics* (Oxford: Clarendon Press, 2006), rather than on the less systematic but stimulating resources to be found in Plato.

12 On ancient and modern democracy, see among other works, John Dunn, *Setting the People Free: the Story of Democracy* (London: Atlantic Books, 2005).

13 For an insightful if ultimately negative assessment of the sociology in Plato's *Republic*, see W. G. Runciman, *Great Books, Bad Arguments: Republic, Leviathan and the Communist Manifesto* (Princeton: Princeton University Press, 2010). This short and stimulating study is flawed in its judgement of the *Republic*, in my view, by its insistence that the rule of the philosophers is 'self-serving' as well as 'self-chosen' (30), ignoring the text's emphasis on the way in which their rule is designed to benefit not themselves but those they rule; and by its reading of Platonic justice as altruism, when in fact it is shown to serve the interests of the just person.

14 Allen, *Why Plato Wrote*, 65: 'shift the landscape of someone's imagination'. See the detailed discussion of Leontius in her first book, *The World of Prometheus*.

15 I have been aided in thinking about these passages by Mark A. Johnstone, 'Tripartition and the Rule of the Soul in Plato's *Republic*', dissertation presented to Princeton University for the degree of PhD, 2009, which he generously shared with me.

16 For a recent popular discussion of self-control as a virtue, see Daniel Akst, *We Have Met the Enemy: Self-Control in an Age of Excess* (New York: Penguin, 2011).

17 Melissa Lane, 'Virtue as the Love of Knowledge in Plato's *Symposium* and *Republic*', in Dominic Scott (ed.) *Maieusis: Essays in Ancient Philosophy in Honour of Myles Burnyeat* (Oxford: Oxford University Press, 2007), 44–67.

18 *Sōphrosunē* ('moderation' or 'self-discipline') is taken by Jacques Rancière to be what replaces freedom in the scheme of the *Republic* (*Disagreement*, 67). See however the more positive view of moderation in the care of the self in Michel Foucault, *History of Sexuality*, vol. 1.

19 Aristotle, *Nicomachean Ethics* VII.2, 1145b21–27, quoting from the translation in Jonathan Barnes, *The Complete Works of Aristotle: the revised Oxford translation*, 2 vols. (Princeton: Princeton University Press, 1984), vol. 2.

20 *Protagoras* transl. Stanley Lombardo and Karen Bell, in Plato, *Complete Works*, ed. Cooper with Hutchinson. The standard position on *akrasia* is summarized well by Christopher Bobonich: 'In the early dialogues, Plato denies the possibility of *akrasia*; in the *Republic*, he accepts its possibility and the *Republic*'s partitioning of the soul is intended to explain how *akrasia* is possible' ('Plato on *Akrasia* and Knowing Your Own Mind', in Christopher Bobonich and Pierre Destrée (eds), *Akrasia in Greek Philosophy: From Socrates to Plotinus* (Leiden and Boston: Brill, 2007), 41–60, at 54. Bobonich himself does not share this view in its most common form, as he argues that tripartition is not introduced primarily to explain *akrasia* (though it serves this function) but for other independent reasons.

21 See for example Aristotle, *Nicomachean Ethics* VII.3, 1147b14–16, and the discussion by Pierre Destrée, 'Aristotle on the Causes of *Akrasia*', in Bobonich and Destrée (eds), *Akrasia in Greek Philosophy*, 139–65.

22 *Republic* 9, 588e5–589a4. I make this case in 'The rule of knowledge as self-knowledge in Plato's *Protagoras*', in Fiona Leigh (ed.), *Self-Knowledge in Ancient Philosophy*.

23 An insightful account of the relation between soul and city in the imperfect cities of Books 8 and 9 is given by Jonathan Lear, 'Inside and Outside the *Republic*', *Phronesis* 37:2 (1992), 184–215, reprinted in Lear, *Open Minded: working out the logic of the soul* (Cambridge, MA: Harvard University Press, 1998), 219–47. A technical critique of part of Lear's argument is offered by G. R. F. Ferrari, *City and Soul in Plato's* Republic (Sankt Augustin: Academia Verlag, 2003; Chicago: University of Chicago Press, 2005), who notes that Lear does not distinguish clearly enough between the accounts given of the timocratic, oligarchic, and democratic individual on the one hand, and city on the other. However, since individuals are also treated *within* the account of each city, Lear's logic of 'internalization' of civic values by individuals

remains illuminating, though as Ferrari also suggests, the evidence for the countervailing logic of 'externalization' is weaker.

24 For example, Kevin Rudd, prime minister of Australia at the time, said that the financial crisis occurred 'because a few thousand financial executives around the world surrendered any pretence of social responsibility in their blind pursuit of absolute greed.' Available at www.abc.net.au/news/stories/2009/10/16/2715667.htm.

25 Lane, 'Introduction' to Plato, *The Republic*, xi.

26 This paragraph echoes and is inspired by Richard Seaford's Presidential Address to the Classical Association, 'Ancient Greece and Global Warming' (London: Classical Association, 2009).

27 Tim Kasser, *The High Price of Materialism* (Cambridge, MA and London: The MIT Press, 2002).

28 Tom Crompton and Tim Kasser, *Meeting Environmental Challenges: The Role of Human Identity* (Godalming, Surrey: WWF-UK, 2009), also available at http://assets.wwf.org.uk/downloads/meeting_environmental_challenges___the_role_of_human_identity.pdf.

29 Offer, *Challenge of Affluence*.

30 For the novelty and significance of money for ancient Greek thought, see Richard Seaford, *Money and the Early Greek Mind: Homer, Philosophy, Tragedy* (Cambridge: Cambridge University Press, 2004). An important discussion of money in the *Republic* to which mine is also indebted is in Malcolm Schofield, *Plato: Political Philosophy* (Oxford: Oxford University Press, 2006), 250–81.

31 See Kasser, *The High Price of Materialism*.

32 Translated by Donald J. Zeyl, in Plato, *Complete Works*, ed. Cooper with Hutchinson.

33 See for example Daniel Kahneman, 'Experienced Utility and Objective Happiness: A Moment-Based Approach', in Daniel Kahneman and Amos Tversky (eds), *Choices, Values and Frames* (New York: Cambridge University Press and the Russell Sage Foundation, 2000), 673–92.

34 On the importance of reinforcing one's commitments through action, see George Ainslie, *Breakdown of Will* (Cambridge: Cambridge University Press, 2001).

PROLOGUE TO CHAPTER 6: PLATO'S IDEA OF THE GOOD

1   On how to understand this claim – we all aim at the good, but are sometimes mistaken, hence aim at apparent goods only – see Rachel Barney, 'Plato on the Desire for the Good', in Sergio Tenenbaum (ed.), *Desire, Practical Reason, and the Good* (New York: Oxford University Press, 2010), 34–64.

2　The leading exponent of the latter view is Gail Fine; her arguments can be surveyed in her *Plato on Knowledge and Forms: Selected Essays* (Oxford and New York: Oxford University Press, 2003).

3　See Lane, *Plato's Progeny*, ch. 3.

4　Robert Merrihew Adams, *Finite and Infinite Goods* (Oxford: Oxford University Press, 2002), 188; see 186–203 and *passim*.

6　THE IDEA OF THE GOOD

1　So Plato's argument escapes the strictures of certain modern-day philosophers, who object that 'goodness' is merely redundant, a place-holder for some more specific category of value. They would say that for Sophia to consider education good, for example, must mean for her to consider it useful, or ennobling, or some other concrete and particular understanding of the value of education. In fact, this move is not inconsistent with the Platonic one, up to this point. For something to be called good, according to Plato, is to identify it as a genuine source of ultimate justificatory value in instrumental pursuit. Plato need not be taken to hold that good education and good tennis are good for the same reasons; the point is rather that the goodness of each identifies it as something worth pursuing. A further question is whether Plato is discussing absolute goodness versus always treating goodness as *for* someone: the latter view is defended by Richard Kraut, *What Is Good and Why: The Ethics of Well-Being* (Cambridge, MA and London: Harvard University Press, 2007).

2　For an overview of these issues, see Kraut, *What is Good and Why*.

3　William McDonough and Michael Braungart, *Cradle to Cradle: Remaking the Way We Make Things* (New York: North Point Press, 2002), 31.

4　'The Age of Stupid', directed by Franny Armstrong, released in London on 15 March 2009.

5　McDonough and Braungart, *Cradle to Cradle*, 67.

6　Ibid. Plato's view that matter limits the realization of the intelligibility of the Forms means that for him, nothing mortal or phenomenal could be 100 percent good.

7　Plato's *Timaeus* develops this view in far more detail than the *Republic*. See Carone, *Plato's Cosmology*, and for a stimulating modern appropriation, Shimon Malin, *Nature Loves to Hide: Quantum Physics and Reality, a Western Perspective* (New York: Oxford University Press, 2001).

8　Phil Edwards and Ian Roberts, 'Population Adiposity and Climate Change', *International Journal of Epidemiology* (2009), 1–4, advance access published 19 April 2009, quoting from 3.

9 Aristotle, *Nicomachean Ethics* I.4.1096a26. On the key role played by the *kairos* in Plato's *Statesman*, see M. S. Lane, *Method and Politics in Plato's Statesman*. I argue there that the *Republic* fails to accommodate the role of the *kairos*, seeing particular decisions of the rulers in time as ultimately their Achilles' heel, whereas for the *Statesman* knowledge of the *kairos* will be definitional of the true ruler.

10 The *9/11 Commission Staff Report on the pre-9/11 failings of the FAA* [Federal Aviation Administration], dated 26 August 2004 in the declassified version released in response to Freedom of Information request, states on 76: 'the air carriers had successfully fought off the FAA's efforts to change the standard [of screening at security checkpoints] to "prevent and detect"' [from the existing 'prevent-or-deter' standard at that time]. This report is available at: http://www.gwu.edu/~nsarchiv/NSAEBB/NSAEBB148/911%20 Commission%20Four%20Flights%20Monograph.pdf.

11 See Carlo Petrini, *Slow Food Nation: Why Our Food Should be Good, Clean, and Fair* (New York: Rizzoli Ex Libris, 2007) and www.slowfood.com among many other sources, and the discussion by political theorist Bonnie Honig in her *Emergency Politics: paradox, law, democracy* (Princeton: Princeton University Press, 2009), 40–65.

12 This is argued in Philip G. Zimbardo and John Boyd, *The Time Paradox: The New Psychology of Time That Will Change Your Life* (New York: Free Press, 2008).

13 See for example Barry Schwartz, *The Paradox of Choice: Why Less is More* (New York: HarperCollins, 2004), and also the discussion in Scitovsky, *Joyless Economy*.

14 See http://www.longnow.org/clock/, last accessed 14 January 2011.

15 Hugh Cleary and Richard Reeves, 'The "culture of churn" for UK Ministers and the price we all pay', *Demos* research briefing, 12 June 2009, available at http://www.demos.co.uk/files/Ministerial_Churn.pdf?1244760978.

16 Translated by Alexander Nehamas and Paul Woodruff, in Plato, *Complete Works*, ed. Cooper with Hutchinson.

17 Viktor E. Frankl, *Man's Search for Meaning: An Introduction to Logotherapy*, transl. Ilse Lasch, preface by Gordon W. Allport (London: Hodder and Stoughton, 1962). The tombstone inscriptions were imagined by the syndicate group which I led for the Prince of Wales's Business and the Environment Programme Madingley Seminar 2009.

18 The Oxford study is by a team led by Angela Wilkinson, 'Beyond the Financial Crisis: The Oxford Scenarios', Institute for Science, Innovation and Society, Saïd Business School, University of Oxford, published 15 February 2010 (a reference I owe to Catherine Cameron). The 'Growth' and 'Health' scenarios are of course only stylized as alternative choices: my moral is not

so far from that of the report overall, but its mode of presentation can be misleading.

19   Herman E. Daly, 'A Steady-State Economy', opinion piece for the Sustainable Development Commission (UK), 24 July 2008, available online at: http://www. sd-commission.org.uk/publications.php?id=775 as of 21 January 2011, but with the British Government's withdrawal of funding for this Commission, this link may not last.

PROLOGUE TO CHAPTER 7: REVISITING PLATO'S CAVE

1   Malcolm Schofield, *Plato. Political Philosophy* (Oxford: Oxford University Press, 2006).
2   Literally, 'see' in the sense of 'envision' – an imperative.
3   This is a literal translation: Glaucon avers that he 'sees' the cave in answer to Socrates' opening command to do so.
4   Again, 'see' as a command: at this point in Plato's writing, he presents what we would call imagination as if it were a literal, actual act of ocular seeing.

7 INITIATIVE AND INDIVIDUALS: A (PARTLY) PLATONIC POLITICAL PROJECT

1   Hannah Arendt, *The Human Condition* (Chicago: University of Chicago Press, 1958).
2   The question 'which way will you lean' was formulated by my friend and former colleague Adam Tooze in our work together with BP (British Petroleum) on behalf of the Cambridge Programme for Industry: my major role in this regard was as a faculty member and speaker employed by the University of Cambridge, but I have also engaged in paid consulting work with BP and later with GSK and Shell (disclosure).
3   Of course, dividing up these goods so starkly is an oversimplification. Philip Pettit's articulation of republican freedom from domination has recently been refined to focus on a dimension of control, for example; see Pettit, *Republicanism: a theory of freedom and government* (New York and Oxford: Oxford University Press and the Clarendon Press, 1997), together with the focus on control in a recent refinement of the theory: Philip Pettit, 'Republican Freedom: Three Axioms, Four Theorems', in Cécile Laborde and John Maynor (eds), *Republicanism and Political Theory* (Oxford: Blackwell, 2008), 102–30.

4 The quotation is from Robert C. Ellickson, 'The Evolution of Social Norms: A Perspective from the Legal Academy', in Michael Hechter and Karl-Dieter Opp (eds), *Social Norms* (New York: Russell Sage Foundation, 2001), 35–75, at 38. This paragraph is generally expounding Ellickson's argument.

5 Ellickson, 'The Evolution of Social Norms', 52.

6 I discuss the distinctive philosophical nature in Lane, 'Virtue as the Love of Knowledge in Plato's *Symposium* and *Republic*', in *Maieusis: Essays in Ancient Philosophy in Honour of Myles Burnyeat*, ed. Dominic Scott (Oxford: Oxford University Press, 2007), 44–67.

7 Here the Lee translation – 'best and quickest' – is literally incorrect; 'quickest and easiest' is my own translation. I owe the emphasis on this caveat to S. Sara Monoson, whose subtle work on what she calls Plato's democratic entanglements is not sufficiently reflected in the broad argument of this book.

8 The point and the example are taken from Robert B. Cialdini, *Influence: science and practice*, 4th edn (Boston and London: Allyn and Bacon, 2001), 65–7, quoting research by J. L. Freedman and S. C. Fraser, 'Compliance without pressure: the foot-in-the-door technique', *Journal of Personality and Social Psychology* 4 (1966), 195–203.

9 Cialdini, *Influence*, 84–5: the example elided in the quotation is that of people coming to see themselves as public-minded citizens, but Cialdini immediately identifies the same effect in the car salesman's technique of 'throwing a low-ball', or offering a low price to elicit commitment, before withdrawing that special offer in the expectation that the self-confirming reasons which it had elicited will still persist (85). On 87–90 he reports a study which used this technique successfully to improve practices of conservation among families: they were initially offered newspaper publicity which altered their behaviour, yet after the publicity ended they continued and even increased their conservation efforts. The study is M. S. Pallak, D. A. Cook and J. J. Sullivan, 'Commitment and energy conservation', *Applied Social Psychology Annual* 1 (1980), 235–53.

10 Ellickson, 'The Evolution of Social Norms', 42.

11 David J. C. MacKay, *Sustainable Energy – Without the Hot Air* (Cambridge: UIT Cambridge, 2008).

12 Gary Kendall, *Plugged In: The End of the Oil Age*, WWF-UK report, available at http://wwf.panda.org/what_we_do/how_we_work/businesses/climate/climate_savers/climate_savers_publications/?151723/Plugged-in-the-End-of-the-Oil-Age.

13 Alison Craig, 'Your Daily Poison: The Second UK Pesticide Exposure Report' (London: Pesticide Action Network UK, 2006), 45, available at http://www.pan-uk.org/publications/your-daily-poison.

14 For the argument that political unity is a key to Plato's political thought, see Jean-François Pradeau, *Plato and the City: A New Introduction to Plato's Political Thought*, transl. Janet Lloyd, foreword by Christopher Gill (Exeter: University of Exeter Press, 2002).

15 Quoted without further attribution in Tom Crompton, *Weathercocks and Signposts: the environment movement at a crossroads* (WWF-UK's Strategies for Change Project, April 2008: available at wwf.org.uk/strategiesforchange), 3.

16 Robert Reich's blog, 26 January 2009, available at http://robertreich.blogspot.com/2009/01/how-you-and-i-are-paying-wall-street-to.html. Part of this section of the book derives from my article 'Corporate Ethics, Post-Crunch', posted on the website of Das Progressive Zentrum on 13 February 2009 in English and in German translation by Danilo Scholz (http://www.progressives-zentrum.org/dpz.php/cat/90/aid/356/title/Post-Crunch for the English version).

17 This is a point stressed by Emma Rothschild in *Economic Sentiments*.

18 The statement is reputedly by Lord Chancellor Thurlow (Edward, 1st Baron Thurlow; 1731–1806): 'Did you ever expect a corporation to have a conscience, when it has no soul to be damned, and no body to be kicked?' It is quoted in many sources on corporate and organizational law and behaviour. I came across it originally in Mark Bovens, *The Quest for Responsibility: Accountability and Citizenship in Complex Organizations* (Cambridge: Cambridge University Press, 1998), 53, n. 1 (where he attributes it to John C. Coffee, '"No Soul to Damn, No Body to Kick": An Unscandalized Inquiry into the Problem of Corporate Punishment', *Michigan Law Review* 79 (1981) 386–459, at 386, n. 1).

19 For the Corporate Leaders Group, which is (disclosure) staffed by the Cambridge Programme for Sustainability Leadership of which I am a Senior Associate and have been a longtime faculty and sometime board member, see: http://www.cpsl.cam.ac.uk/leaders_groups/clgcc.aspx.

20 Ray C. Anderson, *Mid-Course Correction: Toward a Sustainable Enterprise. The Interface Model* (Atlanta: Peregrinzilla Press, 1998), quoting in this paragraph from 7, 43, 43, 45, and 40 respectively.

21 Anderson, *Mid-Course Correction*, quoting in this paragraph from 15, 16, and 20–1 respectively. I have no access to independent verification of Interface's achievements; my interest here is primarily in the way of thinking demonstrated in Anderson's writing, not in validating specific measures or claims by him or by the company. Anderson has extended the story in a second book: Ray C. Anderson with Robin White, *Confessions of a Radical Industrialist: Profits, People, Purpose – Doing Business by Respecting the Earth* (Toronto: McClelland and Stewart, 2009).

22 I owe this point to Alex Guerrero.

23 In his lecture course at the University of Basel entitled 'Einführung in das Studium der platonischen Dialoge' or 'Introduction to the Study of the Platonic Dialogues', Nietzsche described Plato as an '*agitatorischen Politiker*', a reference which I owe to my student Hugo Halferty-Drochon. It can be found in Friedrich Nietzsche, *Werke: Kritische Gesamtausgabe*, ed. Giorgio Colli and Mazzino Montinari (Berlin: Walter de Gruyter, 1967–), II, 4.

24 John R. Wallach, *The Platonic Political Art: a study of critical reason and democracy* (University Park, PA: Pennsylvania State University Press, 2001), points out that Plato rejected all existing regimes, not democracies only, as radically defective from the standpoint of a true political art.

25 F. M. Cornford, *Microcosmographia Academica* (Cambridge: Bowes and Bowes, 1908), now in Gordon Johnson, *University Politics: F. M. Cornford's Cambridge and his advice to the young academic politicians* (Cambridge: Cambridge University Press, 1994), 85–110, at 105.

26 In Latin, 'da mihi castitatem et continentiam, sed noli modo': cited in English from Augustine of Hippo, *Confessions*, transl. F. J. Sheed (New York: Continuum International Publishing, 1943), 134. On the *kairos* in Plato's *Republic* and *Statesman*, and in Greek thought more generally, see Lane, *Method and Politics in Plato's Statesman*, Part III. Cornford, similarly, went on to caution: 'Time, by the way, is like the medlar [a rare fruit]; it has a trick of going rotten before it is ripe.' See Cornford in Johnson, *University Politics*, 105.

Works Cited

Adam, David and Afua Hirsch. 'Oil giants could soon face lawsuits over climate, says Oxford University scientist'. *Guardian*, 9 December 2008, 1.

Adams, Madonna R. 'Environmental Ethics in Plato's *Timaeus*'. In *The Greeks and the Environment*, ed. Laura Westra and Thomas M. Robinson, 55–72. Lanham, MD: Rowman and Littlefield, 1997.

Adams, Robert Merrihew. *Finite and Infinite Goods*. Oxford: Oxford University Press, 2002.

——. *A Theory of Virtue: Excellence in Being for the Good*. 2nd edn, New York: Oxford University Press, 2009.

Ainslie, George. *Breakdown of Will*. Cambridge: Cambridge University Press, 2001.

Akst, Daniel. *We Have Met the Enemy: Self-Control in an Age of Excess*. New York: Penguin, 2011.

Allen, Danielle S. *The World of Prometheus: The Politics of Punishing in Democratic Athens*. Princeton and Oxford: Princeton University Press, 2000.

——. *Talking to Strangers: Anxieties of Citizenship after Brown v. Board of Education*. Chicago and London: University of Chicago Press, 2004.

——. *Why Plato Wrote*. Chichester, West Sussex: Wiley-Blackwell, 2010.

Anderson, Benedict. *Imagined Communities: Reflections on the Origin and Spread of Nationalism*. London: Verso, 1983.

Anderson, Ray C. *Mid-Course Correction: Toward a Sustainable Enterprise. The Interface Model*. Atlanta: Peregrinzilla Press, 1998.

——, with Robin White. *Confessions of a Radical Industrialist: Profits, People, Purpose – Doing Business by Respecting the Earth*. Toronto: McClelland and Stewart, 2009.

Annas, Julia. *The Morality of Happiness*. New York: Oxford University Press, 1993.

[Anonymous]. 'End of the Runway'. Editorial, *Guardian*, 10 July 2008, 30.

——. 'Heavy baggage'. *Economist*, 31 January 2009, 50.

——. 'Mr Segway's Difficult Path.' *Economist*, 10 June 2010, 25.

Appelbaum, Binyamin and David M. Herszenhorn. 'Financial Oversight Bill Signals Shift on Deregulation.' *New York Times*, 15 July 2010, A1.

Appiah, Kwame Anthony. *The Honor Code: How Moral Revolutions Happen*. New York: W. W. Norton & Company, 2010.

Arendt, Hannah. *The Human Condition*. Chicago: University of Chicago Press, 1958.

Aristotle, *Nicomachean Ethics*. In *The Complete Works of Aristotle: the revised Oxford translation*, 2 vols, ed. Jonathan Barnes. Princeton: Princeton University Press, 1984.

The Associated Press. 'California: Backers of Plastic Bags Prevail'. *New York Times*, 2 September 2010, A21.

Augustine of Hippo. *Confessions*. Translated by R. J. Sheed. New York: Continuum International Publishing, 1943.

Balot, Ryan K. *Greed and Injustice in Classical Athens*. Princeton: Princeton University Press, 2001.

Barkham, Patrick. 'Wouldn't changing our clocks make our lives better?' *guardian.co.uk*, 20 December 2010.

Barney, Rachel. 'Plato on the Desire for the Good.' In *Desire, Practical Reason, and the Good*, ed. Sergio Tenenbaum, 34–64. New York: Oxford University Press, 2010.

Baron, Marcia W., Philip Pettit, and Michael Slote. *Three Methods of Ethics: A Debate*. Malden, MA: Blackwell, 1997.

Barr, Stewart. *Environment and Society: Sustainability, Policy and the Citizen*. Aldershot, Hampshire, UK and Burlington, VT: Ashgate Publishing, 2008.

Bentham, Jeremy. *An Introduction to the Principles of Morals and Legislation*. Oxford: Clarendon Press, 1907. http://oll.libertyfund.org.

Bernanke, Ben S. 'The Great Moderation'. Speech at the meeting of the Eastern Economic Association, Washington, DC, 20 February 2004.

Besley, Tim and Peter Hennessy. Letter from the British Academy to the Queen, 22 July 2009. www.britac.ac.uk/news/newsrelease-economy.cfm.

Bobonich, Christopher. 'Plato on *Akrasia* and Knowing Your Own Mind'. In *Akrasia in Greek Philosophy: From Socrates to Plotinus*, ed. Christopher Bobonich and Pierre Destrée, 41–60. Leiden and Boston: Brill, 2007.

Bovens, Mark. *The Quest for Responsibility: Accountability and Citizenship in Complex Organizations*. Cambridge: Cambridge University Press, 1998.

Brennan, Geoffrey. 'Climate Change: A Rational Choice Politics View'. *Australian Journal of Agricultural and Resource Economics* 53 (2009), 309–26.

Brettschneider, Corey. 'When the State Speaks, What Should It Say? The Dilemmas of Freedom of Expression and Democratic Persuasion'. *Perspectives on Politics* 8 (2010), 1005–19.

Brown, Gordon. 'Budget for Enterprise'. Speech at the TGWU Manufacturing Matters conference, 28 March 2002.

Bundy, Murray Wright. *The Theory of Imagination in Classical and Mediaeval Thought*. University of Illinois Studies in Language and Literature, vol. 2. Urbana, Ill.: University of Illinois Press, 1927.

Burnyeat, M. F. 'Culture and Society in Plato's *Republic*'. In *The Tanner Lectures on Human Values*, vol. 20, ed. Grethe B. Peterson, 217–324. Salt Lake City: University of Utah Press, 1999.

Burke, Edmund. *Reflections on the Revolution in France*. London: Penguin Books, 2004.

Caballero, Maria Christina. 'Academic turns city into a social experiment'. *Harvard Magazine*, 11 March 2004. www.news.Harvard.edu/gazette/2004/03.11/01-mockus.html.

Caplan, Bryan. *The Myth of the Rational Voter*. Princeton: Princeton University Press, 2007.

Carone, Gabriela Roxana. *Plato's Cosmology and Its Ethical Dimensions*. Cambridge: Cambridge University Press, 2005.

Cartledge, Paul. *The Spartans: An Epic History*. London: Pan Books, 2003.

Castoriadis, Cornelius. *The Imaginary Institution of Society*. Translated by Kathleen Blaney. Cambridge: Polity Press, 1987.

Chakravarty, S., Ananth Chikkatur, Heleen de Coninck, Stephen Pacala, Robert Socolow, and Massimo Tavoni. 'Sharing Global CO_2 Emission Reductions Among One Billion High Emitters'. *Proceedings of National Academy of Science* 106:29 (2009), 11884–8.

Chappell, Timothy D. J., ed. *Values and Virtues: Aristotelianism in Contemporary Ethics*. Oxford: Clarendon Press, 2006.

Cialdini, Robert B. *Influence: science and practice*, 4th edn. Boston and London: Allyn and Bacon, 2001.

——. 'Crafting Normative Messages to Protect the Environment'. *Current Directions in Psychological Science* 4 (2003), 105–9.

——, R. R. Reno and C. A. Kallgren. 'A focus theory of normative conduct: Recycling the concept of norms to reduce littering in public places'. *Journal of Personality and Social Psychology* 58 (1990), 1015–26.

Cleary, Hugh and Richard Reeves. 'The "culture of churn" for UK Ministers and the price we all pay'. *Demos* research briefing, 12 June 2009. http://www.demos.co.uk/files/Ministerial_Churn.pdf?1244760978.

Coffee, John C. '"No Soul to Damn, No Body to Kick": An Unscandalized Inquiry into the Problem of Corporate Punishment.' *Michigan Law Review* 79 (1981), 386–459.

Cohen, G. A. *Rescuing Justice and Equality*. Cambridge, MA: Harvard University Press, 2008.

Connelly, James. *Sustainability and the Virtues of Environmental Citizenship*. New York and London: Routledge, forthcoming.

Constant, Benjamin. 'The Liberty of the Ancients Compared with that of the Moderns'. *Political Writings*, transl. and ed. Biancamaria Fontana. Cambridge: Cambridge University Press, 1988.

Cornford, F. M. *Microcosmographia Academica*. Cambridge: Bowes and Bowes, 1908, now in Johnson, *University Politics*, 85–110.

Cowie, Jonathan. *Climate Change: Biological and Human Aspects*. Cambridge: Cambridge University Press, 2007.

Craig, Alison. 'Your Daily Poison: The Second UK Pesticide Exposure Report.' London: Pesticide Action Network UK, 2006. http://www.pan-uk.org/publications/your-daily-poison.

Crompton, Tom. *Weathercocks and Signposts: the environment movement at a crossroads*. WWF-UK's Strategies for Change Project, April 2008. Available at wwf.org.uk/strategiesforchange.

—— and Tim Kasser. *Meeting Environmental Challenges: The Role of Human Identity*. Godalming, Surrey: WWF-UK, 2009. http://assets.wwf.org.uk/downloads/meeting_environmental_challenges___the_role_of_human_identity.pdf.

Daly, Herman E. 'A Steady-State Economy'. Editorial, The Sustainable Development Commission (UK), 24 July 2008. www.sd-commission.org.uk/publications.php?id=775

Darling, Rt. Hon. Alastair. 'Speech by the Chancellor of the Exchequer.' Speech, Mansion House, 17 June 2009. www.hm-treasury.gov.uk/press_57_09.htm.

Delgado, Martin. 'An energy saving bulb has gone – evacuate the room now!' *Daily Mail*, 6 January 2009. www.dailymail.co.uk/sciencetech/article-506347/An-energy-saving-bulb-gone--evacuate-room-now.html.

Denyer, Nicholas. 'Sun and Line: The Role of the Good'. In *The Cambridge Companion to Plato's* Republic, ed. G. R. F. Ferrari, 284–309. Cambridge: Cambridge University Press, 2007),

Derbyshire, David. 'The low-energy bulbs that won't fit your light sockets'. *Daily Mail*, 7 January 2009. www.dailymail.co.uk/news/article-1108775/The-low-energy-bulbs-wont-fit-light-sockets.html.

——. 'Revolt! Robbed of their right to buy traditional light bulbs, millions are clearing shelves of last supplies'. *Daily Mail*, 7 January 2009. www.dailymail.

co.uk/news/article-1107290/Revolt-Robbed-right-buy-traditional-light-bulbs-millions-clearing-shelves-supplies.html

Destrée, Pierre. 'Aristotle on the Causes of *Akrasia*'. In *Akrasia in Greek Philosophy: From Socrates to Plotinus,* ed. Christopher Bobonich and Pierre Destrée, 139–65. Leiden and Boston: Brill, 2007.

Diamond, Jared. *Collapse: How Societies Choose to Fail or Survive.* London: Allen Lane, 2005.

Dobson, Andrew. *Green Political Thought.* 4th edn. London and New York: Routledge, 2007.

—— and Robin Eckersley, eds. *Political Theory and the Ecological Challenge.* Cambridge: Cambridge University Press, 2006.

Douglas, Mary and Aaron Wildavsky. *Risk and Culture: An essay on the selection of technical and environmental dangers.* Berkeley: University of California Press, 1982.

Downs, Anthony. *An Economic Theory of Democracy.* New York: Harper and Row, 1957.

Dunn, John. *Setting the People Free: the Story of Democracy.* London: Atlantic Books, 2005.

Easterbrook, Frank H., and Daniel R. Fischel. 'Antitrust Suits by Targets of Tender Offers'. *Michigan Law Review* 80 (1982), 1155–78.

Edwards, Phil and Ian Roberts. 'Population Adiposity and Climate Change'. *International Journal of Epidemiology* 38:4 (2009), 1137–40.

Ellerman, A. Denny, Frank J. Convery, and Christian de Perthuis. *Pricing Carbon: The European Emissions Trading Scheme.* Cambridge: Cambridge University Press, 2010.

Ellickson, Robert C. 'The Evolution of Social Norms: A Perspective from the Legal Academy'. In *Social Norms,* ed. Michael Hechter and Karl-Dieter Opp, 35–75. New York: Russell Sage Foundation, 2001.

Elster, Jon. *Ulysses Unbound: Studies in Rationality, Precommitment, and Constraints.* Cambridge: Cambridge University Press, 2000.

—— and John E. Roemer, eds. *Interpersonal Comparisons of Well-Being.* Cambridge and New York: Cambridge University Press, 1991.

Emerson, Ralph Waldo. 'Self-Reliance'. *Essays: First Series.* 1841. www.emerson-central.com/selfreliance.htm.

Fehr, Ernst and Simon Gächter. 'Fairness and Retaliation: The Economics of Reciprocity'. *Journal of Economic Perspectives* 14:3 (2000), 159–81.

Ferrari, G. R. F. *City and Soul in Plato's Republic.* Sankt Augustin: Academia Verlag, 2003; Chicago: University of Chicago Press, 2005.

Fine, Gail. *Plato on Knowledge and Forms: Selected Essays.* Oxford and New York: Oxford University Press, 2003.

Foot, Philippa. *Virtues and Vices.* Oxford: Blackwell, 1978.

Forum for the Future. 'What is sustainable development?' Accessed 29 June 2009. www.forumforthefuture.org/what-is-sd.

Foucault, Michel. *History of Sexuality*, vol. 1. Translated by Robert Hurley. New York: Vintage Books, 1990.

Frank, Jill. *A Democracy of Distinction: Aristotle and the Work of Politics*. Chicago and London: University of Chicago Press, 2005.

———. 'Wages of War: On Judgment in Plato's *Republic*'. *Political Theory* 35 (2007), 443–67.

Frankl, Viktor E. *Man's Search for Meaning: An Introduction to Logotherapy*. Translated by Ilse Lasch. London: Hodder and Stoughton, 1962.

Freedman, J. L., and S. C. Fraser. 'Compliance without pressure: the foot-in-the-door technique'. *Journal of Personality and Social Psychology* 4 (1966), 195–203.

Frey, Bruno S. *Not Just for the Money: An Economic Theory of Personal Motivation*. Cheltenham, UK: Edward Elgar Publishing, 1997.

Garvey, James. *The Ethics of Climate Change: Right and Wrong in a Warming World*. London and New York: Continuum, 2008.

Gawande, Atul. 'The Hot Spotters'. *The New Yorker*, 24 January 2011, 40–51.

Geach, Peter. *The Virtues*. Cambridge: Cambridge University Press, 1977.

Geuss, Raymond. *Politics and the Imagination*. Princeton: Princeton University Press, 2010.

Gill, Mary Louise. 'Models in Plato's *Sophist* and *Statesman*'. *Plato: The Internet Journal of the International Plato Society* 6 (2006). http://gramata.univ-paris1.fr/Plato/spip.php?article27.

Goldin, Owen. 'The Ecology of the *Critias* and Platonic Metaphysics'. In *The Greeks and the Environment*, ed. Laura Westra and Thomas M. Robinson, 73–80. Lanham, MD: Rowman and Littlefield, 1997.

Goodin, Robert E. *Utilitarianism as a Public Philosophy*. Cambridge and New York: Cambridge University Press, 1995.

Grant, John. *The Green Marketing Manifesto*. London: John Wiley and Sons, 2007.

Guerrero, Alexander A. 'The Paradox of Voting and the Ethics of Political Representation'. *Philosophy and Public Affairs* 38:3 (2010), 272–306.

Hale, Beth. 'Yes I found some … but it wasn't light work'. *Daily Mail*, 6 January 2009. www.dailymail.co.uk/news/article-1107293/Reporter-BETH-HALE-great-bulb-hunt-Yes-I--wasnt-light-work.html.

Halpern, David. *The Hidden Wealth of Nations*. Cambridge: Polity Press, 2010.

Hamilton, Lawrence. *The Political Philosophy of Needs*. Cambridge: Cambridge University Press, 2003.

Hanlon, Michael. 'Analysis: So are these really such a bright idea?' *Daily Mail*, 7 January 2009. www.dailymail.co.uk/news/article-1107296/MICHAEL-HANLON-Are-energy-saving-bulbs-really-going-save-planet.html.

Hansen, Mogens Herman. 'The Ancient Athenian and the Modern Liberal View of Liberty as a Democratic Ideal'. In *Demokratia: A Conversation on Democracies, Ancient and Modern*, ed. Josiah Ober and Charles W. Hedrick. Princeton: Princeton University Press, 1996.

Harman, Gilbert. 'Moral Philosophy Meets Social Psychology: Virtue Ethics and the Fundamental Attribution Error'. *Proceedings of the Aristotelian Society* 99 (1999), 315–31.

Hechter, Michael and Karl-Dieter Opp. Introduction to *Social Norms*, ed. Michael Hechter and Karl-Dieter Opp, xi–xx. New York: Russell Sage Foundation, 2001.

Himmelfarb, Gertrude. *The Moral Imagination*. New York: Ivan R. Dee, 2006.

Hirschman, Albert O. *The Passions and the Interests: Political Arguments for Capitalism before its Triumph*. Princeton: Princeton University Press, 1977.

Honig, Bonnie. *Emergency Politics: paradox, law, democracy*. Princeton: Princeton University Press, 2009.

Horne, Christine. 'Sociological Perspectives on the Emergence of Norms'. In *Social Norms*, ed. Michael Hechter and Karl-Dieter Opp, 3–34. New York: Russell Sage Foundation, 2001.

Hulme, Mike. *Why We Disagree about Climate Change: Understanding Controversy, Inaction and Opportunity*

Huppert, Felicia A., Nick Baylis, and Barry Keverne, eds. *The Science of Well-Being*. Oxford and New York: Oxford University Press, 2005.

Hursthouse, Rosalind. *On Virtue Ethics*. Oxford: Oxford University Press, 1999.

Huxley, Aldous. 'Inaugural Address'. Speech at the International Fisheries Exhibition, London, 1883. alepho.clarku.edu/huxley/SM5/fish.html.

Intergovernmental Panel on Climate Change. *Aviation and the Global Atmosphere*. Cambridge: Cambridge University Press, 1999.

Jackson, Tim. *Prosperity without Growth? The transition to a sustainable economy*. Sustainable Development Commission of the United Kingdom, 2009.

Jamieson, Dale. 'Ethics, Public Policy, and Global Warming'. *Science, Technology, and Human Values* 17 (1992), 139–53.

——. 'Ethics, Public Policy, and Global Warming'. In Jamieson, Dale (ed.), *Morality's Progress: Essays on Humans, Other Animals, and the Rest of Nature*, 282–95. Oxford: Clarendon Press, 2002.

——. *Ethics and the Environment: An Introduction*. Cambridge: Cambridge University Press, 2008.

Johnson, Gordon. *University Politics: F. M. Cornford's Cambridge and his advice to the young academic politicians*. Cambridge: Cambridge University Press, 1994.

Johnstone, Mark A. 'Tripartition and the Rule of the Soul in Plato's *Republic*'. PhD diss., Princeton University, 2009.

Kahan, Dan M. 'Gentle Nudges vs. Hard Shoves: Solving the Sticky Norms Problem'. *University of Chicago Law Review* 67 (2000), 607–45.

Kahneman, Daniel. 'Experienced Utility and Objective Happiness: A Moment-Based Approach'. In *Choices, Values and Frames*, ed. Daniel Kahneman and Amos Tversky, 673–92. New York: Cambridge University Press and the Russell Sage Foundation, 2000.

——, Jack I. Knetsch, and Richard H. Thaler. 'The Endowment Effect, Loss Aversion, and Status Quo Bias: Anomalies'. *The Journal of Economic Perspectives* 5, no. 1 (1991), 193–206.

Kakutani, Michiko. 'Greed Layered on Greed, Frosted with Recklessness'. *New York Times,* 16 June 2009.

Kamtekar, Rachana. 'Situationism and Virtue Ethics on the Content of Our Character,' *Ethics* 114 (2004), 458–91.

Kasser, Tim. *The High Price of Materialism*. Cambridge, MA and London: The MIT Press, 2002.

Katznelson, Ira and Gareth Stedman Jones, eds. *Religion and the Political Imagination*. Cambridge: Cambridge University Press, 2010.

Kendall, Gary. *Plugged In: The End of the Oil Age*. WWF-UK report, 2008. http://wwf.panda.org/what_we_do/how_we_work/businesses/climate/climate_savers/climate_savers_publications/?151723/Plugged-in-the-End-of-the-Oil-Age.

Kintisch, Eli. *Hack the Planet. Hack the Planet*. Hoboken, NJ: John Wiley and Sons, 2010.

Kraut, Richard. *What is Good and Why: The Ethics of Well-Being*. Cambridge, MA: Harvard University Press, 2007.

Kyburg, Henry. *Probability and the Logic of Rational Belief*. Middletown, CT: Wesleyan University Press, 1961.

Lane, Melissa [as M. S. Lane]. *Method and Politics in Plato's* Statesman. Cambridge: Cambridge University Press, 1998.

——. 'Plato, Popper, Strauss, and Utopianism: Open Secrets?' *History of Philosophy Quarterly* 16 (1999), 119–42.

——. *Plato's Progeny: How Plato and Socrates still captivate the modern mind*. London: Duckworth, 2001.

——. 'The Moral Dimension of Corporate Accountability'. In *Global Responsibilities: Who Must Deliver on Human Rights?*, ed. Andrew Kuper, 229–50. New York: Routledge, 2005.

——. 'Introduction'. In Plato, *The Republic*, transl. Desmond Lee. London and New York: Penguin, 2007.

——. 'Virtue as the Love of Knowledge in Plato's *Symposium* and *Republic*'. In *Maieusis: Essays in Ancient Philosophy in Honour of Myles Burnyeat*, ed. Dominic Scott, 44–67. Oxford: Oxford University Press, 2007.

——. 'Corporate Ethics, Post-Crunch'. Posted on the website of Das Progressive Zentrum on 13 February 2009 in English and in German translation by Danilo Scholz. English version: http://www.progressives-zentrum.org/dpz. php/cat/90/aid/356/title/Post-Crunch.

——. 'Constraint, freedom, and exemplar: history and theory without teleology'. In *Political Philosophy versus History? Contextualism and Real Politics in Contemporary Political Thought*, ed. Jonathan Floyd and Marc Stears. Cambridge: Cambridge University Press, forthcoming.

——. 'Founding as legislating: the figure of the lawgiver in Plato's *Republic*'. In *Plato's Politeia. Proceedings of the IX Symposium Platonicum*, ed. L. Brisson and N. Notomi. Berlin: Akademie Verlag, forthcoming.

——[as Melissa S. Lane]. 'The Platonic politics of the George-Kreis: a reconsideration'. In *A Poet's Reich: Politics and Culture in the George Circle*, ed. Melissa S. Lane and Martin A. Ruehl. Rochester, NY: Camden House, forthcoming.

——. 'The rule of knowledge as self-knowledge in Plato's *Protagoras*'. In *Self-Knowledge in Ancient Philosophy: Proceedings of the Eighth Keeling Memorial Colloquium*, ed. Fiona Leigh. Leiden: E. J. Brill, forthcoming.

Layard, Richard. *Happiness: Lessons from a New Science*. Harmondsworth: Penguin, 2005.

Lear, Jonathan. 'Inside and Outside the *Republic*'. *Phronesis* 37:2 (1992), 184–215.

Lederach, John Paul. *The Moral Imagination*. Oxford: Oxford University Press, 2004.

Lucardie, Paul. 'Why Would Egocentrists Become Ecocentrists? On individualism and holism in green political theory'. In *The Politics of Nature: explorations in green political theory*, ed. Andrew Dobson and Paul Lucardie, 21–35. London and New York: Routledge, 1993.

Macedo, Stephen. *Liberal Virtues: Citizenship, Virtue, and Community in Liberal Constitutionalism*. Oxford: Clarendon Press, 1990.

MacKay, David J. C. *Sustainable Energy – Without the Hot Air*. Cambridge: UIT Cambridge, 2008.

Mackie, Gerry. 'Ending Footbinding and Infibulation: A Convention Account'. *American Sociological Review* 61 (1996), 999–1017.

——. 'Why It's Rational to Vote'. Forthcoming.

MacKinnon, Catriona. 'Climate Change and Corrective Justice'. *Jahrbuch für Recht und Ethik/Annual Review of Law and Ethics* 17 (2009), 259–77.

Mahoney, Timothy A. 'Platonic Ecology, Deep Ecology.' In *The Greeks and the Environment*, ed. Laura Westra and Thomas M. Robinson, 45–54. Lanham, MD: Rowman and Littlefield, 1997.

Malin, Shimon. *Nature Loves to Hide: Quantum Physics and Reality, a Western Perspective*. New York: Oxford University Press, 2001.

Mandeville, Bernard. *The Fable of the Bees*, ed. F. B. Kaye. Indianapolis: Liberty Fund, 1988.

Marshall, George. *Carbon Detox: Your Step-by-Step Guide to Getting Real about Climate Change*. London: Gaia Books, 2007.

McClosky, Deirdre N. *The Bourgeois Virtues: Ethics for an Age of Commerce*. Chicago: University of Chicago Press, 2006.

McDonough, William and Michael Braungart. *Cradle to Cradle: Remaking the Way We Make Things*. New York: North Point Press, 2002.

McIntosh, Alastair. *Hell and High Water: Climate Change, Hope and the Human Condition*. Edinburgh: Birlinn, 2008.

Mill, John Stuart. *On Liberty*. In *On Liberty and Other Essays*, ed. John Gray, 1–128. Oxford: Oxford University Press, 1998.

Millennium Ecosystem Assessment. *Ecosystems and Human Well-Being: Synthesis*. Washington, DC: Island Press, 2005.

Milmo, Dan. 'Airlines stage fightback on environmental criticism.' *guardian. co.uk*, 3 June 2008.

Monbiot, George. 'We spend millions on smallpox, but nothing on the far greater threat of peak oil.' *Guardian*, 14 April 2009, 27.

Morgan, Kathryn A., ed. *Popular Tyranny: Sovereignty and Its Discontents in Ancient Greece*. Austin, TX: University of Texas Press, 2003.

Mount, Ferdinand. *Full Circle: How the Classical World Came Back To Us*. London: Simon and Schuster, 2010.

Mulgan, Tim. *The Demands of Consequentialism*. Oxford: Clarendon Press, 2001.

Mulligan, Casey B. and Charles G. Hunter. 'The Empirical Frequency of a Pivotal Vote.' *Public Choice* 116 (2003), 31–54.

Nails, Debra. *The People of Plato: a prosopography of Plato and other Socratics*. Indianapolis: Hackett, 2002.

Nelkin, Dana K. 'The Lottery Paradox, Knowledge, and Rationality.' *The Philosophical Review* 109 (2000), 373–408.

Nietzsche, Friedrich. 'Einführung in das Studium der platonischen Dialoge.' In Nietzsche, *Werke: Kritische Gesamtausgabe*, ed. Giorgio Colli and Mazzino Montinari, vol. II. Berlin: Walter de Gruyter, 1967–.

——. 'What I Owe to the Ancients.' In Nietzsche, *Twilight of the Idols/The Antichrist*, transl. R. J. Hollingdale. Harmondsworth: Penguin, 1999.

Nussbaum, Martha C. *Love's Knowledge: Essays on Philosophy and Literature*. New York and Oxford: Oxford University Press, 1990.

Obama, Barack. 'Remarks of the President at the Acceptance of the Nobel Peace Prize'. Speech, Oslo, Norway, 10 December 2009. www.whitehouse.gov/the-press-office/remarks-president-acceptance-nobel-peace-prize.

——. 'Remarks by the President at a Memorial Service for the Victims of the Shooting in Tuscon, Arizona.' Speech, Tuscon, Arizona, 12 January 2011. www.whitehouse.gov/the-press-office/2011/01/12/remarks-president-obama-memorial-service-victims-shooting-tuscon.

Offer, Avner. *The Challenge of Affluence: Self-Control and Well-Being in the United States and Britain since 1950*. Oxford: Oxford University Press, 2006.

Pacala, Stephen S. and Robert Socolow. 'Stabilization Wedges'. *Science* 305 (2004), 968–72.

Pallak, M. S., D. A. Cook, and J. J. Sullivan, 'Commitment and energy conservation', *Applied Social Psychology Annual* 1 (1980) 235–53.

Parfit, Derek. *Reasons and Persons*. Oxford: Clarendon Press, 1984.

Peck, Jules. Open Letter to the Queen, 26 August 2009. Available at http://www.abundancypartners.co.uk/2009/08/open-letter-to-the-queen/.

Petrini, Carlo. *Slow Food Nation: Why Our Food Should be Good, Clean, and Fair*. New York: Rizzoli Ex Libris, 2007.

Pettit, Philip. *Republicanism: a theory of freedom and government*. New York and Oxford: Oxford University Press and the Clarendon Press, 1997.

——. 'Republican Freedom: Three Axioms, Four Theorems.' In *Republicanism and Political Theory*, ed. Cécile Laborde and John Maynor, 102–30. Oxford: Blackwell, 2008.

—— and Victoria McGeer. 'The Self-Regulating Mind'. *Language and Communication* 22 (2002), 281–99.

Plato. *Republic*, ed. G. R. F. Ferrari, transl. Tom Griffith. Cambridge: Cambridge University Press, 2000.

Plato. *Republic*, transl. Desmond Lee, introduction by Melissa Lane. 2nd edn. London and New York: Penguin, 2007.

Plato. *Complete Works*, ed. John M. Cooper with D. S. Hutchinson. Indianapolis: Hackett, 1997.

Plutarch, *Life of Lycurgus*, in Plutarch, *On Sparta*, 3–38. Transl. and ed. R. J. A. Talbert. New York: Penguin, 1988.

Pocock, J. G. A. 'Quentin Skinner: the history of politics and the politics of history (2004)'. In J. G. A. Pocock, *Political Thought and History: Essays on Theory and Method*, 123–42. Cambridge: Cambridge University Press, 2009.

Popper, Karl. *The Open Society and Its Enemies*, vol. I: *The Spell of Plato*. London: Routledge, 2003 [1945].

Porritt, Jonathon. *Capitalism as if the World Matters*. London: Earthscan, 2005.

Posner, Eric A. *Law and Social Norms*. Cambridge, MA: Harvard University Press, 2000.

Pradeau, Jean-François. *Plato and the City: A New Introduction to Plato's Political Thought*, transl. Janet Lloyd, foreword by Christopher Gill. Exeter: University of Exeter Press, 2002.

Rancière, Jacques. *Disagreement: Politics and Philosophy*, transl. Julie Rose. Minneapolis: University of Minnesota Press, 1998.

Rappaport, Helen. *Joseph Stalin: A Biographical Companion*. New York: ABC-CLIO, 1999.

Rawls, John. *Political Liberalism*. New York: Columbia University Press, 1993.

——. *A Theory of Justice*. Cambridge, MA: Harvard University Press, 1971.

Reich, Robert. 'How You and I Are Paying Wall Street to Lobby Congress To Go Easy On Wall Street'. Blog entry 26 January 2009. http://robertreich.blogspot.com/2009/01/how-you-and-i-are-paying-wall-street-to.html.

Revesz, Richard L. and Michael A. Livermore. *Retaking Rationality: How Cost-Benefit Analysis Can Better Protect the Environment and Our Health*. Oxford: Oxford University Press, 2008.

Rist, John M. 'Why Greek Philosophers Might Have Been Concerned About the Environment'. In *The Greeks and the Environment*, ed. Laura Westra and Thomas M. Robinson, 19–32. Lanham, MD: Rowman and Littlefield, 1997.

Rothschild, Emma. *Economic Sentiments: Adam Smith, Condorcet, and the Enlightenment*. Cambridge, MA and London: Harvard University Press, 2001.

Rousseau, Jean-Jacques. *Emile or On Education*, transl. and ed. Allan Bloom. New York: Basic Books, 1979.

——. *Letter to D'Alembert and writings for the theatre*, transl. and ed. Allan Bloom, Charles Butterworth, and Christopher Kelly. Hanover, NH and London: University Press of New England, 2004.

Runciman, W. G. *Great Books, Bad Arguments: Republic, Leviathan and the Communist Manifesto*. Princeton: Princeton University Press, 2010.

Sagan, Eli. 'Citizenship as a Form of Psycho-Social Identity'. In *The Good Idea: democracy in ancient Greece*, ed. John A. Koumoulides, 47–60. New Rochelle, NY: A. D. Caratzas Press, 1995.

Samuelson, William and Richard Zeckhauser. 'Status Quo Bias in Decision Making'. *Journal of Risk and Uncertainty* 1 (1998), 7–59.

Scheffler, Samuel. *The Rejection of Consequentialism: A Philosophical Investigation of the Considerations Underlying Rival Moral Conceptions*. Rev. edn. Oxford: Clarendon Press, 1994.

Schofield, Malcolm. *Plato: Political Philosophy*. Oxford: Oxford University Press, 2006.

Schumpeter, Joseph Alois. *Capitalism, Socialism, and Democracy*. 6th edn. London: Unwin Paperbacks, 1987.

Schwartz, Barry. *The Paradox of Choice: Why Less is More*. New York: HarperCollins, 2004.

Scitovsky, Tibor. *The Joyless Economy: An Inquiry into Human Satisfaction and Consumer Dissatisfaction*. New York: Oxford University Press, 1976.

Seaford, Richard. *Money and the Early Greek Mind: Homer, Philosophy, Tragedy*. Cambridge: Cambridge University Press, 2004.

——. 'Ancient Greece and Global Warming'. Presidential Address to the Classical Association. London: Classical Association, 2009.

Sedley, David. 'Socratic intellectualism in the central books of the *Republic*'. Forthcoming in a festschrift for Christopher Rowe, ed. Christopher Gill, Dimitri El Murr, and George Boys-Stones.

Seligman, Martin E. P. *Authenic Happiness: Using the New Positive Psychology to Realize Your Potential For Lasting Fulfillment*. New York: Free Press, 2004.

Sen, Amartya. 'Freedom and Coercion'. *University of Chicago Law Review* 63 (1996), 1035–61.

——. 'Why Exactly is Commitment Important for Rationality?' In *Rationality and Commitment*, ed. Fabienne Peter and Hans Bernhard Schmid, 17–27. Oxford: Oxford University Press, 2007.

Sinnott-Armstrong, Walter. 'It's not *my* fault: global warming and individual moral obligations'. In *Perspectives on Climate Change: Science, Economics, Politics, Ethics*, ed. Walter Sinnott-Armstrong and Richard B. Howarth, 285–307. Advances in the Economics of Environmental Resources, vol. 5. Amsterdam: Elsevier, 2005.

Smith, Adam. *An Inquiry into the Nature and Causes of the Wealth of Nations*, ed. R. H. Campbell and A. S. Skinner. Indianapolis: Liberty Fund, 1981.

——. *The Theory of Moral Sentiments*, ed. D. D. Raphael and A. L. Macfie. Indianapolis: Liberty Fund, 1982.

Sonenscher, Michael. *Sans-Culottes: An Eighteenth-Century Emblem in the French Revolution*. Princeton: Princeton University Press, 2008.

Stern, Nicholas. *The Economics of Climate Change: The Stern Review*. Cambridge: Cambridge University Press, 2007.

Stock, James H. and Mark W. Watson. 'Has the Business Cycle Changed and Why?' *NBER Macroeconomics Annual* 17 (2002), 159–218.

Stone, Christopher D. *Should Trees Have Standing?: Law, Morality and the Environment*. 3rd edn. Oxford: Oxford University Press, 2010.

Sunstein, Cass. 'Preferences, Paternalism, and Liberty'. In *Preferences and Well-Being: Royal Institute of Philosophy Supplement* 81. Cambridge: Cambridge University Press, 2006.

Tarnopolsky, Christina H. '*Mimêsis,* Persuasion, and Manipulation in Plato's *Republic*'. In *Manipulating Democracy*, ed. John Parrish and Wayne S. LeCherminant. New York: Routledge, 2010.

———. *Prudes, Perverts, and Tyrants: Plato's* Gorgias *and the Politics of Shame*. Princeton and Oxford: Princeton University Press, 2010.

———. 'Plato's Politics of Distributing and Disrupting the Sensible'. *Theory and Event* 13:4 (2010).

Taylor, Charles. *Modern Social Imaginaries*. Durham, NC, and London: Duke University Press, 2004.

Tress, Daryl McGowan. 'The Philosophical Genesis of Ecology and Environmentalism'. In *The Greeks and the Environment*, ed. Laura Westra and Thomas M. Robinson, 33–42. Lanham, MD: Rowman and Littlefield, 1997.

Tuck, Richard. *Free Riding*. Cambridge, MA and London: Harvard University Press, 2008.

Tversky, Amos and Eldar Shafir. 'Choice under Conflict: The Dynamics of Deferred Decision'. *Psychological Science* 3 (1992), 358–61.

Tyler, Tom R. *Why People Obey the Law*. 2nd edn. Princeton: Princeton University Press, 2006.

Unger, Peter. *Living High and Letting Die: Our Illusion of Innocence*. New York and Oxford: Oxford University Press, 1996.

Urbinati, Nadia. 'Thucydides the Thermidorian: democracy on trial in the making of modern liberalism'. In *Thucydides: Reception, Reinterpretation, Influence*, ed. Katharine Harloe and Neville Morley. Cambridge: Cambridge University Press, forthcoming.

Van Wensveen, Louke. *Dirty Virtues: The Emergence of Ecological Virtue Ethics*. Amherst, NY: Humanity Books, 1999.

Wallach, John R. *The Platonic Political Art: a study of critical reason and democracy*. University Park, PA: Pennsylvania State University Press, 2001.

Whitford, Margaret. 'Feminism and Psychoanalysis'. In *The Routledge Encyclopedia of Philosophy*, vol. 3, ed. Edward Craig, 583–8. London and New York: Routledge, 1998.

Wilkinson, Angela. *Beyond the Financial Crisis: The Oxford Scenarios*. Undated report of the Institute for Science, Innovation and Society, Oxford University. http://www.sbs.ox.ac.uk/centres/insis/projects/Pages/financial-scenarios.aspx.

Williams, Bernard. *Shame and Necessity*. Berkeley, CA: University of California Press, 2008.

Wolin, Sheldon S. *Politics and Vision: Continuity and Innovation in Western Political Thought.* Boston and Toronto: Little, Brown and Company, 1960.

World Commission on Environment and Development. *Our Common Future.* Oxford: Oxford University Press, 1987.

WWF. *Living Planet Report 2010: Biodiversity, biocapacity and development.* wwf. panda.org/about_our_earth/all_publications/living_planet_report/.

Zimbardo, Philip G. and John Boyd. *The Time Paradox: The New Psychology of Time That Will Change Your Life.* New York: Free Press, 2008.

Index